The Silents Go to War

The Silents Go to War
American World War I Propaganda Films, 1915–1930

ANITA R. APPELBAUM

Foreword by Anthony Slide

McFarland & Company, Inc., Publishers
Jefferson, North Carolina

LIBRARY OF CONGRESS CATALOGUING-IN-PUBLICATION DATA

Names: Appelbaum, Anita R., 1950– author. | Slide, Anthony, author of foreword.
Title: The silents go to war : American World War I propaganda films, 1915-1930 / Anita R. Appelbaum ; foreword by Anthony Slide.
Description: Jefferson, North Carolina : McFarland & Company, Inc., Publishers, 2024. | Includes bibliographical references and index.
Identifiers: LCCN 2024029700 | ISBN 9781476690346 (paperback : acid free paper) ∞
ISBN 9781476652726 (ebook)
Subjects: LCSH: World War, 1914-1918—Motion pictures and the war. | Motion pictures in propaganda—United States—History. | Silent films—United States—History and criticism. | Propaganda—United States—History. | Motion pictures—United States—History and criticism.
Classification: LCC D522.23 .A67 2024 | DDC 791.43/658—dc23/eng/20240702
LC record available at https://lccn.loc.gov/2024029700

BRITISH LIBRARY CATALOGUING DATA ARE AVAILABLE

ISBN (print) 978-1-4766-9034-6
ISBN (ebook) 978-1-4766-5272-6

© 2024 Anita R. Appelbaum. All rights reserved

No part of this book may be reproduced or transmitted in any form or by any means, electronic or mechanical, including photocopying or recording, or by any information storage and retrieval system, without permission in writing from the publisher.

Front cover image:: Poster art for the 1930 film
All Quiet on the Western Front (Universal Pictures)

Printed in the United States of America

*McFarland & Company, Inc., Publishers
Box 611, Jefferson, North Carolina 28640
www.mcfarlandpub.com*

To my beloved high school teacher,
Mr. Philip Seuling (1934–1984),
who opened my eyes to the magical
world of silent films.

Table of Contents

Acknowledgments	viii
Foreword by Anthony Slide	1
Preface	5
Introduction: Influential Propaganda Movies During the First World War	7
1. Watchful Waiting: Antiwar and Pro-War Films of 1915 and 1916	19
2. The War Begins: The Committee on Public Information and Films of 1917	35
3. "Horrible Hun" Films of 1918	55
4. "Kaiserphobia" Films of 1918: Dramas and Comedies	72
5. Documentaries of 1918	95
6. Postwar Films of 1919	105
7. Antiwar and War Trauma Films of 1921–1930	118
Epilogue: Lost and Found	149
Chapter Notes	161
Bibliography	185
Index	195

Acknowledgments

I would like to thank the following people for their kind assistance. I am indebted to noted film historian Anthony Slide for the foreword to this book, as well as for his encouragement and suggestions to a first-time author. I would also like to thank Cheyenne Dawson of Alamy Inc. for patiently assisting me in the selection of photographs for this book. Thank you also to the late Mr. Philip Seuling of Lafayette High School for his wonderful course in theater, television, and film that sparked my intense interest in American World War I propaganda films, and for the wonderful Saturday mornings spent in a little theater in Greenwich Village in New York City watching many of these films. A special "thank you" to the late Mrs. Madeleine Verne of LIM College in New York City, who taught me the importance of fashion as propaganda. Many thanks to my dear friend, author Elizabeth Splaine, for her steadfast friendship and encouragement. Thank you also to my editor Layla Milholen for her critical comments that added to the content of the book.

Last, and most important of all, a heartfelt "thank you" to my patient husband of 37 years, Dr. Peter Appelbaum, himself the author and/or translator of 13 books dealing with Jewish participation in the military on the side of Austria-Hungary in the First World War. He constantly prodded me to write this book, always telling me that I had a book in me. Well, I guess I did.

Foreword

BY ANTHONY SLIDE

It is known as World War I, the Great War, and the War to End All Wars. Only the first seems an accurate description of a conflict that certainly did not end all wars and has somehow faded into partial insignificance thanks to the brutal conflicts that have followed and continue to the present. Where World War I does stand out is as the first to thoroughly embrace the motion picture to present the war as it took place and how it continues to be used as background for films of later years. Above all, World War I illustrates the power of the motion picture as a propaganda tool, and, appropriately, Anita R. Appelbaum has undertaken an examination of propaganda films from 1915 through 1930. (I cannot help but note that two of the greatest, and many might argue the most inflammatory and controversial, films of all time are propaganda efforts: D.W. Griffith's *The Birth of a Nation* and Leni Riefenstahl's *Triumph of the Will*. One documents a nationwide conflict, the American Civil War, and the other may well be considered a lead-up to a worldwide conflagration.)

The Silents Go to War is divided into chapters with specific themes, such as films with pro- or antiwar sentiment leading up to America's entry into the conflict, George Creel and the Committee on Public Information, documentaries, and the "Horrible Hun" (a lovely chapter title). The principal actor referenced in the last is (as one might expect) Erich von Stroheim. The next chapter discusses "Kaiserphobia," and the actor most referenced here is New Zealand–born Rupert Julian, who starred in *The Kaiser, the Beast of Berlin* and is the personification of the German leader on film. It has always amused me that despite his villainous appearance, one of his leading ladies told me that he was the kindest and gentlest of performers.

While documentaries, including newsreels, are discussed in a separate chapter, there is not an entire chapter devoted to comedy, but

Foreword by Anthony Slide

comedic contributions to the war effort are not ignored, in particular, as one might expect, Chaplin's *Shoulder Arms* and female impersonator Bothwell Browne's outrageous *Yankee Doodle in Berlin*.

The book concludes with a very interesting chapter discussing antiwar films from 1921 through 1930, which are described as "Trauma Films," a description with which I was not familiar. The epilogue provides the reader with information as to whether a production has survived, its preservation status, and its availability to the viewer at large. The chapter on "Trauma Films" primarily discusses *The Four Horsemen of the Apocalypse*, *The Big Parade*, and *All Quiet on the Western Front*. There are obviously many—perhaps too many—later films that might have been included in the book. And the new (2022) German version of *All Quiet on the Western Front* reminds one that World War I is still a subject of major interest, and, of course, is important in that it tells the horror of the war from a totally German perspective, being a German film of a German novel. And, yes, *All Quiet on the Western Front* is a German-language novel, despite its immediate and lasting appeal in the English-language world.

This is not a catalog of film titles but rather a narrative history. However, such an approach does not prevent Ms. Appelbaum from providing thorough documentation of each of the films under discussion, with information on casts, storylines, critical contemporary commentary, and (most important) the backstory of each of the productions.

In the course of her commentary on specific, related films, she also manages to provide the reader with a useful history of silent filmmaking in general, touching upon many individuals (both in front of and behind the camera) and titles unrelated to the basic theme. Rather than interfering with the narrative, this discussion is not irrelevant, but rather provides background to the main text.

I am a great believer in endnotes that do not merely provide a citation for a quote within the text, but rather add to our knowledge on a topic within the chapter. And Anita Appelbaum does not disappoint with endnotes that are as readable as the chapters themselves—and equally enjoyable.

I must emphasize that this is a volume devoid of academic jargon and easily readable by all. (I suspect, however, that its main use will be as a textbook for courses on "the war film.")

Obviously, the author does not discuss all relevant films. There are just too many. But she does examine all major ones and quite a few that I suspect will be unknown to even the most enthusiastic film fan or scholar of the period.

Foreword by Anthony Slide

World War I may not have been the war to end all wars, but, hopefully, with her discussion of the conflict on film, Anita Appelbaum will have provided a stunning revelation as to its impact on American, and perhaps world, audiences, and make us stop and think that enough really is enough as far as war is concerned. There should be no need for a volume such as this on wars of the twenty-first century.

Anthony Slide is the author or editor of more than 200 books on the history of popular entertainment, publishing his first work, Early American Cinema, *in 1970, and being described by the* Los Angeles Times *as "a one-man publishing phenomenon." In 1990, he was awarded an honorary doctorate of letters by Bowling Green State University, at which time he was hailed by Lillian Gish as "our pre-eminent historian of the silent film."*

Preface

I wrote this book out of my love for silent films. I saw my first silent film at age nine in 1959: it was an old, grainy version of *The Four Horsemen of the Apocalypse*. I didn't understand the entire plot, but I was mesmerized by Rudolph Valentino, and the shots of the Four Horsemen (War, Death, Famine, and Disease) riding across the screen gave me cold shivers.

As I grew up, I saw a variety of silent films on TV in my formative years, and when I attended Lafayette High School in Brooklyn as a teenager, I was privileged to take a course on theater, television, and film taught by Mr. Philip Seuling, a true silent film buff. Mr. Seuling would take members of our class to monthly Saturday viewings of old silent films in a Greenwich Village theater, and that's how I came to be familiar with First World War propaganda films including *Hearts of the World* (1918), *The Heart of Humanity* (1918), *The Enchanted Cottage* (1924), *The Big Parade* (1925), and *All Quiet on the Western Front* (1930 silent version). In college (the Laboratory Institute of Merchandising), I took a course in costume history, and my teacher, the elegant Mrs. Madeleine Verne, introduced our class to the history of fashion propaganda from ancient times up to the First World War, both in class and through visits to the Costume Institute at the Metropolitan Museum of Art. She was the inspiration for my introduction's channeling of history's early propagandists including Rome's fashion trendsetter Gaius Augustus Caesar (toga power!), dueling jewelry queens Catherine de Medici of France and Elizabeth I of England (diamonds were a girl's best friend!), and the astute Napoleon Bonaparte of France (the ladies loved his fashion medallions)!

Over the next 50 years, I watched silent film specials and retrospectives on TV and attended silent film showings. I read books on the subject by noted film historians including Anthony Slide and Kevin Brownlow, as well as biographies of many of the great silent film stars— John Gilbert, Mary Pickford, comedienne Mabel Normand, Richard

Preface

Barthelmess, Lillian Gish, Rudolph Valentino, Ramon Novarro—and such great directors as D.W. Griffith, Cecil B. DeMille, Erich von Stroheim, and Rex Ingram.

I began to realize that some writers, commentators, and filmgoers of the present generation now view some films like D.W. Griffith's *Birth of a Nation* as racist (and it is, but it is also landmark filmmaking) as well as regard many silents as out of date and not worthy of respect. So I decided to write this book as a salute to these films, their stars, and their directors. Many films are as relevant today as they were when they were made: 1916's *War Brides* dealt with a woman's reproductive rights; *The Secret Game* (1917) accurately portrayed Japan as America's ally during the First World War; the documentary *Our Colored Fighters* (1918) showed the heroism of African American troops under fire in France; and *The Enchanted Cottage* (1924) depicted the plight of a First World War veteran suffering from post-traumatic stress syndrome.

While my book does not cover every American First World War propaganda film, it does highlight 45 films and documentaries, ending with an epilogue on the fate of these films in the present day.

My research over three years included endless hours on film websites and so much reading: century-old newspaper, movie magazine, and movie journal reviews; books and articles on the cause of the First World War; articles on propaganda from ancient times up to the twentieth century; and, of course, books on the great directors and stars of the silent era. The era of the American First World War propaganda film was relatively short, but its impact on film history remains to this day on people who value the major contribution of the stars, writers, and directors during the heyday of the silent film.

Introduction

*Influential Propaganda Movies
During the First World War*

American propaganda movies from the period 1915–1918 (and beyond) tapped into various elements of the American psyche at the time: suspicion of German Americans as less-than-loyal American citizens; suspicion of Asian Americans as agents of both Germany and Mexico (long considered an enemy of the United States), and a dislike of Germans in general, with a special loathing for Kaiser Wilhelm II. Added to that potent mix was "Hun" hatred of German soldiers as heartless barbarians after their atrocities against Belgian citizens (especially women) in the first six weeks of the war. Filmmakers were quick to capitalize on these fears, and the movies during this time period reflected the mood of the American public.

However, the use of propaganda to influence a "particular point of view" (as defined by the Oxford English Dictionary) started thousands of years before the first propaganda movie was ever made. An enterprising ruler by the name of Darius I of Persia started the ball rolling back in 515 BCE by carving his victories over his enemies on a large cliff now known as the Behistun Inscription—probably the first example of billboard advertising.[1] His son Xerxes I ultimately won the Battle of Thermopylae in September 480 BCE (it was the 300 Spartans against 20,000 Persians, holding out for three days) but lost the propaganda war when, one month later, the Athenian navy destroyed the Persian navy.[2] The great Greek playwright Aeschylus mocked Xerxes and company in his standing-room-only play *The Persians*, which won him the "Dionysus award," the ancient equivalent of Broadway's Tony Award, giving the Greeks a big win in the propaganda war.[3] Caesar Augustus, the grandnephew of Julius Caesar, became one of the first fashion influencers, using toga-power propaganda to influence men's fashions in Rome, not

Introduction

to mention his self-promotion via political propaganda: his own autobiography, *The Deeds of the Divine Augustus*, was distributed throughout the Roman empire.[4] Fast-forward to the Middle Ages, when the church made sure to avail themselves of the "propaganda of the saints," setting up fan clubs for wonder-working saints via holy shrines throughout the Christian world.[5] This also helped the early tourist industry ... after all, travelers to these sites needed a place to stay (inns), bought food and souvenirs, and changed money via local money changers (early versions of ATM machines). Then, another form of propaganda reappeared: clothing propaganda. For many ruling monarchs and ladies of fashion, it was dress for success! Queen Elizabeth I of England (1533–1603), noted for her extravagant dresses, was one of the chief jewelry propagandists, having her image reproduced in miniature cameos and pendants to be worn by an adoring public. Not to be outdone, her rival queen, Catherine de Medici of France (1519–1589), dressed in basic black gowns as a form of piety propaganda, but accented the plainness of her gowns with simple jewelry—only your average diamonds, rubies, sapphires, and pearls.[6] Over in the New World in the early 1600s, the Pilgrim fathers and the Wampanoag Indians celebrated with one of the earliest pieces of food propaganda—the first Thanksgiving, which featured seafood platters of shellfish plus mains of roasted wild turkey and grilled meats. (No pies, since there was no butter, flour, or sugar available.) By the time the American Revolution came around in 1776, publishing propaganda took center stage: pamphlets including Thomas Paine's *Common Sense* inspired starving American troops under General George Washington to defeat the British on Christmas Day, 1776. As news of Washington's victories during the course of the revolution continued, *Common Sense* became one of the first colonial bestsellers[7]; within a short time, it was translated into French and helped light the fire of the French Revolution of 1789. The French Revolution inspired another kind of propaganda: cartoons explicitly depicting the French king (Louis XVI) and queen (Marie Antoinette) wiping their behinds with Royalist newspapers.[8] This did not go over well with the majority of Frenchmen (poor and hungry) and, inevitably, they were guillotined during the 1792–93 Reign of Terror. Eventually, Frenchmen revolted against the excesses of the Reign of Terror, and a new leader arose: Napoleon Bonaparte (1769–1821), France's greatest military leader and emperor of France from 1804 to 1814. Napoleon was no slouch in the art of self-propaganda: he used pictures and sculptures to depict his military triumphs, had bulletins published to make the French public aware of his many victories,

Introduction

and capitalized on the popularity of medallions (a fashion accessory since ancient times) to celebrate his reign. No self-respecting French lady was without her stylish medallion to make a fashion statement![9] Over in India in the 1850s, the British used virulent newspaper propaganda to depict the Sepoy Rebellion of 1857 as the work of "savages in great need of enlightenment and beneficent rule of Britain."[10] In actuality, the Sepoys were proud professional soldiers who took great pride in their military prowess and loyalty to their British officers. Relations had reached a low point in 1857, however: not only were the Sepoys (a mix of Hindu and Muslim soldiers) denied promotional opportunities and better pay, but the British also violated religious Muslim and Hindu traditions by using pig fat (Muslims considered pigs unclean) and cow fat (Hindus considered cows sacred) to grease rifle cartridges. The soldiers were required not only to handle cartridges but also to bite off the ends of cartridges before loading the rifles. The Sepoys revolted; atrocities on both sides were committed against Indian and British civilians until British control was re-established in 1858. Due to the virulent racist cartoons and articles in British newspapers that were published worldwide, the propaganda of the press succeeded in tarnishing the Indian culture for decades.[11] Then came the American Civil War, which was fought not only on the battlefields but in the print media as well: posters, periodicals, and newspaper articles were used to demonize both sides, and musical propaganda ("The Battle Cry of Freedom"; "Maryland, My Maryland"; "Dixie's Land"; "The Battle Hymn of the Republic") was used on both sides to encourage young men to enlist. Ultimately, the South lost the war, but enmity between North and South continued to resonate for decades to come. In the 1870s, all eyes were on the Franco-Prussian War (1870–1871), which was eventually lost by the French, giving the Germans a military and national propaganda triumph. Mercilessly (and unfairly) ridiculing the courage of French soldiers via newspaper articles, Germany forced France to cede them not only a large cash indemnity but also the French provinces of Alsace and Lorraine. The Germans, however, did not go unscathed: the European press published damaging (true) propaganda articles on the German mistreatment of French civilians as well as the bombardment and starvation tactics used during their Siege of Paris at the end of the war. French hatred of the Germans would come to a head decades later in the armed conflict of World War I. In faraway South Africa, the British would again use virulent newspaper propaganda to stir up hatred against the South African Republic and its sister republic, the Orange

Introduction

Free State. The Boers (originally Dutch, French Huguenot, and German settlers from the 1600s) fought and defeated the British in the first Anglo-Boer War (1880–1881). After gold was discovered in the South African Republic in 1886, it was only a matter of time before the British would try again. The *London Times* used a quote from Queen Victoria calling the Boers "a horrid people, cruel and overbearing" to inflame the general opinion of the public, and in 1899, they again invaded South Africa in the Second Anglo-Boer War (1899–1902). This time, the British used overwhelming force to defeat the Boers and facilitated one of the most devasting pieces of atrocity propaganda against helpless Boer women and children: the concentration camp. Imprisoning 120,000 Boer women and children after the British burned their farms and destroyed their crops in an effort to halt food and supplies to Boer fighters, the camps had no proper housing, appalling sanitary facilities, dwindling food supplies, and rampant disease. In total, 4,000 women and 22,000 children died.[12]

But then ... across the sea in France, something revolutionary would happen to shift the trajectory of the propaganda sphere: in 1902, the first silent film was premiered in Paris, and the use of film as propaganda would explode during the First World War.

At the beginning of the First World War in 1914 (Chapter 1), Americans had other things on their minds: the endless troubles with the pesky Mexicans on America's southern border; working hard to keep their families fed; celebrating the first Mother's Day (by presidential proclamation) on May 14, 1914; and following the all–American sport of baseball, with home run hero Honus Wagner of the Pittsburgh Pirates getting 3,000 hits in one season. The relatively new pastime of going to the "flickers" (silent movies) gave audiences the chance to laugh at the antics of comedian Charlie Chaplin and the adventures of all–American girl Mary Pickford. The far-off war in Europe was not high on the average person's list of concerns, but all that would change when word came in the late autumn of 1914 of the atrocities committed by the Germans against innocent Belgian civilians. In January of 1915, newspaper mogul William Randolph Hearst would release the documentary *The History of the World's Greatest War* to American theaters nationwide, with footage shot on location highlighting the plight of the Belgian people under the onslaught of the German army, including the deliberate destruction of the old university city and library of Louvain, with the burning of hundreds of precious Gothic and Renaissance manuscripts. May 1915 brought the sinking of the passenger ship *Lusitania* (1,198

Introduction

people, including 128 Americans, drowned) by a German submarine, and acts of German espionage in the United States were uncovered, causing intense suspicion of German Americans possibly aiding the German cause. To try to counteract the anti–German feelings emerging in the United States, some enterprising movie theaters (with backing from wealthy German Americans) showed newsreels shot by American cameramen in France depicting the German perspective: *The German Side of the War*, compiled and released by the *Chicago Tribune*, which played to sold-out crowds for weeks in late 1915. Film studios began to tentatively take sides: should America prepare for war, or should she remain cautiously neutral? On the pro-preparedness propaganda side, 1915's *The Battle Cry of Peace* advocated for a strong stance on preparing for a sneak attack by Teutonic-like forces, which happens midway through the film; 1916's *Civilization* flips the coin and shows a German submarine captain having second thoughts about sinking the "ProPatria" (*Lusitania*) and instead sinking his own ship; and *The Fall of a Nation* has Germany invading the United States and executing citizens (luckily a secret rebel group organized by suffragettes and a rebel army led by a young congressman unite to drive out the invaders). Three other 1916 films approach war from a woman's point of view: *If My Country Calls* has a mother who poisons her son to stop him from enlisting to fight in Mexico; *War Brides* finds a German widow fighting for reproductive rights against the German state which tries to compel her to birth sons for future conflicts; and the Cecil B. DeMille extravaganza *Joan the Woman* has a British soldier finding Joan of Arc's sword in a trench in France, conjuring up Joan to tell her story, and then, with the ghost of Joan at his side, leading a suicide mission against the Germans.

On April 6, 1917 (Chapter 2), the United States declared war on Germany after the Germans, in their infamous Zimmermann Telegram, offered Mexico the American states of Texas, Arizona, and New Mexico for their commitment to the German cause (wisely, Mexico declined). America went to war, and so did the film industry under the guidance of the Committee on Public Information (CPI), authorized by President Wilson and organized by America's first propaganda czar, George Creel (1876–1953). Creel was a crusading journalist with extensive investigative experience, working as an editor for the *Rocky Mountain News* in Denver, Colorado, from 1911 to 1913, championing the rights of women and mine workers and helping to break the power of corrupt politicians. Serving briefly as Denver's police commissioner, he would hire Denver's first policewoman, Josephine Roche (1886–1976), and together

Introduction

they would curb rampant prostitution in Denver. Moving to New York City in 1913 to be with his wife, Broadway star Blanche Bates, Creel would gain fame as an independent journalist, writing articles to help secure the confirmation of Louis Brandeis as the first Jewish member of the United States Supreme Court, a book exposing child labor abuses, and then a series of pamphlets in favor of women's suffrage. A staunch supporter of Woodrow Wilson, Creel would go to work for Wilson's chief strategist Bob Woolsey, writing a series of articles supporting Wilson's neutrality policy, and then, in 1916, a best-selling book called *Wilson and the Issues*. When Creel was appointed the head of the CPI in April of 1917, he knew that he would need to reach the four corners of the United States through a vast propaganda network. Working out of Washington, D.C., with a force of handpicked journalists, scholars, artists, and political figures to head the various departments of the CPI, Creel also went into the movie business. He would "draft" directors (including D.W. Griffith, Cecil B. DeMille, and Thomas Ince) and stars (cowboy hero William S. Hart, screen idols Mary Pickford, Douglas Fairbanks, Sessue Hayakawa, and Charlie Chaplin) to make movies to help spread the message of the CPI: support the war effort. The film industry responded with three big hits on three very different subjects: *Womanhood, the Glory of the Nation* (J. Stuart Blackton's sequel to his 1915 hit *The Battle Cry of Peace*), with the heroine stealing secrets from a besotted German prince and helping to lead U.S. forces to victory against invading Teutonic forces; *The Little American*, starring Mary Pickford as a plucky (what else?) American girl stranded in France and forced to fight off lecherous German officers; and *The Secret Game*, starring matinee idol Sessue Hayakawa as a resourceful Japanese agent hot on the trail of German saboteurs in the United States. William Randolph Hearst, still convinced that Japan would connive with Mexico (and Germany) against the United States, would finance the anti–Japanese propaganda serial *Patria*, creating even more suspicion of Asian Americans and earning the wrath of the CPI, the State Department, and President Woodrow Wilson.

By 1918, Hollywood would be churning out movies vilifying the behavior of German soldiers (Chapter 3): *The Cross Bearer* tells the true story of Cardinal Mercier of Belgium defending his people against looting Germans; King Albert of Belgium inspires a little Belgian boy to outwit the Germans in Paramount's *Till I Come Back to You*. But nobody embodied the "Horrible Hun" more than legendary character actor (and later director) Erich von Stroheim (1885–1957). With his menacing

Introduction

demeanor and serpentine charm, he was the very essence of the arrogant Prussian officer. Still, fact was stranger than fiction ... he wasn't a Prussian (he was born in Vienna, Austria), he wasn't a Hun (he was 4F in the Austrian army), and he certainly wasn't a "von" (he was from a Jewish, middle-class family). He arrived in the United States in 1909, presented himself at Ellis Island as "Count Erich Oswald Hans Maria von Stroheim und Nordenwald" and proceeded to build himself a new identity. After two early failed marriages and dead-end jobs, he arrived in Hollywood. Realizing that he was not the leading man type (tall, dark, and handsome) he capitalized on his other attributes: he shaved his head to highlight the scar on his forehead (a kick in the head from a horse during his brief time in the Austrian army) and his dark, piercing eyes, and he attired himself in a natty suit, white gloves, a long dark coat, and a monocle. With his charming European manners, accent, and knowledge of continental customs, he began to be noticed, and soon obtained work as an assistant director/actor on productions including 1915's *Old Heidelberg* for actor/director John Emerson and 1916's *The Social Secretary*, again directed by Emerson and starring the gorgeous Norma Talmadge, who became a lifelong friend of von Stroheim. She recommended him as an assistant director/actor in her next picture, *Panthea*; he was noticed by critics in a small role as a nasty young "lieutenant of police," and he was on his way. As the war progressed, he found himself typecast as an arrogant Prussian officer, hitting his stride in 1918 in a series of memorable roles. He played brutal officer Kurt von Schnieditz—so nasty that his own soldiers kill him!—in *The Unbeliever*; a bald-headed Hun—a small-but-eye-catching role—kicking a poor French peasant (played by British playwright Noël Coward) in D.W. Griffith's all-star *Hearts of the World*; a German spy master in *The Hun Within*; and finally, in *The Heart of Humanity*, a lecherous German officer attempting to rape a Red Cross nurse (he tears off most of her clothes) while disposing of a crying baby by throwing it out of a window! In the 1920s, von Stroheim would become one of the great directors of the silent screen era, whose body of work would rank in the same class as D.W. Griffith and Cecil B. DeMille.

If the American film public hated the Germans (Chapter 4), it was their kaiser, Wilhelm II, who was the actual personification of the overbearing Hun. In reality, Wilhelm was a mercurial, emotionally unstable man who projected arrogance to hide his withered left arm. In addition, suspicion of German Americans ran high during the war years. Hollywood filmmakers were quick to capitalize on both perceptions, and

Introduction

turned out a series of "Kaiser-hating" films and "Huns-in-the-Hometown" propaganda films. *Lest We Forget* channels the exploits of a French opera star condemned to death by the kaiser as a spy, escaping a firing squad and sailing on the ill-fated *Lusitania* (the opera star is played by French actress Rita Jolivet, an actual survivor of the *Lusitania*). *The Road Through the Dark* gives a bleak look at a French girl forced to become the mistress of a murderous German officer while sneaking spy documents to the American Secret Service. *Kaiser's Finish* poses a question: What if the kaiser had an illegitimate son who looked just like the crown prince? Whose side would he be on? *My Four Years in Germany* was a based-on-fact depiction of the kaiser and his plans to conquer Europe during the First World War. Ambassador to Germany James W. Gerard, whose book depicted Wilhelm's erratic behavior and physical deformity (a shortened left arm), served as technical advisor to the film, which proved to be a big hit with the public. *To Hell with the Kaiser* gives a mocking look at the kaiser (he makes a deal with the devil for world conquest, loses, and gets sent to hell). *The Kaiser, the Beast of Berlin* featured an all-star cast (including not-yet horror star Lon Chaney as German chancellor von Bethmann-Hollweg) and an over-the-top performance by Rupert Julian as the fiendish kaiser. Really poking fun at the kaiser came in the form of Charlie Chaplin's *Shoulder Arms*, with Charlie capturing the kaiser and his whole general staff!

"Huns in the Hometown" films *Claws of the Hun* and *Me und Gott* depict conflicted loyalties of young German American men (true-blue in the end), and real-life German counterintelligence agent Horst von der Goltz basically portrays himself in the aptly-titled *The Prussian Cur*. *Joan of Plattsburg* (starring Keystone Cops comedienne Mabel Normand) not only spoofs the Joan of Arc legend but has Mabel capturing German spies in the basement of her orphanage! And *Johanna Enlists* has farmgirl Mary Pickford inspiring a regiment of "doughboys" to go fight the Huns, while acquiring a future husband in the process.

War documentaries from 1918 (Chapter 5) were vital to influence and support American participation during World War I. Short documentaries produced by independent film studios spotlighted the contributions of both the public and private sector: *I'll Help Every Willing Worker Find a Job* (the U.S. Employment Service), *Solving the Farm Problem in the Nation* (mobilizing the Boy Scouts to help harvest crops), *Feeding the Fighter* (the work of the U.S. Food Administration), and *I Run the Biggest Life Insurance Company on Earth* (the contributions of the government's War Risk Bureau). Under the aegis of the

Introduction

Committee on Public Information (CPI), the United States Signal Corps produced documentaries on the heroics of soldiers fighting in France designed to appeal to the patriotism of people from all corners of the United States: *Pershing's Crusaders* (raw recruits from around the country become fighting soldiers on the fields of France), *America's Answer to the Hun* (how American manpower and machines are transferred across the Atlantic, culminating in the American and French victory at Château-Thierry), *Our Colored Fighters* (the heroics of African American soldiers in France, specifically the famous "Harlem Hellfighters"), and *Under Four Flags* (documenting American, French, Italian, and British soldiers fighting together to liberate Europe from the Germans).

World War I ended on November 11, 1918, and the American public welcomed peace. Still, antipathy and bitterness toward wartime German behavior was slow to fade, and Hollywood would release six postwar propaganda films (five dramas and one comedy) that reflected these negative feelings (Chapter 6): *The Great Victory* or *The Great Victory: Wilson or the Kaiser? The Fall of the Hohenzollerns* (German atrocities in France and Belgium with a young Alsatian soldier deserting the Germans and joining the United States army by special permission of Woodrow Wilson), *The Lost Battalion* (weaving a fictitious love story around the actual heroics of the 77th Infantry Division's legendary "Lost Battalion"), *The False Faces* (famous British jewel thief Michael Lanyard pursues fellow jewel thief/German assassin Karl Eckstrom, played by makeup marvel Lon Chaney, across the Atlantic to New York City for a climactic battle involving the American Secret Service), *The Unpardonable Sin* (twin sisters and their mother, menaced by violent German officer, flee to freedom in Holland), *Behind the Door* (loyal German American ship's captain pursues murderous German U-boat captain who rapes and murders the captain's wife), and the uproarious *Yankee Doodle in Berlin* (downed American flyer in Berlin cross-dresses as an exotic dancer and seduces the kaiser and his entire High Command).

The 1920s came roaring in (Chapter 7), and the nation looked forward to a time of peace and prosperity. They were not interested in the fractured European society ... why should they be? After all, America had been dragged into the war with 117,000 men killed and 234,000 returning home wounded in body and mind. They wanted escapist movies, and Hollywood began to oblige with romantic melodramas, historical epics, crowd-pleasing Westerns, and laugh-out-loud comedies.

Still, the deep psychological and physical wounds of the war intruded on the public conscience. In 1921, the first antiwar propaganda

Introduction

picture premiered: *The Four Horseman of the Apocalypse* (Argentinian/French playboy—Rudolph Valentino—tangos his way to Paris, falls in love with a married woman, becomes a soldier, and sees the futility of war). An unusual Western war trauma film arrived in 1923: *Shootin' for Love* starred legendary cowboy star Hoot Gibson (himself a World War I tank corps sergeant) as a shell-shocked veteran involved in a modern-day range war. *The Enchanted Cottage* (1924) was an exploration of the physical and psychological damage experienced by a young returning veteran played by Richard Barthelmess.

In 1925, the blockbuster hit *The Big Parade* grabbed audiences as they watched spoiled young man John Gilbert becoming a soldier and enduring the mental and physical horrors of World War I, including losing a leg and watching his buddies die in front of him. That same year saw dashing Ronald Colman as an English soldier blinded in battle and unable to cope with his disability in *The Dark Angel*.

Two antiwar films came to the screen in 1927: *Barbed Wire* opened to critical acclaim, but the general public stayed away due to the controversial topic: a French farmgirl, whose brother is blinded by Germans, falls in love with a German POW and returns to Germany with him at the end of the war. *The Patent Leather Kid* tells the story of a young boxer who is revealed as a war-time slacker and shamed into enlisting, ultimately finding his courage on the battlefield and sustaining a crippling wound that ends his career. The film channels elements of the famous slacking charges during World War I against world heavyweight champion Jack Dempsey. That same year also brought the high-flying aviation movie *Wings* (featuring a nude scene with gorgeous Clara Bow) to theaters across the country, glorifying the exploits of American pilots during the Great War.

In 1928, the sentimental *Four Sons* took an antiwar (Hollywood) look at the German side of the war, with a noble Bavarian widow seeing her sons fighting on opposite sides. The improbable gender-bending *She Goes to War* (1929) looks at war from the feminine side: a spoiled young socialite goes to France as an aid worker, puts on her cowardly boyfriend's uniform when he gets drunk, goes to the front, impersonates him, goes into battle, and kills Germans.

Finally, in 1930, 12 years after the end of the war, America was able to look at the war from a true German perspective: the silent film version of German author Erich Maria Remarque's *All Quiet on the Western Front*, with the story of a young German soldier experiencing the horrors of war, resonating with worldwide audiences and critics alike.

Introduction

Sadly, the movie was outlawed for its perceived antiwar message in Germany by Adolf Hitler and the Nazi Party and would not be seen again by Germans until long after their defeat in the Second World War.

With the coming of sound, silent movies began to fade from the memory of the movie-going public (Epilogue). What happened to these once-famous propaganda movies? Which of these movies, filmed on unstable, highly flammable cellulose silver nitrate, were recycled by their respective studios for their silver content? Which films were destroyed in studio vault fires or junked to save space? Which films were rescued and restored by the ongoing efforts of dedicated film historians, archivists, international cinémathèques, and nonprofit organizations? And which films were selected for preservation in the United States National Film Registry by the Library of Congress as being "culturally, historically or aesthetically significant"? Read on.

1

Watchful Waiting

Antiwar and Pro-War Films of 1915 and 1916

Nearly 50 years after the end of the bloody American Civil War, the country lay at peace.

When World War I erupted in Europe on July 28, 1914, the opinion of average Americans echoed that of President Woodrow Wilson (1856–1924), which was that the United States should maintain neutrality.

Of what concern was a faraway war to a rural farmer in the South? Or a poor African American struggling to eke out a living for his family? What about the eight million German Americans out of 92 million Americans living in the United States? Wouldn't they be frightened of receiving negative treatment if they expressed support for the German side in Europe? Or a poor Jewish or Italian immigrant working in a New York sweatshop? And what wife or mother would even want to contemplate sending a husband or son off to war in a foreign land? Bad enough that the United States had trouble on the southern border[1] with Mexican insurrectionists. The average American was far more interested in President Wilson's proclamation making May 14 Mother's Day. Or reading in the newspapers that Pittsburgh powerhouse hitter Honus Wagner (1874–1955) became the first baseball player to achieve 3,000 hits!

What about the new medium of film, rapidly becoming an important means of communicating new ideas to the American public? Some film companies were located on the East Coast: Edison Studios, founded by the great inventor Thomas Edison (1847–1931); Manhattan's Biograph Studios, founded by Harry Marvin (1862–1940); Brooklyn's Vitagraph Studios, founded by Englishmen J. Stuart Blackton (1875–1941) and Albert E. Smith (1875–1958). All of these companies used and paid enormous fees for Edison's patented film process.

The Silents Go to War

Other companies, unwilling to pay these fees, fled west to sunny California and developed their own movie-making processes.[2] Wherever the studio was located, however, there was silence on the European conflict. Studios made entertaining movies that Americans enjoyed: melodramas, comedies, Westerns. Audiences thrilled to cowboy star William Hart (1854–1946) in *The Bad Buck of Santa Ynez*, laughed at Charlie Chaplin (1889–1977) in *Kid Auto Races*, and cried over the Mary Pickford weepie melodrama *Hearts Adrift*. Female moviegoers mooned over the exotic Asian heartthrob Sessue Hayakawa as a seductive Japanese secret agent in *The Typhoon*, and men adored sexy Grace Cunard in Universal's first serial, *Lucille Love: The Girl of Mystery*. Popular too were movies about the recent invention of the airplane: *Across the Atlantic*, *The Aviator Spy*, and *The Aviator Traitor*, all centering on aviators and spies stealing planes, plans, and girls from one another.[3]

American opinion began to change when word came down in the late autumn of 1914 via newsreels and newspaper articles of real[4] or imagined atrocities committed by German troops against helpless Belgian and French civilians. Views were exaggerated, but because the American public had no outside means of communicating with Europe (the transatlantic cable between the United States and Europe had been cut at the outset of the war),[5] they believed the worst of German behavior. Some films shipped from European studios to American theater owners were openly anti–German: in the French-made *Horrors of War* a French family suffers at the hands of the Germans during the Franco-Prussian War; in the Italian-made *Woe to the Conqueror* a countess retrieves stolen plans from an enemy lieutenant (Teutonic) and causes his death. From England came *England's Menace*, with a "foreign" emperor deciding to invade England but having his spy code foiled by quick-thinking English children. The Germans responded with films deriding the French: *The Fall of France* depicting the triumph of German forces over the French in the Franco-Prussian War, and *Famous Battles of Napoleon* depicting Napoleon's defeat at the Battle of Waterloo with the help of German forces.[6] But to most of the American movie public, war in Europe was still a faraway occurrence, and at the end of 1914, they preferred light holiday fare: Charlie Chaplin cavorting in *His Prehistoric Past*, Mack Sennett's first comedy feature film *Tillie's Punctured Romance*, and the lovely Mary Pickford as *Cinderella*.

1. Watchful Waiting

1915

In January of 1915, the General Film Company (owned by publisher William Randolph Hearst) released the documentary *The History of the World's Greatest War*, highlighting both the plight of the Belgian people under the onslaught of the German army and the destruction of the Belgian city of Louvain, with actual footage of German troops destroying the old university's library containing priceless Gothic and Renaissance manuscripts.[7]

American public opinion worsened even more when the passenger ship *Lusitania* was sunk by a German U-boat[8] in the North Atlantic on May 7, 1915. A total of 1,198 people—including 128 Americans—were drowned. Although several New York newspapers published a warning by the German embassy in early May that Americans traveling on British ships in a war zone would do so at their own risk, the American public was outraged at the loss of life; the dead included women, children, and infants. President Woodrow Wilson issued a warning to Germany that it would face "strict accountability" if it continued to sink neutral United States passenger ships; Germany acquiesced, ordering submarines to avoid all passenger ships.

On July 24, 1915, the first case of German espionage in the United States was uncovered:

While shadowing German commercial attaché Heinrich Albert (1874–1960) on a New York City train, Secret Service agent Frank Burke (1869–1942) picked up the briefcase Albert left behind on the train. Documents in the briefcase indicated Germany was systematically funding United States pro–German newspapers as well as trying to block British purchases of war materials. President Wilson allowed newspapers to publish this information, setting off more fear and distrust of not only German spies operating in the United States, but the possibility that German Americans were aiding their efforts.

The film industry would now respond, but their opinions (as will be seen) were divided on the subject of about whether the United States should prepare for war or continue with the policy of cautious neutrality.

In August of 1915, the first anti–German, pro-preparedness film premiered: *The Battle Cry of Peace*, released August 6, 1915, by Vitagraph Pictures, co-directed by J. Stuart Blackton and Wilfred North. Cast: Charles Richman (John Harrison), L. Rogers Lytton (Mr. Emanon),[9] James W. Morrison (Charley Harrison), Mary Maurice (Mrs.

The Silents Go to War

Harrison), Louise Beaudet (Mrs. Vandergriff), Harold Hubert (Mr. Vandergriff), Captain John Crawford (Poet Scout), Charles Kent (The Master), Julia Swayne Gordon (Magdalen), Belle Bruce (Alice Harrison), Norma Talmadge (Virginia Vandergriff), Lucille Hammill (Dorothy Vandergriff), Thais Lawton (Columbia), Lionel Braham (The War Monster), William J. Ferguson (Abraham Lincoln), Paul Scardon (Ulysses S. Grant), Joseph Kilgour (George Washington). Plot[10]: Mr. Vandergriff is a prominent peace activist who refuses to see the possibility of an invasion by an unnamed country that has already invaded parts of Europe. His daughter Virginia's sweetheart, John, tries to persuade Mr. Vandergriff that the United States must prepare and stand ready to repel an invasion if necessary. Mr. Vandergriff has taken into his confidence a mysterious international diplomat named Mr. Emanon, who in reality is the mastermind of a network of enemy spies. At a peace rally chaired by Mr. Vandergriff, a naval attack is launched by enemy forces, who sail into New York City harbor and force the city to capitulate. Airplanes bomb Washington, D.C. John is killed defending Virginia from assault by enemy troops. Mrs. Harrison then kills Virginia, Virginia's sister Dorothy, and herself to avoid rape by enemy troops. In a coda, the National Guard (inspired by the ghosts of General Ulysses S. Grant, Abraham Lincoln, and George Washington) and with aid from the United States Army and Navy, defeat enemy forces and take back New York City and the rest of the country.

The backstory: English-born director J. Stuart Blackton was one of the founders of Vitagraph Studios and the father of American animation.[11] Blackton believed that the United States should join the Allies involved in World War I overseas and resolved to make a film highlighting the dangers of being unprepared for such a conflict, as well as the possibility of German espionage and sabotage within the United States. He enlisted the aid of former President Theodore Roosevelt, who persuaded his friend General Leonard Wood (United States Army) to lend Blackton an entire regiment of Marines to use in the climactic battle scenes. Although Blackton never explicitly identified the invaders as Germans, their battle dress and actions were distinctly Teutonic. The film was well received by the filmgoing public upon release due to the timely subject matters of preparedness and espionage/sabotage.

Critical response: *The New York Times*, in a August 7, 1915, review, noted that the picture has "the accent of authority by the presence on screen of Admiral Dewey, General Wood and Secretary

1. Watchful Waiting

Garrison." The review also mentioned battle scenes including "the advancing fleet of the enemy and the Capitol at Washington crumbling." While praising the special effects, the review noted that "'The Battle Cry of Peace' was a sometimes lurid argument for the immediate and radical improvement of our national defenses."[12] *Variety*'s review noted: "'The Battle Cry of Peace" came into the field at a moment when every American is faced with the realization [that] this country is in a general state of what is termed 'unpreparedness.'" As such, the review continued, "it is a film that will come in for nation-wide discussion."[13]

As for the reaction of prominent German American newspapers, which were read throughout the nation, the pro–German weekly *Fatherland*[14] kept silent until June of 1916, when it issued a scathing review. The editor, George Sylvester Viereck,[15] then editorialized that the film was an "atrocity" bankrolled by a "secret British propaganda fund."[16] The conservative *Staats-Zeitung* had no comment at all.[17] William Randolph Hearst's German language newspaper *Deutsches Journal*, with its large German American readership, opted to state in its September 1915 review that the film was "a sensational photoplay, by far the most tremendous film" ever shown at New York's Vitagraph Theater.[18] German American newspaper reviews aside, *The Battle Cry of Peace* was a big moneymaker, grossing more than $1 million.[19]

American filmgoers were then given a look at the German perspective in September of 1915: *The German Side of the War*, an American news film compiled from newsreels released by the *Chicago Tribune* shot by cameramen Edwin F. Weigle and Joseph Patterson in Belgium. The film premiered to sold-out crowds at the 44th Street Theatre in New York City. It generated such interest that the line for tickets extended several blocks, and many moviegoers were forced to buy tickets from scalpers. *The New York Times* estimated that 150,000 people saw the film in the first three weeks of its engagement.[20]

Filmgoer movie tastes in the late fall were titillated by the November release of Mutual Film Corporation's *Inspiration*, featuring actress Audrey Munson[21] posing nude, and the December release by Paramount Pictures of *The Cheat*, featuring Japanese-born matinee idol Sessue Hayakawa[22] as the villain, a mysterious rich Burmese ivory merchant who uses a branding iron on a woman when she refuses his advances.

The Silents Go to War

1916

On March 24, 1916, the French cross-channel passenger ferry *Sussex* was torpedoed without warning by a German submarine. The ship was severely damaged and 80 people died, with numerous passengers injured, including three Americans. This prompted President Wilson to declare that if Germany continued the practice of sinking unarmed passenger ships, the United States would sever relations with Germany. Germany tried to appease the United States by issuing on May 4, 1916, the *Sussex* pledge, which promised that passenger ships would not be targeted, merchant ships would not be sunk until the presence of weapons had been established, and merchant ships would not be sunk without provision for the safety of passengers and crew.

April of 1916 saw the release of the first major antiwar/pacifist themed movie: *Civilization*, released on April 17, 1916,[23] by Triangle Film Corporation, directed by Thomas Ince, Reginald Barker, and Raymond West. Cast: Howard C. Hickman (Count Ferdinand), Herschel Mayall (The King of Wredpryd), George Fisher (The Christ), Enid Markey (Katheryn Haldemann), Lola May (Queen Eugenie), J. Frank Burke (the peace advocate), Charles K. French (the prime minister), J. Barney Sherry (the blacksmith), Jerome Storm (the blacksmith's son), Ethel Ullman (The blacksmith's daughter), Kate Bruce (a mother). Plot[24]: In the peaceful kingdom of Wredpryd, war breaks out when the king decides he wants to acquire more territory and increase his power. The women start a peace movement called the Mothers of Men. Count Ferdinand (one of the king's courtiers), the inventor of a new submarine, is assigned to command the new ship in battle. The king orders the count to sink the *ProPatricia*, a civilian ship that is believed to be carrying munitions as well as civilian passengers. On board the submarine, the count has a vision of what will happen if he sends a torpedo crashing into ship, and balks at the thought, knowing that his crew will carry out the order. The count fights with the crew and blows up his own submarine, sending it (and the crew) to the bottom of the sea. The count's soul descends into Purgatory, where he meets Jesus Christ. Jesus tells the count that he can find redemption by returning to the living world as a voice for peace. Jesus inhabits the count's body and goes back to earth. Once there, the king orders the count's execution for failing to follow his orders to sink the ship. The women's peace movement holds a rally and pleads with the king to end the war. The king decides to visit the count's cell before execution. The count is found dead in his cell, but the

1. Watchful Waiting

spirit of Jesus emerges and takes the king on a walk through the battlefields to show him the carnage of war. The king repents, stops the war, and signs a peace treaty with his enemies, the soldiers return home, and peace is declared.

The backstory: Director Thomas Ince (1880–1924) was a pioneering director/producer. By 1916, Ince had his own production company (called Inceville) and had complete say over all his films.[25] Ince secured President Woodrow Wilson's appearance in the film's prologue, photographed in Ince's private home, Shadow Hills. Ince also commissioned a "Peace Song" and a march, both composed by Victor Schertzinger,[26] to be included in the film score and issued as sheet music for the public. In an interview with the *Los Angeles Times* before the film's preview, George Fisher (1891–1960), who played The Christ in the film, told the paper that, in order to get into the proper mood for the role, "he lived the life of a recluse, spending his time in study and meditation."[27] The film was a popular success with filmgoers (making $800,000 in profits) and was used by the Democratic National Convention to help re-elect Wilson as the United States president in 1916.[28]

Critical response: The film received decidedly mixed reviews. Upon its premiere in Los Angeles in April 1916, *Los Angeles Times* critic Henry Christeen Warnack was troubled by the depiction of The Christ and wrote that the film "is not daring, it is only in poor taste." He opined that it was offensive to the belief of Christians, Jews, and atheists alike:

> The play will ... be popular with everyone with the exception of three classes: It will probably prove offensive to Christians because they are likely to think of it as irreverent; to the Hebrew it will seem mystical and exaggerated; the non-churchgoer will find it absurd and undramatic. Outside of the Christian, the Jew and the unbeliever, I haven't the slightest doubt of its appeal.[29]

In their October 21, 1916, review, *The La Crosse Tribune* of Wisconsin called the film "a masterpiece" and the "Biggest Spectacle in History of Motion Pictures."[30] The September 15, 1916, review from *The Fairbanks Daily Times* declared: "Had such a picture as 'Civilization' been shown to the people of Europe before the war started there would have been no war."[31]

The reaction of the two prominent German American newspapers was surprisingly muted. In his June 24, 1916, issue George Sylvester Viereck of *The Fatherland* noted only that "a film is now exhibited under the title of '*Civilization*.'"[32] The *Staats-Zeitung* wrote: "The film is harmless in this realm compared to what has been achieved by others."[33]

The Silents Go to War

Hearst's *Deutches Journal* applauded: "The skills on display [in *Civilization*], both in terms of acting and its overall staging, provide genuine pleasure and the film as a whole is an achievement worthy of respect."[34]

Next up in June came a movie that directly attacked pacifism: *The Fall of a Nation*, released on June 2, 1916, by Dixon Studios, directed by Thomas Dixon, Jr. Cast: Lorraine Huling (Virginia Holland), Percy Standing (Charles Waldron/Prince Karl Von Waldron), Arthur Shirley (John Vassar), Flora Macdonald (Angela Benda), Paul Willis (Billy), Phil Gastrock (Tomasso Bendo), Clarence Geldert (General Arnold). Plot[35]: After the sinking of the *Lusitania*, American millionaire Charles Waldron (actually Prince Karl Von Waldron) assists a German conspiracy (helped by German immigrant traitors) to overthrow the American government. America is caught unprepared, and a large German force, known as the European Confederation Army, invades the country and begins executing citizens. After suffering under German rule for two years, a suffragette named Virginia Holland, with the aid of former Congressman John Vassar, organizes a secret rebel army known as the Daughters of Jael.[36]

Designated female members seduce German officers for vital information.[37] Armed with this information, the army members stage a revolt against the occupying soldiers, drive out the Germans, and restore the country back to American rule. Virginia and John make plans to marry.

The backstory: Director Thomas Dixon Jr. (1864–1946) considered *The Fall of a Nation* to be the sequel to D. W. Griffith's great 1915 success *Birth of a Nation*. Dixon was a good friend of D. W. Griffith, who had adapted Dixon's 1905 novel *The Klansman* into *Birth of a Nation*. Dixon was able to persuade well-known operetta composer Victor Herbert[38] to compose the score. He was not successful in persuading President Woodrow Wilson, a personal friend, to endorse the movie. Upon reading the plot synopsis, the president wrote to Dixon that "the thing is a great mistake."[39] Dixon also caricatures (without naming them) peace advocates William Jennings Bryan and Henry Ford in the movie.[40] After its initial release, the film did not attract large numbers of filmgoers, and was considered a commercial failure.

Critical response: *The New York Times* in a June 7, 1916, review said that there are "a few points that offend against good taste and several points that outrage the intelligence, but many stretches of the film are finely spectacular, and it is full of battlefields and such pictures of avenging cavalry sweeping across moonlit country roads as the movies do particularly well."[41] *Variety* noted that the film caricatured German

1. Watchful Waiting

invaders and immigrant traitors, "twenty thousand [of whom] rise and capture New York from the National Guard."[42]

The German American press had no problem in condemning the film. George Sylvester Viereck of *The Fatherland* called the movie

> an abortion whose one purpose is to traduce the German race and make the German people appear as enemies of the United States. Any American with a drop of German blood in his veins must have his feelings outraged by the attempts to show Germans as invaders resorting to the most fiendish violations of humanity.... Nothing in the category of bestiality is omitted in order to incense public sentiment against the German people."[43]

William Randolph Hearst's *Deutsches Journal* wrote that, "following the general *Zeitgeist*,[44] it is once again the evil 'Hyphens'[45] who were cast as the villains," but that the film was compelling "because the battle sequences have been achieved through incredible technical expertise" and offered "splendid military scenes."[46]

On July 30, 1916, Black Tom Island[47] in New York Harbor, a repository for U.S.-made munitions, was the site of an explosion that killed four people and destroyed some $20 million worth of arms and ammunitions destined for Russia. In addition, the blast damaged the nearby Statue of Liberty. Initially, the police determined that the explosion was likely an accident, but an investigation was launched by the nascent United States Intelligence Service. Eventually, German saboteurs were found to be responsible.[48]

The end of September 1916 brought a movie that asked the question: To what lengths would a mother go to prevent her son from serving in a foreign war?

If My Country Should Call, released on September 25, 1916, by Universal Pictures, directed by Joseph De Grasse. Cast: Dorothy Phillips (Margaret Ardrath), Jack Nelson (Donald), Lon Chaney Jr. (Dr. George Ardrath), Helen Leslie (Patricia Landon), Frank Whitson (Robert Ogden), Albert MacQuarrie (Colonel Belden), Gretchen Lederer (Mrs. Ardrath), Adele Farrington (Mrs. Landon). Plot[49]: Mrs. Ardrath calls a family meeting to discuss the proposed marriage of her daughter Margaret to Englishman Robert Ogden. Colonel Beldon, a family friend, is also there and remarks that Robert would make a good soldier if his country should need him. Margaret has an aversion to war and fighting and dreams that one day, Robert will be called back to fight for his country. Right before their wedding, Margaret has a fainting fit, and her uncle Dr. George Ardrath gives her a special tonic. He also tells her of a new drug, a cardiac depressant, that can produce the symptoms of a weak heart, but that too large a dose can kill. Margaret and Robert marry and have a son, Donald. Robert is overseas when the war begins, and he writes home that he has enlisted to fight for his mother country. Donald temporarily takes over the family business and becomes engaged to Patricia Landon. When Margaret learns that Donald plans to enlist in the armed forces to fight the Mexican army down at the border,[50] she panics and takes matters into her own hands. She steals a small bottle of the heart depressant from the medical bag of her uncle George when he leaves the bag unattended. She begins to slip small amounts of the drug into Donald's drinks, which begins to cause Donald heart problems. Mrs. Landon tells Patricia that she cannot think of marrying an invalid, and Patricia breaks their engagement, marrying a millionaire not long after. Donald becomes a drunkard. When Dr. Ardrath examines Donald, he finds his heart in perfect health and realizes the symptoms are caused by the cardiac depressant. Donald finally realizes that his mother's scheme has cost him Patricia's love. Then, a messenger arrives with news that Robert has died overseas. Margaret decides to kill herself using the remnants of the medication. She goes downstairs, but trips and falls down the stairs. When she wakes up, she realizes that she has been dreaming, and rushes into Robert's arms just as a newsboy shouts that the war has ended.

The backstory: Director Joseph De Grasse (1873–1940) tapped into the topicality of the movie's theme, as many American men were then signing up to fight in Mexico and overseas in the European conflict. This was the 44th film that De Grasse and star Lon Chaney (1883–1930) had worked on together between 1914 and 1916.[51]

Critical response: In the October 7, 1916, issue, *Moving Picture World* said: "This rather harrows the feelings at times, but is modern and dramatic. It presents problems that have been threshed out in the hearts of many women during the past two years. The presentation is acceptable throughout. The cast is pleasing."[52]

On October 16, 1916, birth control activist Margaret Sanger opened a family planning and birth control clinic at 46 Amboy Street in Brooklyn, New York, the first of its kind in the United States. Nine Days after the clinic opened, Sanger was arrested for breaking a New York State law that prohibited distribution of contraceptives.

Less than one month later, a pacifist movie opened with the same controversial topic: does a woman have the right to decide on her own reproductive rights, or does the state decide for her?

War Brides, released on November 12, 1916, by Selznick Pictures,

1. Watchful Waiting

directed by Herbert Brenon. Cast: Alla Nazimova (Joan),[53] Charles Hutchison (George), Charles Bryant (Franz), William Bailey (Eric), Richard Barthelmess (Arno),[54] Nila Mack (Amelia), Gertrude Berkeley (the mother), Alex Shannon (the king), Robert Whitworth (Lieutenant Hoffman), Ned Burton (Captain Bragg), Theodora Warfield (Minna, the sister), Charles Chailles (a financier). Plot[55]: Joan is a worker who has successfully led a strike against the grasping owner of the factory in which she and her fellow peasants work. She meets a young farmer named Franz at a picnic; they fall in love and then marry soon after. She and Franz are newlyweds when war breaks out. Franz and his brothers George, Eric, and youngest brother Arno are called to the front. They leave behind Joan, their mother, and their sister Minna. All four brothers die in battle and Joan considers suicide but decides against it because she is pregnant; a sewing basket filled with baby garments reminds Joan that she must be responsible for a child who will be born fatherless. Then, the government decrees that all unmarried women (including widows) must be compelled to marry returning soldiers to ensure a new generation of manpower for future wars. Joan goes among the women of her village, arguing against permitting themselves to be made victims and tools of the ruling powers. This action brings Joan under the displeasure of the military authorities, and when she persuades her sister-in-law Minna not to become the war bride of the village commander Lieutenant Hoffman, she is arrested and ordered to be shot. When the authorities learn that she is to be a mother, the order is rescinded and she is sent to jail. She learns from her female jailer that the king is to pass through her village. She escapes and leads a procession of women to protest the war and the government decree. Soldiers try to hold her back and threaten to shoot her, but she manages to come face to face with the king and, in protest, kills herself in front of him. Her final words are: "If you will not give us women the right to vote for or against the war, I shall not bear a child for such a country."

The backstory: The film was based on the play by poet/playwright/suffragist Marion Craig Wentworth (1872–1942) and was a success on the Broadway stage in 1915. Alla Nazimova, who played the part of Joan on the stage, was enticed by producer Lewis J. Selznick[56] to recreate her role of Joan in the film for the salary of $1,000 a day. Selznick invested heavily to publicize the film, taking ads in the influential trade journals *Motion Picture News*[57] and *Moving Picture World*,[58] as well as targeting the large immigrant German population in the Wisconsin area with a full-page ad in the influential *Sheboygan Press*.[59] Selznick's investment

The Silents Go to War

Alla Nazimova (second from right) as German war widow Joan defending her fellow war widows from lustful German soldiers in the 1916 Selznick Pictures production of *War Brides*. The movie created considerable controversy due to its theme of women's reproductive rights (World History Archive/Alamy Stock Photo).

paid off; when the film opened at New York's Broadway Theatre on November 12, 1916 (at two dollars a ticket), it was a huge hit with filmgoers (especially women, who espoused Nazimova as a champion of women's rights) and made Selznick Pictures a profit of $300,000. Women around the country flocked to see the picture, considering the theme of a female as a "woman troop breeder" to be an afront to American womanhood. Nazimova herself told a reporter from *The New York American* that her decision to appear as a figure of suffrage in *War Brides* was intended to be a contribution to "the womanhood of the world."[60]

Critical response: *The New York Times* in a November 13, 1916, review was full of praise for Nazimova's performance, raving that "Mme. Nazimova's marvelously mobile face, capable of indicating varying shades of emotion, especially those of sorrow, is a priceless asset for the dumb show of the screen." They were less enamored of the film's attempt to expand itself beyond the stage original, and were critical of director Herbert Brenon's attempt at filming battle scenes: "With such

1. Watchful Waiting

pictures as those of the battle of the Somme on view there should be a law against photoplay directors photographing sham martial scenes, or else to force them to make scenes approximating reality." Nonetheless, the review did feel that Mme. Nazimova "screens well, which, translated, means that she is a good object for motion picture photography, always a consummation devoutly to be wished for; and what is more to her credit, since it is the result of her intelligence and not her good fortune, she knows how to express herself in terms of the film."[61]

Moving Picture World was also highly complimentary of the film, with their December 21 review by Edward Weitzel stating that the drama of *War Brides* "reaches a tragic height never before attained by a moving picture." It considered the ending "like a flash of lightening and one of the most powerful ever seen on film."[62]

On November 10, Woodrow Wilson was certified for a second term as president of the United States. His slogan "he kept us out of war" helped him eke out a narrow victory against Republican Charles Evans Hughes, a former justice of the Supreme Court.

American filmmakers ushered in the holiday season with offerings including rising young comedian Harold Lloyd (as his Chaplin knock-off character Lonesome Luke) cavorting in a short film titled *Luke's Preparedness Preparations*; *Less Than Dust*, a Mary Pickford melodrama set in India (she plays a white girl raised as a boy in colonial India); and Jules Verne's fantasy adventure *20,000 Leagues Under the Sea* (featuring a super submarine named the *Nautilus*).

On Christmas day, a pro-war movie spectacle premiered that would use the story of the warrior maid Joan of Arc as an accolade to France, bookending sequences set during World War I involving an English soldier inspired by Joan's bravery: *Joan the Woman*, released on December 25, 1916, by Paramount Pictures, directed by Cecil B. DeMille. Cast: Geraldine Farrar (Jeanne d'Arc, a.k.a. Joan of Arc), Raymond Hatton (Charles VII), Hobart Bosworth (General La Hire), Theodore Roberts (Bishop Cauchon), Wallace Reid (Eric Trent 1431/Eric Trent 1916), Charles Clary (La Tremouille), James Neill (Laxart), Tully Marshall (L'Oiseleur), Lawrence Peyton (Gaspard), Horace B. Carpenter (Jacques d'Arc), Cleo Ridgley (the king's favorite), Lillian Leighton (Isambeau), Marjorie Daw (Katherine), Ernest Joy (Robert de Beaudricourt), John Oaker (Jean de Metz), Hugo B. Koch (Duke of Burgundy), William Conklin (John of Luxembourg), Walter Long (the executioner), William Elmer (Guy Townes), Emilius Jorgensen (Michael). Small uncredited roles: Donald Crisp, Jack Hoxie, Lucien Littlefield (English soldiers),

The Silents Go to War

Nigel De Brulier (man at Joan's trial), Fred Kohler (L'Oiseleur's henchman), Ramon Novarro (starving peasant). Plot[63]: In 1916, Eric Trent is a young British soldier digging a trench near German lines. He pulls a sword out of the wall of the trench. When he removes it, the ghost of Joan of Arc is conjured up, and she tells him her story. Jeanne d'Arc is a peasant girl living on her parents' farm in Domrémy-la-Pucelle, France. France is at war with the English, and English soldiers come to pillage the farm, where one of the Englishmen is knocked out by a French deserter hiding in the barn. Jeanne takes pity on him, nurses him back to health, and they fall in love. However, just as Trent proposes to Jeanne she has a vision: an angel appears to her to tell her of her mission to go to King Charles VII and rally French forces to fight the English in the name of God. Trent leaves in frustration as Jeanne goes to the local governor, who believes in her and arranges an audience with the king. The king is dissolute, holding wild parties at court while under the influence of a shady financier called "the Spider." When Jeanne arrives, "the Spider" tries to convince the king that she is a phony and suggests "testing her" by leading her into a room without telling her who the king is and seeing if she can identify him without his crown. She does so and persuades the king to give her soldiers and weapons to fight the English. Some of the nobles rebel, but Jeanne convinces them of her patriotism and zeal. Jeanne leads her forces, including the loyal General La Hire, in lifting the siege of the town of Orleans and routs the English. Among the English prisoners captured is Eric Trent, but Jeanne sees to it that he is well treated. "The Spider" conspires with Bishop Cauchon to discredit Jeanne by spreading rumors that Jeanne plans to usurp the throne and become queen of France. This isn't enough to stop the coronation, so the bishop tries poisoning the king's wine. Jeanne has another vision and warns the king of the poisoned wine. The king tries it on a servant, who dies instantly. The king dismisses the bishop but can't execute him for fear of offending the Church. Jeanne and her forces continue to win victories in France and drive out the English. When the king offers her anything she asks as a reward, she requests two boons: free Eric Trent and grant her home village freedom from taxation forever. The king complies. Trent thanks her for saving his life a second time, and they nearly confess their love for each other, but Jeanne's devotion to the cause of France prevents it. She knows from her visions that she has only a short time to live. When Cauchon informs the English that Jeanne will be traveling with a small party of soldiers on a certain road, they send Trent and his men to capture her. Trent initially refuses, but he

1. Watchful Waiting

must obey orders from his English king. Jeanne is put up for ransom, with the English agreeing to give her to the highest bidder. Jeanne hopes that Charles VII will ransom her, but instead, Cauchon buys her and brings her to trial before the church on charges of heresy for hearing saints' voices, having visions, and wearing men's clothing. She denies being a heretic, but when the ecclesiastical interrogators use torture, she breaks down and signs a document condemning herself. Trent tries to rescue her, but the attempt fails. General La Hire and some of his soldiers appeal to the king for help during a wild orgy, but he appears too drunk and debauched to understand. Joan is convicted of heresy and is sentenced to burn at the stake. Trent attends the burning, and as Jeanne walks up to the pyre, he gives her a small cross. As she burns, he cries out, "We have burned a saint!"

The story returns to 1916, and the young British soldier, inspired by Joan's story, accepts a suicide mission to carry a bomb across no man's land and into enemy trenches. He is caught in a German searchlight and shot, but with his dying strength he hurls the bomb and destroys the enemy trench as the ghost of Joan triumphantly hovers over him.

The backstory: When director Cecile B. DeMille (1881–1959) decided to film an epic on Joan of Arc, he and his screenwriter Jeanie MacPherson (1886–1946) ignored all of the historical documentation dating from the medieval period detailing Joan's life and achievements. Instead, their main sources of information were the *Encyclopædia Britannica* and Friedrich Schiller's 1801 play *The Maid of Orleans,* in which Schiller (falsely) asserts that Joan refrains from killing an English soldier when she falls in love with him. DeMille and MacPherson took Schiller's soldier as their inspiration for Joan's love interest, the fictitious English soldier Eric Trent. DeMille cast film heartthrob Wallace Reid (1891–1923)[64] as Eric Trent, and for the role of Joan, he chose Metropolitan Opera soprano Geraldine Farrar (1882–1967). Farrar had previously starred in DeMille's 1915 silent adaptation of Georges Bizet's opera *Carmen,* earning good reviews. She was, however, a suspected Germanophile; she'd been educated in Berlin, and made her operatic debut in 1901 at the *Berlin Hofoper.* Reputed to have had a love affair with German Crown Prince Wilhelm, she hoped that her performance as Joan of Arc would result in filmgoers regarding her in a more favorable light.[65] DeMille had been given a budget of $300,000 for his epic, partially as the result of the success of D. W. Griffith's 1915 *Birth of a Nation,* with the hope that the picture would resonate with audiences as a piece of patriotic propaganda. DeMille used a new color process[66] invented for him by his studio technicians, engravers Max Handschiegl and Alvin W. Wyckoff, which allowed for the striking use of color against a monochrome background to highlight key sections of the film, especially the fiery scene of Joan being burned at the stake while her erstwhile boyfriend Eric Trent looks on. DeMille hired theatrical impresario David Belasco's composer William Furst to write an orchestral score that would be synchronized with various projection speeds. To promote the picture, exhibitors decorated the lobbies of first-run theaters with suits of armor, historical costumes, colorful banners, and murals framed by drapery embroidered with the French fleur-de-lis.[67] DeMille traveled to New York City for the 1916 Christmas Eve premiere at the 44th Street Theatre, and Farrar went to Boston to promote the film, but it was not considered a box office success, earning only $600,000 nationwide. Many theater owners complained of the film's length—13 reels, making the film over two hours in running time—which meant that they could not schedule the customary two matinees and two evening shows per day, cutting into their profits. Eventually, DeMille agreed to cut the film to eight reels.[68] Additionally, the egregious inclusion of the latter day Eric Trent as Joan's lover offended numerous religious filmgoers, and the film had little resonance with audiences around the country.[69]

Critical reviews: *Variety*'s December 29, 1916,[70] review lauded the film, saying that "it is impossible to describe in detail what producer DeMille accomplished with such a wealth of material. Suffice it to say that no one else could have done more and few, if any, could have done as much." Writing for *The Motion Picture News* issue of January 6, 1917,[71] columnist Peter Milne declared: "'Joan the Woman' is a triumph for Geraldine Farrar but equally for Cecil DeMille. Through his long picture he has interpolated the personal and the spectacular with the fine result of dramatic contrast." George Blaisdell of *Moving Picture World* concurred, stating in his January 13, 1917, review[72]: "If anything in the way of evidence were needed to convince the photoplay-going public that Cecil B. DeMille belongs in the front rank of the day, 'Joan the Woman' should supply it in full measure."

The year 1916 had been a tumultuous one for the United States, with both antiwar and pro-war opinions dividing the country. Still, America maintained a fragile international neutrality stance as 1917 was about to begin.

2

The War Begins

The Committee on Public Information and Films of 1917

On January 31, 1917, the German government declared its decision to resume unrestricted submarine warfare against neutral shipping. By March 1917, five American merchant ships had been sunk, resulting in the loss of many lives and outraging the American public. Further inflaming American wrath was the March munitions explosion at the Mare Island Naval Shipyard in Vallejo, California, the work of German saboteur Lothar Witzke (1895–1962).[1] But the final catalyst for the entry of the United States into World War I was the Zimmermann Telegram,[2] which proposed a military alliance between Germany and Mexico, offering the American states of Texas, Arizona, and New Mexico to Mexico in return for their commitment to the German cause. The contents of the telegram were released to the American public on March 1, 1917, generating tremendous indignation and support for an American declaration of war against Germany. On April 2, 1917, President Woodrow Wilson asked a joint session of Congress to declare war on the German Empire, citing that the war would "make the world safe for democracy." On April 6, 1917, Congress declared war.

Adding to the war fever was a militant propaganda epic released a few days later that reinforced the need for preparedness: *Womanhood, the Glory of the Nation*, released on April 9, 1917, produced by Vitagraph Pictures, directed by J. Stuart Blackton and William P. S. Earle. Cast: Alice Joyce (Mary Ward), Harry T. Morey (Paul Strong), Joseph Kilgour (Marshal Prince Dario), Walter McGrail (Count Dario), James Morrison (Phillip Ward), Naomi Childers (Jane Strong), Mary Maurice (Julia Strong), Templar Saxe (Baron Reyva), Bobby Connelly (the little boy), Edward Elkas (Ortos), Bernard Siegel (Carl, the spy), Theodore Roosevelt (himself). Plot[3]: Mary Ward, returning from Ruritania (Germany)

The Silents Go to War

to the United States by way of the Orient, learns in Manila that war has been declared, New York captured, and her mother and sister killed. Paul Strong, in Manila at the time, is called home, and he and Mary travel together, he being appointed minister of energies on his arrival. Count Dario of Ruritania has sought Mary's hand in marriage, and she had promised to give him an answer when they meet in New York, not knowing of the war plans; she finds him an officer of the invaders. To help her country, she joins forces with the count, and does valuable service as a spy, but is compelled to witness the shooting of Paul's sister, who had won the title of the "American Joan of Arc" for her recruiting of arms and soldiers to fight against the invaders. Count Dario is shot by his father, the prince, for disobedience of orders. Paul rallies the troops, and with a new naval war engine called the "firebugs," the Ruritanian army and navy are wiped out. Mary's brother Phillip, blinded during the war, is cared for by Paul's sister Jane, disfigured by enemy troops. Paul and Mary are reunited and look forward to peace and prosperity once again.

The backstory: This was another propaganda epic by J. Stuart Blackton, considered to be a sequel to his 1915 film *The Battle Cry of Peace*. So compelling was the film that it was endorsed by the Daughters of the American Revolution, the National Preparedness Society, The American Defense League, the National Security Society, and the Navy League, with plans for a nationwide publicity campaign by these organizations to make sure that every able-bodied man would see this film.[4] As he did in *The Battle Cry of Peace*, former President Theodore Roosevelt makes a guest appearance as himself in the film. Vitagraph's publicity department mounted a massive campaign aimed at film exhibitors nationwide, sending out extensive publicity and advertising plan books, including advertising advanced seat sales, having tickets printed so that they were only good for one particular performance, plus advertising matinee tickets at discount prices. The strategies proved successful, and the film was a rousing success.[5]

Critical response: *The New York Times* excoriated the film in a April 2, 1917, review[6] headlined "Feeble War Film Shown. 'Womanhood The Glory Of The Nation,' Is A Plea For Preparedness":

> The most interesting part of the first exhibition of a new preparedness picture called "Womanhood, the Glory of the Nation" at the Broadway Theatre was not the eight reels of melodramatic film, but the interlude of speeches provided by J. Stuart Blackton and Burr MacIntosh. Mr. Blackton spoke of the Bryans, Stones, and La Follettes as mollycoddles, and asked his auditors

2. The War Begins

to consider what a nation of 100,000,000 Bryans would be compared with a like number of Roosevelts. Mr. McIntosh gave excerpts from the preparedness speech he has been making at intervals in the last ten years.

There was no denying the psychological aspect of the occasion, with its flags, its patriotic tunes and speeches on the eve of the meeting of what will probably be a war Congress, and the audience clapped and cheered and hissed with great abandon. The loudest cheers came with the mention of Theodore Roosevelt's name or the showing of his picture, and for Mr. McIntosh's suggestion that when Major General [Leonard] Wood reached Washington on his way South he should receive an order to report to the War Department to become its Secretary, and that Mr. Roosevelt be made Secretary of the Navy.

"Womanhood, the Glory of the Nation" is an inartistic and ineffective picture. It purports to show what might happen to the United States in its present unprepared condition, and for the purposes of its argument assumes that an alien army of 150,000 men has landed on these shores and captured New York. Hidden trick trenches, vast "invisible" mines, and a fleet of wireless controlled "firebugs" which are full of an inflammable substance that surrounds the enemy fleets and consumes them, conspire to rout the "Ruthanians." It is to be hoped that no enemy spies in the audience will send these secrets abroad.

Variety's April 6, 1917,[7] review was also on the negative side:

In an effort to put out a wonderful photodrama and at the same time an effective and compelling argument for preparedness, Vitagraph in "Womanhood" has overshot the mark, and overplayed the game, thereby weakening the effort as a whole. The scenario by H.W. Bergman, leads to plenty of heavy dramatic work, with a love episode an impressive feature and the hinge on which the development of the plot hangs, but with the memory of other preparedness plays comparatively fresh it is easy to see where the blowing up of fake battleships, and the bombing of trenches, and the lurid glare of burning villages, and the marching and fighting of armies, and the general wreck, ruin and devastation of a campaign of invasion, have had their force lessened by too constant and insistent repetition, and when in an attack by airships of New York the whole lower part of the city is shattered, it seems rather strange that enemy marksmen moving swiftly through the air should be able to spare such notable structures as the Woolworth tower and the big municipal buildings. Preparedness is sorely needed, but much stronger arguments can be made for it than "Womanhood" represents. The cast leaves nothing to be desired. As propaganda of a certain kind it is excellent, but in spite of all its hurrah it leaves a feeling of disappointment that no more powerful argument has been presented for the cause that has been shown along not dissimilar lines many times before.

Both the *New York Dramatic Mirror* and *Moving Picture World* held entirely different views. The *New York Dramatic Mirror* lauded the film in a April 7, 1917, review,[8] heaping praise on the photodrama:

> "Womanhood, the Glory of the Nation," Greater Vitagraph's militant film spectacle which began an indefinite run at the Broadway Theatre, New York, last Sunday night, will be one of the most convincing evidences of the value of motion pictures in a time like the present. It is the most powerful of arguments for preparedness and the least enthusiastic American could scarcely fail to be stirred by the fervor of its patriotic purpose. The producers are to be congratulated upon having, at a vital time, released a spectacle which should aid recruiting and bring home to the people of this country the necessity of preparing against the possibility of alien invasion.
>
> The premiere was an occasion for a patriotic outburst. When J. Stuart Blackton was introduced by Burr McIntosh and gave a rapid-fire talk on preparedness he was applauded to the echo. Burr McIntosh followed with a smashing address, in which pacifist leaders were flayed and the cause of patriotism given a stirring impetus. His speech brought cheers. All this occurred during intermission.
>
> As a picture "Womanhood" ranks with the best of its kind. It tells of the capture of New York and Philadelphia by a foreign power, whose identity was thinly veiled under the name "Ruritania." An American girl, inspired as was Joan of Arc, aids recruiting and is captured and murdered by the invaders. Her brother becomes Director of Energies and through him, and by the aid of Mary Ward, serving as a spy, the tables are finally turned and the invading army annihilated. The battle scenes are immense; the incidental action vivid, the pathos convincing. Alice Joyce as Mary gives a sympathetic portrayal and Harry Morey presents a powerful characterization in the role of Paul Strong. Naomi Childers is a pathetic and appealing figure as the martyred modern Joan. The others in their respective roles are excellent. The photoplay is clear throughout and the scenes effective. The direction results in the swift and inspiring development of a story which is fraught with calamitous moments, but which ends with America triumphant, as she must ever be. "There is a tone of sincerity to the film which deserves the success it will undoubtedly receive."

In the April 21, 1917, issue,[9] *Moving Picture World* columnist Louis Reeves Harrison echoed the same view:

> "Womanhood" is in every respect a finer example of artistry than "The Battle Cry of Peace," primarily because the story is not continually broken by preachment. The subtitles of great vigor fit naturally into the composition, a harmonious part of it, enhancing rather than destroying interest. With the same obvious purpose in view, "Womanhood" reaches deeper into the sympathies of an audience and will on that very account make a more profound impression. "The Battle Cry of Peace" was an intellectual argument. "Womanhood" is an inspiring appeal to chivalry, to manhood, to ennobling

2. The War Begins

sentiments which lie deep and strong in the American heart, though almost smothered by material prosperity.

High tension is set up from the start by the elimination of all but essential activities among the main characters, the story scenes flashing along at high speed, with an occasional relief of large assemblies from real life, one intensifying the other in cleverly arranged structure. The unrelaxed grip on emotion is especially valuable in driving home imprinted sentiment—the mind of the spectator is reached through his heart. There is a story continuously and successfully presented in the midst of a grand spectacle.

There is no fault to find with Mr. Blackton's sincerity, none with his structure, none with his treatment; but it becomes quite obvious as the development proceeds that he is actuated largely by a sense of justice and a desire to arouse a fuller conception of the wrongs perpetrated by a mentally cunning and warlike nation—wrongs which may be brought home to us in bitter experience. The motif of the play is involved in a warning to prepare, with only a suggestion as to our deeper motives for entering a world conflict. There is no doubt that our people are deeply moved by the terrible wrong and injustice being done by a powerful autocracy in Europe—the fact that we have sent millions to relieve distress shows how we feel—but we have realized our own impotence, and have held aloof, with a hope that some adjustment might be reached in the European situation without our direct interference.

The Russian revolution has done much to transform our passive attitude into an active one, because the issue is fast becoming that of our own Revolutionary War, the issue of our Civil War. Those are issues we cannot evade, and they are suggested all too mildly in "Womanhood." The great world issue becomes ours when it is clearly defined as that of democracy in opposition to organized tyranny. Here and there, Mr. Blackton makes this point, and whenever he does the audience storms its approval. "As it is never too late to add an effective subtitle, he might interpolate that when this Gibraltar of democracy goes into the world war it will stay until there is neither Hohenzollern nor Hapsburg left to break world peace."

On April 13, 1917, Woodrow Wilson established the Committee on Public Information (CPI), the first state bureau covering propaganda in the history of the United States. Wilson selected experienced journalist George Creel to head the committee.

George Creel (1876–1953) was the son of Henry Clay Creel (1829–1907) and Virginia Fackler Creel (1845–1937). His father had served as a captain in the Confederate army during the American Civil War and became an alcoholic, squandering a $10,000 inheritance left to him by his father. His family (including two brothers, Wylie and Hal) moved periodically across Missouri, with their mother running a boarding house in Kansas City, Missouri, to support her family. Creel and his brothers were educated both at local public schools and later at home by Mrs. Creel, who received a classical education by tutors and teachers before her marriage. His mother ingrained in Creel belief in the power of the written word and love of literature: he read poetry, novels, newspapers, and American and English periodicals. In 1896, at the age of 21, George Creel got himself hired as a "society reporter" for the Kansas City *World*, churning out articles on lurid local scandals. Realizing that his qualifications would not have gained him "admission to the kindergarten class of modern journalism" he nonetheless decided to try his luck in New York City as a journalist. With no money or prospects he left Kansas City and arrived In New York in early February 1897.[10]

He found work as a joke writer for the *Evening Journal*, eventually selling freelance articles to the *Evening World* and the *American*. Creel came face to face with the "yellow journalism" reporting of William Randolph Hearst's *New York Journal* and declined a job at his paper. Creel disliked Hearst's newspaper style of emphasizing sensationalism over facts. In 1898, he struck up a friendship with a young poet named Arthur Grissom, who persuaded him to join him as an associate editor of a brand new opinion journal to be called *The Independent*, headquartered in Kanas City. It turned out to be a success, but Grissom returned to New York. He left Creel as the sole proprietor and editor-in-chief. Creel would transform *The Independent* into a voice for social activism for a faction of the local Democratic Party (the Rabbits) who advocated for worker's rights and lower taxes against another faction (the Goats), who were in the pay of big business. Creel's paper became the semi-official organ of the local reform movement, linking his weekly paper to the national reform movement of Theodore Roosevelt. He became a "muckraker[11] knight errant," doing battle against crooked cops, crooked judges, and crooked businessmen with the power of the pen.

By 1909, *The Independent* had crusaded on behalf of women's suffrage and women's rights and against medical hucksters, with Creel engaging in genuine investigative journalism to expose dangerous frauds and con artists. Growing bored, he looked for greener pastures, and found another paper he hoped to transform—the Denver *Post*, which offered him the position of editor-in-chief. The *Post* had acquired a reputation as "the Coney Island of journalism," permeated by yellow journalism. As editor, Creel hoped to remedy that with hard-hitting articles on the city's corrupt mayoral system, using written imagery to promote public initiative referendums, the right of recall, and a direct primary to elect senators. Unfortunately, his efforts yielded no results.

2. The War Begins

The power of the Denver political machine was such that he resigned and headed for New York City in the spring of 1911 to work as an independent journalist.[12] His well-intentioned muckraking efforts preceded him, and he was only able to find work with William Randolph Hearst's publication *Cosmopolitan*, which sent Creel to cover powerful political demagogues of the day including Mississippi Senator James K. Vardaman, known as the Great White Chief because of his advocacy of white supremacy. Creel had the intuition to see through not only the right-wing likes of Vardaman, but also through the left-wing rants of anarchist Emma Goldman, a neighbor in his Greenwich Village neighborhood. His distaste for covering unsavory personalities made him highly receptive to an offer to join the *Rocky Mountain News* in Denver, Colorado, as an editorial writer in September of 1911.[13] Tapped by former Democratic Senator Thomas M. Patterson to lead a newspaper campaign to bring down the corrupt utility corporations collectively known as the "Big Mitt" (public officials, including court judges were on their payrolls) that controlled Denver, Creel used the paper to collect 30 thousand signatures on a petition to vote on instituting a commission government to investigate the Big Mitt. A special election instituting the commission was held in December 1911, and the political power of the Big Mitt was effectively broken. With Patterson's backing, Creel himself was elected to serve as the new police commissioner.[14]

Creel would now launch one of his most important crusades: the curbing of prostitution in Denver. In Denver, prostitution took the form of the "crib system" in which an improvised street was fashioned, featuring a row of cubicles (cribs), each displaying a half-nude woman seated on a tumbled bed with a dirty washbasin for client cleanup. Creel, instead of arresting these women, proposed taking over a large farm owned by the city and building public hospitals and dormitories to rehabilitate prostitutes, as well as drug addicts and drunkards who frequented the cribs. He issued orders barring minors from the crib district and barring the sale of alcohol there. Knowing that certain amusement establishments (dance halls, social clubs, amusement parks, skating rinks) were connected with channeling customers to the cribs, Creel took a bold step: the use of feminine propaganda in the form of Josephine Roche (1886–1976), Denver's first woman police officer and the new inspector of public amusement. Educated at Vassar and Columbia colleges, Roche had proven herself as a hard-driving social worker in the slums of New York. She approached her new job with heart, compassion, and imagination: instead of arresting the owners of these prostitution-fronting groups, she spoke woman-to-man with every proprietor, pointing out to him the evil effects on children and appealing to his family values. Instead of forcing and coercing change, Roche became the friend and confidante of every dance hall and skating rink owner. Creel used the psychological propaganda of influencing, coaxing, and molding public behavior rather than forced compliance. Public opinion (through well-placed newspaper articles in the *Rocky Mountain News*) supported his efforts. Creel also developed a crusade against the spread of venereal disease, which was a taboo subject both in the press and public conversation. He dispatched police officers to arrest prostitutes, who were arraigned in court, with judges automatically continuing each case for 10 days so that blood tests could be done. Women found to be infected were committed to the county hospital for treatment. Creel believed that nothing "was more necessary than to gain the co-operation of the sullen resentful women by convincing them that this was not a mere 'moral crusade,' but a reclamatory movement largely in their own interest." In this he had the assistance of Josephine Roche, whose "sympathy and understanding won the great majority (of arrested prostitutes) to the hope of a new and better life, many coming in voluntarily."[15] Creel felt that if people were in full possession of all the facts, they would make the right decision, so he carefully compiled relevant statistics on arrests, voluntary surrenders, diagnoses, and treatments, and then published them.[16] He was correct: the public again supported his efforts, and his policies were adopted by local government officials.[17]

In 1913, George Creel left Denver to try his luck again in New York City. His impetus was his 1911 marriage to Broadway star Blanche Bates. Although he had made a name for himself as a crusading reporter, she hated life in Denver. She had given up her career on the stage only to encounter the social ostracism that the politicians of the Big Mitt still wielded against Creel and his friends. The Creels were barred from fashionable clubs and prominent homes and subject to public and personal attacks (orchestrated by the Big Mitt) via obscene, anonymous letters. Creel had depleted his personal savings for his crusades, and the $60-a-week Denver newspaperman's salary was not enough to support the glamorous lifestyle of a famous actress. New York beckoned once more.[18]

When Creel and his wife came to New York in 1913, there were no editorial openings on papers that shared his crusading political beliefs. Back he went to freelancing, writing articles for *Harper's Weekly* on the subject of medical quacks. He wrote numerous political articles for the

2. The War Begins

magazines *Everybody's* and *Century*. In April 1914, he was called back to Denver by the *Rocky Mountain News* to report on the great Colorado coal strike by immigrant miners, which eventually turned into the Ludlow Massacre.[19] During ensuing investigations into the origins of the Ludlow Massacre, Creel was able to observe the first "crisis communications" propagandist, Ivy Ledbetter Lee (1877–1934). Lee specialized in handling the way corporate blunders, disasters, and scandals were presented to the public; his client in this case was Colorado coal and oil magnate John D. Rockefeller (1839–1937), considered one of those responsible for the massacre. Lee counseled Rockefeller to "tell the truth, because sooner or later the public will find out anyway. If the public doesn't like your policies, change them and bring them in line with what people want." To counter the adverse publicity generated by the Ludlow Massacre, Lee created a pamphlet for Rockefeller, titled *Facts*, filled with provable propaganda based on truth and absolving Rockefeller's part in the massacre. The public, flooded with thousands of pamphlets, swallowed it hook, line, and sinker. Creel saw firsthand the potential power of public relations propaganda in the hands of a master manipulator.[20]

Back in New York, and with the agreement of his wife, Creel began to lace the flavor of his journalism with outright crusading, including a series of articles to help secure the confirmation of Louis D. Brandeis (1856–1941) as the first Jewish member of the United States Supreme Court. He also collaborated on a book exposing child labor abuses, *Children in Bondage*, and wrote a series of pamphlets doing battle for the cause of women's suffrage.[21]

When Woodrow Wilson stood for reelection in 1916, Creel, a staunch admirer of Wilson's progressive government reforms, offered his services to Bob Wooley, Wilson's clever chief strategist. While Wilson's neutrality policy still found favor with the American public, Wooley knew that sentiment was changing, and he needed to shore up support for the upcoming election. Wooley assigned Creel a series of articles to paint the president in the most glowing terms possible, and Creel's first newspaper feature centered around support for Wilson from Thomas Alva Edison (1847–1931), one of the most admired men in America. A lifelong Republican, Edison threw his support to Wilson: "They say Wilson blundered. Well, I reckon he has, but I notice he always blunders *forward*." Creel fully understood that this was a public relations coup: having one of the most influential men in America espousing the aristocratic Wilson's policy in folksy, homespun terms with which the average American could identify.[22] This was public relations gold, but more was to follow: a fact-based book written by Creel called *Wilson and the Issues* highlighting Wilson's policies regarding the hostilities with Mexico, the sinking of the *Lusitania*, the German invasion, the ravaging of Belgium, and other issues related to the "European War." Ten chapters long and written in plain, down-home prose, the book was a commercial success and Creel donated his copyright to the Democratic Committee.[23]

Wilson's opinion of the book was favorable; when, in 1917, the United States declared war on Germany, Wilson called on George Creel to form the Committee on Public Information (CPI) as an independent agency of the government of the United States to influence public opinion to support the U.S. entry into World War I. Creel would merge democracy and propaganda into a fact-based juggernaut to influence the American people's home-front thinking on the need to support American participation in the European conflict. Joining Creel on the committee were the secretaries of state (Robert Lansing, 1864–1928), war (Newton D. Baker, 1871–1937), and the navy (Josephus Daniels, 1862–1948). All three men knew Creel personally and realized that Creel would take Wilson's view of the war and transform it so that every citizen in the four corners of the United States would be imbued by the need to win a war "as shall bring peace and safety to all nations and make the world itself at last free."[24]

Creel's first task was to find space for the CPI to function: that was accomplished when a young major by the name of Douglas MacArthur (1880–1964) located a house at 10 Jackson Place right across the street from the White House. Creel went to work, and within one week, he recruited some of the best and brightest journalists, scholars, artists, and political figures to head the various departments of the CPI, which included:

1. The Division of News, responsible for news gathering and news publishing by CPI journalists, led by Leigh Reilly (1866–1954), former managing editor of the *Chicago Herald*. By the end of the war, Reilly's division had issued approximately 6,000 articles published in about 20,000 newspaper columns per week. They would work hand in hand with the *Official Bulletin*, the first official daily newspaper of the United States government, intended to be a record of the nation's participation in the war.[25]

2. The Division of Pictorial Publicity, overseen by respected graphic artist Charles Dana Gibson (1867–1944), creator of the

2. The War Begins

world-famous "Gibson Girl" image. Gibson would recruit an army of famous artists to create paintings and posters glorifying America's participation in World War I. Many of these posters would be used in lobbies of theaters across the country to aid in recruitment activities.[26]

3. The Division of Advertising, responsible for purchasing advertising space in newspapers, magazines, and billboards, headed by advertising executive William H. Johns (1868–1944), joined by publisher Herbert Houston (1866–1955) and billboard specialist Thomas Cusack (1858–1926).[27]

4. The Division of Civic and Educational Cooperation, responsible for commissioning, editing, and publishing books and pamphlets on America's war efforts, distributed through schools and colleges with a circulation of 75 million by the war's end. Guy Stanton Ford (1873–1962), distinguished historian and dean of the Graduate School of the University of Minnesota, led the division. Future Pulitzer Prize–winning novelist Booth Tarkington (1869–1946) and notable muckraker Ida Tarbell (1857–1944) were among the most well-known contributors.[28]

5. The Foreign Language Newspaper Division, which was established to monitor every foreign language newspaper printed and sold in the United States, as well as translate CPI pamphlets and publications into foreign languages.[29]

6. The Foreign Press

Committee on Public Information poster (1918) with the message "Don't Talk, Spies Are Listening," and depicting the kaiser as a spider weaving his web of deceit (World History Archive/Alamy Stock Photo).

The Silents Go to War

Bureau, directed by Ernest Poole (1880–1950), provided CPI agents stationed abroad with feature articles and photographs to be offered to friendly foreign newspapers and magazines.[30]

7. The Bureau of War Expositions, established to organize, mount, manage, and circulate exhibits of the weapons of war as well as battle trophies captured by United States armed forces. The bureau would also sponsor patriotic parades nationwide.[31]

8. The Division of Work with the Foreign Born, directed by Creel's trusted colleague Josephine Roche, established contact with racial groups including Italians, Hungarians, Lithuanians, Russians, Yugoslavs, Czechoslovaks, Poles, Germans, Ukrainians, Danes, Swedes, Norwegians, Finns, Dutch, Chinese, Japanese, Croatians, Jews, and Spaniards through bureaus, each headed by a chief who was not only of the same nationality but also fluent in the culture and language. Each nationality was provided with an ongoing stream of speakers, news stories, translated CPI pamphlets, publications, posters, advertisements, and Liberty Bond appeals. In addition, Roche personally made sure that each bureau chief conveyed customized messages showing President Wilson's special interest and appreciation for each group's patriotism to the United States.[32]

9. The Division of Films, which would go into the movie business. Supervised by Louis B. Mack for the first six months and then by Charles S. Hart,[33] the film division would cooperate with the Signal Corps and navy filmmakers to create documentaries, write original scripts, produce original feature-length films, and distribute and promote all war films, whether produced by the United States government or commercial studios. Lastly, all commercial filmmakers would be issued permits of approval by the CPI for their war pictures.[34] In 1917 alone, the Division of Films produced *The 1917 Recruit, Submarines, Army and Navy Sports, Labor's Part in Democracy's War, Making of Big Guns,* and *Woman's Part in the War,* all short subject films designed to be shown with feature-length films in the nation's movie houses.

10. To promote its message to all American citizens to support the war effort, the CPI established the Division of the Four-Minute Men, a cadre of 75,000 volunteer speakers from every faith and ethnicity to speak in union halls, churches, synagogues, lodges, fraternal organizations, labor unions, logging camps, assemblies of Indian tribes, and movie theaters on the need for patriotic Americans to either enlist or join their hometown war efforts. Speeches were

2. The War Begins

mostly in English, but ethnic groups—Italians, Jews, Czechs, Poles, Hungarians, Ukrainians, Armenians, Chinese, Japanese—were reached in their own languages. The brainchild of publicist Donald Ryerson, each volunteer attended training sessions through local schools and universities and was given pamphlets and speaking tips on topics including registering for the draft, buying Liberty Bonds, recruiting workers for munitions jobs, and supporting Red Cross programs.[35]

First and foremost, Creel and the CPI focused on establishing itself as the source of guidance for a voluntary censorship program. The press was initially outraged at the idea of censorship, and Creel needed a program that would satisfy the bureaucrats and the military so that outright censorship of the press would not be included in the Espionage Act[36] being debated in Congress in May and June 1917. Creel launched a series of statements designed to mollify the members of the press, as well as outline the need for "keeping information from our own people in order to keep it from the enemy." He cited European censorship, which betrayed "distrust of democratic common sense." Creel pledged that only information "that is of direct military use to the enemy would be censored. Everything else would be left to the patriotic sense of the editors." This mollified the press somewhat, but President Wilson then issued a statement saying that he had not withdrawn his support for a full-blown censorship law. Editors felt that a full-blown censorship law would effectively gag them, but Creel gave them the alternative: an authoritative policy fully defining voluntary censorship as requested by the government.[37] The policy, printed on a 10-by-12-inch card, was distributed to every editor in the nation. It was accepted in lieu of outright censorship, although the press tried to put a spin on the outcome by stating that the espionage bill was an anti-spy law, not press censorship, and declared victory.[38]

Creel would next turn to the picture business. A letter drafted by Creel and signed by President Wilson was sent in June of 1917 to the National Association of the Motion Picture Industry (NAMPI) asking that the industry be organized in cooperation with the CPI. In July, NAMPI's chair, actor/producer William A. Brady, deputized the newly created War Co-operation Committee to handle liaising with the CPI; representatives went to Washington, D.C., and met with almost every department and agency of the CPI. Designated representatives of the film industry (including directors D. W. Griffith, Cecil B. DeMille, and

The Silents Go to War

Thomas Ince, as well as studio heads Carl Laemmle and Louis J. Selznick), were "drafted" into making films that would support the message of the CPI to the American public: that Americans needed to rally their support for the war effort. Also "signing on" were screen stars (and Liberty Bond[39] salespeople) Mary Pickford, Sessue Hayakawa, Charlie Chaplin, Douglas Fairbanks, cowboy star William Hart, and vamp Theda Bara. While the CPI technically had no statutory censorship authority over film content (that was handled by censors at local and state levels), they were able to work with these censors to ensure that films that discouraged enlistment, lacked patriotism, or maligned allies could result in scenes being cut.[40]

Shortly after the first American troops landed in France on June 28, 1917, the film industry would begin to enfold movie audiences in films (features, shorts, and documentaries) that would demonize the Germans and stir up home-front feelings of patriotism. Two big propaganda feature films came out in the summer and winter of 1917, becoming box office hits. The films were directed by two brothers, treated two very different subjects, and starred two very influential American screen idols.

Lovely Mary Pickford (center) as plucky American Angela Moore being questioned by a bevy of German officers in Artcraft Pictures' 1917 production of *The Little American*. That's Jack Holt (as Karl von Austreim) directly behind Pickford (World History Archive/Alamy Stock Photo).

2. The War Begins

In July of 1917, "America's sweetheart" Mary Pickford appeared in a public-shocking, "manhandled heroine" movie unlike any she'd ever played in: *The Little American*, released July 12, 1917, by Artcraft Pictures, co-directed by Cecil B. DeMille and Joseph Levering. Cast: Mary Pickford (Angela Moore), Jack Holt (Karl von Austreim), Raymond Hatton (Count Jules de Destin), Hobart Bosworth (German colonel), Walter Long (German captain), James Neill (Senator John Moore), Ben Alexander (Bobby Moore), Guy Oliver (Frederick von Austreim), Edythe Chapman (Mrs. von Austreim), Lillian Leighton (Angela's aunt), DeWitt Jennings (English barrister). Plot[41]: Two men—German-born Karl von Austreim and Frenchman Count Jules de Destin—court young American Angela Moore. At her birthday party on July 4, 1914, Karl (who is half–American) is summoned back to his regiment in Germany, and Angela is despondent. Shortly afterward, war is declared in Europe and Jules goes back to fight for France against the invading Germans. Angela has had no word from Karl in three months (she doesn't know if he's dead or alive), but her aunt in France sends word to Angela to visit and help her return to the United States. Although word has spread that the German submarines will sink any ship that is thought to be carrying munitions, Angela boards the *Veritania* (carrying arms), and the ship is torpedoed by the Germans. Angela saves herself by climbing onto the wreckage of a floating table, and she and fellow passengers are eventually rescued. Angela makes her way to France and arrives at her aunt's chateau in Vangy, only to discover that her aunt has died. The Germans are bombing Vangy, and Angela is told to flee by concerned French servants. Angela decides to stay and help wounded French soldiers. The Germans attack the chateau and kill the remaining wounded soldiers. The Germans enter the chateau, get drunk, and attack the servant girls. They try to rape Angela, who reveals herself to be a neutral American (she waves a little American flag), but the Germans are not interested in her nationality. Angela tries to run away and hide, only to be discovered and dragged out by a German soldier, who turns out to be Karl. While Karl is willing to save Angela, he refuses to save the other women, responding that he cannot give orders to superior officers who require French girls for "relaxation" purposes. Unable to help the young women, Angela receives permission to leave the chateau. She witnesses the degradation of the women as well as the execution of French civilians. She decides to seek revenge, and after leaving the chateau, gets word to French forces via a hidden telephone and describes three German gun positions near the chateau. The French attack, but

The Silents Go to War

Angela is recaptured by the Germans, led by Karl. He has a change of heart and tries to help her escape, but both are caught. They are sentenced to death, but the French shell the chateau, enabling Angela and Karl to escape. They make their way to a nearby church and collapse in the ruins. They are found by French soldiers, who intend to shoot Karl. Fortunately, their commander is Jules de Destin (he has lost an arm in combat), who spares Karl's life and eventually helps the lovers flee to America.

The backstory: Director Cecil B. DeMille had established himself as a successful filmmaker with a string of hits between 1914 and 1915 including *The Squaw Man, Brewster's Millions, Rose of the Rancho, The Ghost Busters,* and *The Warrens of Virginia,* as well as his first 1916 epic *Joan the Woman.* His most successful film was *The Cheat* (1915) featuring star Sessue Hayakawa branding a woman's shoulder with a hot iron for refusing him promised sexual favors. DeMille was known in Hollywood for his unsavory sexual proclivities,[42] which carried over into his filmmaking. Canadian-born Mary Pickford (1892–1979), in contrast, was "America's Sweetheart" and a potent national symbol of American womanhood—pretty, dainty, plucky, determined, and loveable. Her films, including her 1914 hits *Hearts Adrift, Tess of the Storm Country,* and *Cinderella,* cemented her place as Hollywood's quintessential all–American girl. An astute businesswoman, Pickford signed a contract in 1916 with Famous Players/Paramount Pictures mogul Adolph Zukor to produce her own films, distributed under a special division called Artcraft Pictures.[43] In 1916 came *Less Than Dust* (Pickford playing a girl in India disguised as boy), followed by 1917's *The Poor Little Rich Girl* and *The Pride of the Clan.* Pickford had worked with DeMille in *A Romance of the Redwoods* also in 1917 and looked forward to working with him again. She found herself uncomfortable with the level of brutality and lurid rape scenes, however, and never worked with DeMille again.

Critical response: *Variety*'s July 6, 1917, review said of the film: "It's a Pickford. 'Nuf said. Just Mary Pickford, the same Mary that one has seen in a score of other pictures, only this time she is made the central figure of a war story."[44] The July 21, 1917, review from *Motion Picture News*[45] declared: "As a patriotic spectacle and as an ideal Pickford vehicle, *The Little American* is superb. When Angela Moore, the Little American, announces that she has quit being neutral and has turned human, then came the time for loud applause." To publicize the movie, Famous Players developed and promoted the nickname "Our

2. The War Begins

Mary," which became indelibly associated with the Pickford persona. Additionally, they had special posters featuring the image of Pickford wrapped in an American flag accompanied by the caption "The Greatest Appeal of America's Sweetheart." All the publicity did not help the picture; although it made back the initial costs plus a respectable profit, it became a box office failure, not generating the expected millions of dollars of profit. For many fans of "Our Mary," the violent scenes were not in keeping with the Pickford perception and sufficed to keep them away.[46]

Throughout the summer and early fall, the film industry would release independent short films and documentaries that would focus on American commitment to the war effort on the home front, including food films: *Winning with Wheat, Feeding an Army, Saving the Food of a Nation,* and *On the Farm Where the Food Comes From.* Women's contributions included *Women's Work in Wartime, Patriotic Auntie,* and *Doing Their Bit,*[47] while military preparedness films included *How Uncle Sam Prepares, Our Fighting Forces, Manning Our Navy, Rebuilding America's Merchant Marine, Soldiers of the Sea, Making a War Poster.*[48]

A number of summer-into-fall feature film releases explored the subject of home-front slacking: the July releases of *The Slacker* and *The Man Who Was Afraid,* the August releases of *The Slacker's Heart* and *When the Call Came,* and the September release of *Over There.*[49] Of the five movies, *The Slacker* would be the most popular with the public due to an ad campaign by Metro Pictures[50] and would be used by the U.S. army as a recruitment tool.

Fall of 1917 showcased films featuring heroic home-front women, including *War and the Woman, Her Country's Call, Arms and the Girl, Miss U.S.A., For Liberty,* and *Miss Jackie of the Army.*[51] Even children heeded the call to arms, exposing a German spy in *The Little Patriot.*[52]

Not in keeping with the flow of movies that emphasized American national patriotism, Thomas Ince released his November big-budget spectacle *The Zeppelin's Last Raid* with a plot twist that featured a secret German society crusading for peace (headed by a heroic German woman) vowing to overthrow the kaiser with the aid of a sympathetic zeppelin commander. While the movie generally received good reviews, it was noted that the film featured a storyline recycled from Ince's 1916 pacifist movie *Civilization.*[53]

December 1917 introduced the public to the second great

The Silents Go to War

propaganda film of the year that would not only focus on German espionage at home but also shed light on the pro–American activities of an Asian ally, Japan: *The Secret Game*, released on December 3, 1917, by Paramount Pictures, directed by William C. deMille (1878–1955), elder brother of Cecil B. DeMille.[54] Cast: Sessue Hayakawa (Nara-Nara), Jack Holt (Major John Northfield), Florence Vidor (Kitty Little), Mayme Kelso (Miss Loring), Raymond Hatton (Mr. Harris), Charles Ogle (Dr. Ebell Smith). Plot[55]: Kitty Little is a German spy under the direction of Dr. Ebell Smith. The spies are anxious to obtain information on the sailing dates of American transport ships and have planted Kitty as the secretary of Major John Northfield to obtain covert intelligence plans on U.S. naval operations in the Pacific. Nara-Nara, a clever and resourceful agent of the Japanese Secret Service, is charged with finding the traitor among his country's American allies. Initially suspecting Northfield of betrayal, Nara-Nara obtains a letter that implicates Kitty (whom he has met and fallen in love with) as the spy. Northfield, also suspecting Kitty (and also in love with her) gives her a sealed (blank) letter supposedly containing intelligence plans, which she promptly delivers to Smith. Nara-Nara is trailing her and, in a struggle with Smith, kills him. He then tries to force Kitty to go away with him, but she refuses, reminding him of his pledge as a samurai warrior to never dishonor himself or others. Shamed, Nara-Nara leaves her. While starting to examine the body of Smith for incriminating evidence, Nara-Nara is killed by one of Smith's accomplices. Northfield confronts Kitty, who is in receipt of a letter from her brother (fighting in the trenches in France) telling her that he is to be shot for shielding women and children from German atrocities. Kitty confesses to Northfield that the only reason she is spying for the Germans is to save her brother. Realizing that she helped cause Nara-Nara's death, Kitty helps lead Northfield to the spy network. After the remaining spies are arrested, Kitty becomes engaged to Northfield, and both remember the courage of Nara-Nara.

The backstory: Although Japan had entered the war in 1914 on the side of the allies, perception of the Japanese in newspapers and film was overwhelmingly negative. William Randolph Hearst's July 1917 movie serial *Patria* particularly portrayed the Japanese as evil agents in league with Mexico to sabotage American interests. The 15-chapter serial, starring well-known dancer Irene Castle[56] and featuring Warner Oland as the nefarious Japanese villain,[57] was a huge success with audiences around the country. The Pathé Company, distributor of the serial, was rebuked by President Woodrow Wilson in a letter that read:

2. The War Begins

> Several times in attending Keith's Theater here I have seen portions of ... "*Patria*"... May I not say to you that the character of the story disturbed me very much? It is extremely unfair to the Japanese and I fear that it is calculated to stir up a great deal of hostility which will be ... extremely hurtful. I take the liberty, therefore, of asking whether the Pathé Company would not be willing to withdraw it if it is still being exhibited.[58]

Searching for a movie that would show Japan in a positive light as an American ally, Paramount Pictures came up with *The Secret Game*, with a Japanese secret service agent as the hero. The role was tailor-made for their "exotic" male star, Sessue Hayakawa. By 1917, Hayakawa was one of the screen idols of silent pictures, having first been noticed as a suave Japanese diplomat/spy in 1914's *The Typhoon*, followed by his star-making role as the charismatic, sexually threatening villain in Cecil B. DeMille's 1915 production of *The Cheat*. As one of the most highly paid actors in Hollywood, he commanded a salary of $5,000 per week, and his female fans were legion. The power and elegance of his performances elevated him far above the stereotyped "Yellow Peril"[59] roles normally associated with Asians (who were mostly portrayed by white actors in "yellowface" makeup), and his career boomed.

Critical response: In a December 16, 1917, review, the *Exhibitors Herald* noted: "'*The Secret Game*' is a war play that shows no fighting and one that holds the attention of spectators from beginning to end. It is exceedingly well done and should prove a first-class attraction. Sessue Hayakawa is well supported by Jack Holt, Florence Vidor and Charles Ogle, Mayme Kelso and Raymond Hatton. The direction is by William C. deMille."[60] *Moving Picture World* said: "In this story, the representatives of the two countries are not at odds ... they are working hand in hand against a common enemy.... Germany. Sessue Hayakawa has a role of a member of a Japanese secret service organization, co-operating with the United States authorities in an effort to uncover the work of the sleepless Teutons."[61] The film became both a critical and commercial success, allowing Hayakawa to eventually form his own production company.[62]

On November 2, 1917, the American Expeditionary Forces experienced their first casualties: Corporal James Gresham and privates Thomas Enright and Merle Hay of the 16th Infantry became the first American soldiers to die in battle when Germans raided their trenches near Bathelémont, France. The "reel" war had now become reality, and the American public wanted revenge, on the battlefront and on the film

The Silents Go to War

front. Films would reflect the utter hatred of Germans, with the stereotype of the "Horrible Hun" front and center for audiences to hiss and boo at. One actor embodied that vicious, cruel, lecherous, heartless image: Erich von Stroheim. His on-screen villainy will be highlighted in the next chapter, featuring some shocking plots and gleefully deviant behavior.

3

"Horrible Hun" Films of 1918

For centuries, the word "Hun" has denoted unfettered savagery toward conquered nations. The images of terrifying, sword-wielding barbarian hordes, bearing down on innocent victims down through the ages had stayed in the mindset of European nations up until World War I. The image was perpetuated by the exploits of the most famous Hun of all: Attila, King of the Huns, who ruled from 434 to 453. But it wasn't until German Kaiser (Emperor) Wilhelm II decided to reference the Huns in his speech of 1900 during the Boxer Rebellion in China[1] that the term was applied to German mercilessness in battle.

The kaiser's farewell address to his departing soldiers commended them, in the spirit of the Huns, to be merciless in battle:

> Should you encounter the enemy, he will be defeated! No quarter will be given! Prisoners will not be taken! Whoever falls into your hands is forfeited. Just as a thousand years ago the Huns under their King Attila made a name for themselves, one that even today makes them seem mighty in history and legend, may the name German be affirmed by you in such a way in China that no Chinese will ever again dare to look cross-eyed at a German.[2]

By the start of World War I, the German army had been built up into a well-oiled juggernaut that would release its wrath on Belgium. On August 3, 1914, Germany declared war on France, and invaded through Belgium. What followed was the brutal mistreatment and occupation of Belgium by Germans in World War I.

Throughout the first six weeks of the war, German soldiers (some of whom were young and inexperienced and afraid of Belgian guerrilla fighters called *francs-tireurs* or "free shooters") burned homes, executed civilians, raped women, and sent thousands of men, women, and children to Germany to serve as forced laborers. In addition, they faced fierce resistance from the small Belgian army (*Garde Civique*), who, with rudimentary uniforms and outdated guns, were perceived as civilian

The Silents Go to War

Belgian resistance and were shot where they stood and given no chance to surrender. On August 25 the German army burned and ravaged the beautiful old university town of Leuven, deliberately burning the library and destroying approximately 230,000 books and 950 manuscripts. In total, 6,000 Belgians were killed by German soldiers; 17,700 died during expulsion, deportation, imprisonment, or by death sentences imposed by the German military court. One hundred twenty thousand Belgians became forced laborers, with half that number deported to Germany; 25,000 homes and other buildings in 837 communities were destroyed in 1914 alone, and 1.5 million Belgians fled from the invading German army into France and neutral Holland.[3] By the end of September 1914 the atrocities ceased, but the damage in the eyes of the world was done.

As word seeped out through newsreels and firsthand accounts from Belgian survivors, the American public reacted with outrage. America's fourth Liberty Bond drive of 1918 employed a "Remember Belgium" poster (released by the Committee on Public Information) depicting the silhouette of a helpless Belgian girl being dragged by a German soldier to be raped against a background of a burning village. Hollywood would release six memorable films in 1918 depicting German barbarism: two dealing with accounts of the courage of the Belgians in the face of German occupation and four highlighting the actor most associated with the terrifying face and vicious acts of the "Horrible Hun."

In April of 1918, the true story of the staunch resistance of Belgium's Cardinal Mercier against the German occupation premiered: *The Cross Bearer*, released April 1, 1918, by World Film, directed by George Archainbaud. Cast: Montagu Love (Cardinal Mercier), Jeanne Eagels (Liane de Merode), Tony Merlo (Lt. Maurice Lambeaux), George Morgan (Gaston Van Leys), Edward Elkas (Banker Van Leys), Charles Brandt (Baron Spiegelman), Eloise Clement (Jeanne Perrier), Al Hart (Colonel Krause), Alec B. Francis (Brother Joseph), Kate Lester (cardinal's housekeeper), Fanny Cogan (Madame Lambeaux), Henrietta Simpson (Madame Van Leys). Plot[4]: Cardinal Mercier protects the altar of his church from desecration when German forces invade the Belgian city of Leuven during World War I. Although the soldiers commit widespread atrocities, the cardinal does his best to protect the townspeople. Cardinal Mercier's young ward, Liane de Merode, is betrothed to Belgian officer Maurice Lambeaux, but the German governor general tries to force his attentions on her against the cardinal's will. Despite the plotting of the governor general, Maurice breaks through the German lines in a disguise. The cardinal secretly marries the young couple, and with

3. "Horrible Hun" Films of 1918

the aid of some of the townspeople, smuggles them across the border to France.

The backstory: Distinguished British character actor Montagu Love (1877–1943) was cast as the heroic Cardinal Mercier.[5] Beautiful stage actress Jeanne Eagels (1890–1929) was cast as his young ward, although in reality she was just 13 years younger than Love. Before its official release in April 1918, *The Cross Bearer* was given a four-day run at Carnegie Hall to raise funds for the Red Cross. Tickets were priced at 50 cents to one dollar, with box seats at 10 dollars each. The film received a royal endorsement from Albert I, king of the Belgians.

Critical response: *The Michigan Film Review* of April 1918 called the film "an uplifting experience of courage and faith in the face of a ruthless enemy" and recommended it to the clergy, local club women, and the Red Cross for viewing.[6] The *Hattiesburg American*'s April 5, 1918, review raved: "An altogether exceptional, extraordinary picture. Love's Cardinal is quite the best he has contributed to the screen and Jeanne Eagels is charming as Liane de Merode."[7]

August saw the release of a film illustrating the mistreatment of Belgian children by Germans: *Till I Come Back to You*, released August 25, 1918, by Famous Players Lasky/Artcraft, directed by Cecil B. DeMille. Cast: Bryant Washburn (Captain Jefferson Strong), Florence Vidor (Yvonne Von Krutz), G. Butler Clonbough (Karl Von Krutz), Winter Hall (King Albert I of Belgium), George Stone (Jacques), Julia Faye (Susette), Lillian Leighton (Margot), Clarence Geldert (U.S. colonel), Mae Giraci (Rosa), C. Renfield (Rosa's father), Frank Butterworth (Hans), Monte Blue (American doughboy). Plot[8]: Yvonne Von Krutz, a Belgian, lives with her German husband Karl, whom she was forced to marry, and her spirited little brother, Jacques, in a farmhouse in the countryside at the start of World War I. Karl joins the German forces, and during the Belgian retreat, King Albert I stops at the house where he finds little Jacques playing soldier. The king tells him to be brave; wait, he says, "till I come back to you." Shortly afterward, the Germans invade, and Jacques is taken by force to a reformatory with other Belgian orphans to be trained as munitions workers in preparation for their slave labor in munitions plants. The children are beaten and abused by the Germans. America enters the war, and Captain Jefferson Strong is detailed to destroy the German storehouse containing explosives. Strong pretends to be an escaped German soldier and hides in Yvonne's cottage. He learns that the underground supply of explosives is located near the Von Krutz farm, and by means of a tunnel, he and his team will mine and destroy the explosives. The children, led by Jacques, are sent by Armstrong through the tunnel to the Americans, but they lose their way, and to save them, Strong disables the explosives. He is arrested by his superior officer and is brought up on charges of disobedience, tried, and court-martialed. Through the influence of King Albert, who has befriended little Jacques, he is saved from being shot. Yvonne, whose husband has been killed in battle, finds consolation in Strong's love.

The backstory: After directing two films in 1918 in two other genres, a women's weepie (*Old Wives for New*) and a satire on divorce (*We Can't Have Everything*), Cecil B. DeMille went back to World War I with the rousing *Till I Come Back to You*. For his leads, he chose handsome stage actor Bryant Washburn (1889–1963) and Florence Vidor, who had played the lead in DeMille's brother William's 1917 film *The Secret Game*. At the same time, DeMille kept up his own personal military fervor by volunteering his services to the Justice Department's Intelligence Office, offering to investigate friends, neighbors, and other actors at the studio for signs of less-than-patriotic conduct.[9]

Critical response: The August 26, 1918, *New York Times* was laudatory: "There are few directors in this country who have Mr. DeMille's ability to make pictures. He knows what the camera can do, and how to make it do best: *Till I Come Back to You* reveals his power in a succession of amusing, beautiful, vivid pictures."[10]

The *Exhibitor's Herald* review of September 14, 1918, placed an emphasis

The "Horrible Hun" himself, Erich von Stroheim, in full Prussian regalia in a scene from von Stroheim's 1922 hit *Foolish Wives*, produced, written, directed, and starring von Stroheim for Universal Pictures (Picture Lux/The Hollywood Archive/Alamy Stock Photo).

3. "Horrible Hun" Films of 1918

on the fine acting: "It is a story of the conflict in Europe with most of the action taking place in Belgium and presents various phases of the war, as they influence the lives of Belgian children under the German Reign of Terror. Bryant Washburn is excellent in the role of Captain Jefferson Stone; Florence Vidor is especially appealing as the wife of a German soldier, and little Georgie Stone, a most loveable little Jacques, a loyal Son of Belgium. Winter Hall, who impersonated King Albert I of Belgium, had remarkable life-like makeup."[11]

If any actor was the face of the "Horrible Hun" it was the legendary character actor/director Erich von Stroheim. With his menacing demeanor, Prussian posturing, and serpentine charm, he was the very definition of "the man you love to hate." But ... he wasn't a Prussian, he wasn't a Hun ... and he certainly wasn't a "von."

Rare photograph of Sessue Hayakawa (left) and Erich von Stroheim in the French film production of *Macao, l'enfer du jeu* (English title *Gambling Hell*), shot in 1939 and released in France in 1943. Von Stroheim had become a major French film star in the late 1930s, while Hayakawa supported himself by selling his Japanese watercolors and appearing sporadically in French films (Photo 12/Alamy Stock Photo).

The Silents Go to War

Erich Oswald Stroheim was born on September 22, 1885, in Vienna, Austria, to Benno Stroheim and Johanna Bondy, both of whom were Jews. He was circumcised according to the Jewish faith on September 29, 1885, in Vienna, as noted by the Israelitische Kultusgemeinde.[12] His younger brother Bruno followed in 1889. His parents were hatters, manufacturing and selling straw and felt hats and handling imported hats for fashionable ladies. His family lived in comfortable circumstances, and young Erich lived in the center of the Austro-Hungarian Empire: Vienna, city of Johann Strauss waltzes, beautiful women, and mustachioed military men. Music, theater, military bands, visits to the Hofberg Palace, the ornate St. Stephen's Cathedral, and the Volksoper Wien were all part of his childhood experiences. A keen observer with a photographic memory, he watched the behavior of the beautiful people (men and women) of the aristocracy with their rigid set of social rules, soldiers with their colorful beribboned uniforms, and his family's middle- and lower-class customers, who lived life without the burden of social niceties.[13]

Although Stroheim had an endless fascination with the military, his family had other plans for him: to join the family business. Subsequently, they enrolled him in 1901 in *Die Grazer Handelsakadamie*, a business school located in Graz. He loathed the school, and despite the fact that he was a bright, creative young man, he was a terrible student. Although his grade in German was "satisfactory," he was graded poorly in French, English, bookkeeping, economics, and other business subjects. He was, however, outstanding in one area ... playing hooky. Of the 225 hours of absences noted in his school records, 62 did not even have an excuse, and he was labeled a truant. A loner who had trouble making friends, he desperately wanted to be something other than a middle-class hat maker and longed to be a part of upper-crust Viennese society.[14] Or ... a soldier.

When he was given a conscription examination for his compulsory six-months service in the Austrian army in April 1906, he failed his physical examination. He tried again a few months later and was accepted into the Royal and Imperial Training Regiment in Vienna. He became familiar with horses and was, at one point, kicked in the head, resulting in the distinctive scar on his forehead. Proving himself to have some capabilities, he received a commission on December 23, 1906, as a "one-year voluntary soldier-in-training with the title Corporal."[15] The commission didn't last: on April 20, 1907, Stroheim was deemed a "4-F"—not capable of bearing arms—and was discharged from the service on May 29, 1907.[16]

3. "Horrible Hun" Films of 1918

Disconsolate, he worked in the family hat shop for two years, flirting with pretty girls perusing the wares, and dreamed of a better life. But how? He had had a substandard education (he was not a graduate of a *Gymnasium*—academic high school), had failed in the military, hated being a shop clerk, and wanted another kind of life. Feeling inferior because he was of Jewish birth[17] and could not succeed in raising himself from his middle-class origins (what girl would marry a nobody without money or position?), he made a decision. Across the ocean lay the promised land: America. He said goodbye to his family and traveled to Bremen, Germany, where he boarded the SS *Prinz Friedrich-Wilhelm* bound for New York and arrived on November 26, 1909. The process of reinventing himself would now begin. He would no longer be an obscure, ex–Jewish tradesman; he would be a member of the Austrian nobility, a high-ranking officer, and a Catholic.[18]

At Ellis Island, the entry point for incoming immigrants, he presented himself (shabby and penniless) as "Count Erich Oswald Hans Maria von Stroheim und Nordenwall," scion of Austrian nobility. His name was recorded in the Ellis Island records, and he took the ferryboat into New York City on that cold November day.

But ... even a count has to eat, and that meant a job. Working at various menial positions, he finally wound up in San Francisco in 1912 as a traveling salesman; eventually discharged from that job, he stayed in San Francisco and took jobs including a telephone repairman and a flypaper salesman. An avid hiker, he enjoyed the countryside north of Oakland, made the acquaintance of the Austrian proprietor of the West Point Inn, Captain Henry Masjon, and got himself hired as a handyman. There, he met his first wife, Margaret Knox. She introduced him to American literature including Stephen Crane's *Red Badge of Courage* and Edgar Lee Masters's *Spoon River Anthology* and encouraged him to start writing plays. They lived together briefly, eventually marrying at the home of her family on February 13, 1913. The marriage did not last: within two months, it began to fall apart. Stroheim still could not find a good job, and he started to drink. Angry and frustrated, he took out his frustrations on his wife, and she divorced him in May of 1914.[19] In the five years that he had been in the United States, he had accomplished next to nothing, but that was about to change.

Stroheim, with financial backing from a woman whom he had met (and impressed) while working at a job in Lake Tahoe in the summer of 1914, managed to have one of his plays produced in Oakland. The play bombed, but Stroheim made the acquaintance of some actors working as movie extras, and he decided to seek work in the movie business. He knew that he wasn't the "leading man" type (tall, dark, and handsome), but he realized that if he created a unique look for himself, it might result in being noticed. So, he shaved his head to highlight the facial scar and his dark, piercing eyes and put on a natty suit, white gloves, a long dark coat, and a monocle. He was shrewd enough to realize that the combination of his appearance, coupled with his European accent, charming manners, and knowledge of continental customs would eventually get him noticed. And it did. Broadway actor and director John Emerson, preparing his movie *Old Heidelberg*[20] (another variation on *The Student Prince*) for Majestic Studios, picked von Stroheim for a small part in the movie and engaged him as his assistant for his invaluable knowledge of European details and set decoration authenticity. When the movie premiered on October 8, 1915, *Variety*'s review opined: "Whoever is directly responsible for the casting of the other members of the organization is a positive genius for selecting 'types.'" Emerson had a positive review, and Stroheim was on his way as an actor.[21]

His next part was in *The Social Secretary*, directed by Emerson and starring Norma Talmadge, shot on location in New York City. Stroheim was again the assistant director and had a small comedic part as "The Buzzard" (a snoopy society reporter). The film, released on September 8, 1916, was a great success; Talmadge was so pleased with Stroheim's work that she recommended him as an assistant director on her next picture, *Panthea*, to be directed by Allan Dwan. Stroheim worked for Emerson on one more production as an assistant director: 1916's *Less Than Dust* starring Mary Pickford and set in colonial India. Although Stroheim created villages in India and settings in England, the film was not a success; some of the scenes shot by Emerson were not deemed important enough by Pickford, and as the star, she removed them (because she wasn't in them). As a result, the film lacked continuity.[22]

Director Allan Dwan gave Stroheim the small part of an arrogant Russian officer in *Panthea* (a Selznick Pictures production) as well as using him as his directorial assistant. The film opened to excellent reviews; he was listed in the credits as both an assistant director and as a "Lieutenant of Police." The April 1917 *Photoplay* noticed him: "The lieutenant of police who comes to arrest Panthea in the early episodes is the perfect picture of the 'well, it's all in a day's work' type of blasé young militarist."[23]

Actor Douglas Fairbanks formed his own film corporation and for his first film, *In Again, Out Again* (released in May 1917), engaged

3. "Horrible Hun" Films of 1918

John Emerson as director, with Emerson bringing Stroheim along as his assistant director. His experience on the film was not pleasant; when Stroheim went out to research munitions factories (the plot called for the hero to impersonate a spy blowing up a munitions factory) he was ultimately fired because of Fairbanks's fear of having a man with a German name and accent in his employ.[24]

Next came a job as an assistant director and actor in director George Fitzmaurice's film *Sylvia of the Secret Service* (an Astra Films production), released in May of 1917, starring dancing icon Irene Castle. Playing a villainous spy, he was sent by Fitzmaurice to New York City to research the names of different explosives to be painted on munitions boxes. Dressed in his usual style as a dapper gentleman with a Prussian clipped haircut, and asking suspicious questions, he was promptly arrested and thrown into jail. Astra Films immediately came to his rescue, and he was eventually released.

As World War I progressed and virulent Hun hatred mounted, Stroheim found himself typecast as an arrogant Prussian officer, and he made the most of it. Appearing as an evil Hun officer in Vitagraph's *For France* (filmed in Brooklyn, New York, and released in September of 1917), he would finish work and then walk up and down Fifth Avenue in New York City in full uniform, flashing his monocle and flirting with all the pretty girls he encountered. His good friends actresses Norma and Constance Talmadge were constantly worried that he would be pelted with rocks or hauled off and arrested. But he wasn't and went right on enjoying himself.[25]

In 1918, he hit his stride playing Hun officers in such films as *The Unbeliever*, released February 11, 1918, by the Edison Company, directed by Alan Crosland. Cast: Marguerite Courtot (Virginie Harbrok), Raymond McKee (Philip Landicutt), Erich von Stroheim (Lieutenant Kurt von Schnieditz), Kate Lester (Margaret Landicutt), Frank DeVernon (Uncle "Jemmy" Landicutt), Mortimer Martine (Eugene Harbrok), Blanche Davenport (Madam Harbrok), Harold Hollacher (Pierre Harbrok), Darwin Karr ("Lefty"), Earl Schenck (Emanuel Muller), Gertrude Norman (Marianne Marnholm), Lew Hart (Hoffman), Major Thomas Holcomb (the commanding officer), Lieutenant J. F. Rorke (Lieutenant Terence O'Shaughnessy), Sergeant Moss Gill (Albert Mullins), Major Ross E. Rowell (himself), Captain Thomas Sterrett (himself), Corporal Bob Ryland (himself). Plot[26]: Philip Landicutt, a spoiled rich boy with class and race prejudice, dislikes anyone with German blood and is an atheist. Encouraged by his mother, he enlists in the Marine Corps and is sent to France. There, he witnesses both heroism and suffering, including an Irish Catholic soldier who dies on the battlefield in the arms of a Jewish chaplain. Gradually, his viewpoint begins to change. Across the lines in Belgium, the German forces led by the brutal Lieutenant Kurt von Schnieditz execute Madam Harbrok and her little son, believing them guilty of aiding the enemy, but because of Virginie Harbrok's beauty, he spares her. Philip rescues Virginie and, learning that she has lost her family, sends her to live with his mother in America. Shortly afterward, "Lefty," Philip's old chauffeur and close friend on the battlefield, sacrifices his life for Philip, finally dispelling Philip's notions of class and race distinction. In his grief, he reclaims his belief in Christ. At the same time, von Schnieditz is shot by one of the "good" Germans, as his troops rise in revolt with cries of "Long Live Democracy!" Upon his return home, Philip is reunited with Virginie.

The backstory: Actor Raymond McKee (1892–1984) was actually an army lieutenant, having served in France from 1917 to 1918, and wore his uniform throughout the movie. He met and fell in love with actress Marguerite Courtot (1897–1986) on the set of *The Unbeliever*. They married shortly afterward and remained married for nearly 60 years. Erich von Stroheim was dating actress Valerie Germonprez (1897–1988) when he took her to see the movie (at her request) after it had been released to the general public. After seeing the movie, von Stroheim reported, "she took one look at me and ran away. I finally caught up with her and she said, 'I don't think I want to go home with you.'" There was a long argument, but eventually he got his point across: "In real life I am not exactly like in reel life."[27] They were married in 1919 and remained married for 38 years.

Critical response: *The New York Times* in a February 12, 1918, review praised the United States Marine Corps for their cooperation in filming the action scenes in Quantico, Virginia, emphasizing that "many scenes of the marines in action were effectively worked into the story to give the effect of real war." The review also noted that "several scenes depict Prussian brutality in realistically ugly form, but rebellion against it by Germans themselves prevents sweeping condemnation of the Teutonic people."[28]

Variety's February 15, 1918, review praised von Stroheim (even while getting his name wrong): "German cruelty is driven home forcibly by Karl [sic] von Stroheim in the role of a lieutenant of the Prussians. It is true to life in its military bearing. He is the German officer to perfection. So much so that there was a groan and a hiss from the audience at the Rivoli Monday when he committed several heart-rending atrocities."[29]

3. "Horrible Hun" Films of 1918

His next role was not what he expected: *Hearts of the World*, released March 12, 1918,[30] by Paramount Pictures, directed by D. W. Griffith. Cast: Lillian Gish (the girl), Robert Harron (the boy), Dorothy Gish (the little disturber), Ben Alexander (the boy's littlest brother), Noël Coward (the man with the wheelbarrow/a villager in the streets), George Siegmann (Von Strohm), Sir Edward Grey (as himself, uncredited), Anne Harron (a woman with a daughter, uncredited), John Harron (a boy with a barrel, uncredited), Mary Harron (a wounded girl, uncredited), Tessie Harron (a refugee, uncredited), Lady Lavery (a nurse, uncredited), Jules Lemontier (a stretcher bearer, uncredited), Adolph Lestina (the grandfather), David Lloyd George (himself, uncredited), Diana Manners (nurse, uncredited), René Viviani (himself, uncredited), Erich von Stroheim (a Hun, uncredited), Francis Marion (the boy's other brother, uncredited). Plot[31]: Two families live next to each other in a French village on the eve of World War I. The boy of one of the families falls in love with the only daughter in the other family. As they make preparations for the marriage, World War I breaks out, and although the boy is American, he feels that he should fight for the country in which he lives. When the French retreat, the village is shelled. The boy's father and the girl's mother and grandfather are killed. The girl, deranged, wanders aimlessly through the battlefield and comes upon the boy, badly wounded and unconscious. She finds her way back to the village, where she is nursed back to health by the little disturber, who had previously been a rival for the boy's affections. The boy is carried off by the Red Cross. The Germans occupy the village. Von Strohm, a German officer, lusts after the girl and tries to rape her, but she narrowly escapes when he is called away by his commanding officer. Upon his recovery, the boy, disguised as a German officer, infiltrates the enemy-occupied village and finds the girl. The two of them are forced to kill a German sergeant who discovers them. Von Strohm finds the dead sergeant and locates the boy and the girl, who are locked in an upper room at the inn. It's a race against time with the Germans trying to break the door down as the French return to retake the village. The French are triumphant, Von Strohm and the Germans are defeated, and the boy and the girl are saved.

The backstory: The idea for *Hearts of the World* originated at the British War Office Cinematograph Committee at some point in the winter of 1916–1917. Hoping to turn out a film that would inspire Americans to join in the fight against Germany, the office contacted D. W. Griffith (David Wark Griffith, 1875–1948), America's premier filmmaker, with

The Silents Go to War

the idea. Griffith liked the idea and began working on the script sometime in 1917. Although the United States declared war on Germany in April of 1917, the idea of encouraging Americans to enlist was vital, and the film went forward as an inspirational propaganda piece. Griffith went to England, where he was given permission to film footage on actual battlefield locations in France that were still being shelled by the Germans. Griffith was presented to George V and Queen Mary, as well as members of London's aristocracy.[32] Among them were Lady Lavery and Diana Manners, who agreed to appear in uncredited roles. Playwright Noël Coward also appeared as an extra but made sure that he was listed in the credits.[33]

Griffith's cast included his favorite leading lady, Lillian Gish (1893–1993), as well as her sister Dorothy Gish (1898–1968), and young leading man Robert Harron (1893–1920).[34] For the role of the chief German villain, Griffith had rehearsed von Stroheim for the part but ultimately decided on actor George Siegmann, since he thought that the big, burly actor would make a more threatening, menacing rapist. Von Stroheim was bitterly disappointed; he had carefully worked out the nuances of his character, and even Griffith's offering to name the character "von Stroheim" after him was not met with appreciation. Instead, Griffith called the character "Von Strohm." Von Stroheim played a small, uncredited part as a Hun, but he was instantly recognizable in a short scene abusing a poor French peasant played by Noël Coward. Additionally, Griffith had also engaged von Stroheim as a military/costume advisor on the picture but failed to give him any credit as either an actor or advisor. It is possible that Griffith thought that the name "von Stroheim" was too close in name to "Von Strohm" and would confuse audiences, but that is not known for sure.[35] In any event, the picture was a great success, doing sell-out business in its bookings in New York, Los Angeles, Boston, and Chicago. Describing the audience reaction in Atlanta, Georgia, a theater manager stated, "I have never seen such enthusiasm displayed in a playhouse ... the people down here went wild. It was all we could do to keep many persons from standing in their seats."[36] Griffith was so sure of the success of the picture that he wrote a letter to President Wilson's secretary, Joseph Tumulty, urging him to get Wilson to see the movie, saying, "It has been hailed as the biggest propaganda to stir up patriotism yet put forth." Neither Wilson nor his wife Edith shared his viewpoint: after seeing the movie at the Washington, D.C., premiere, Mrs. Wilson wrote a highly critical letter to Griffith expressing displeasure with some of the more violent scenes. Griffith replied

3. "Horrible Hun" Films of 1918

that he would eliminate two of the scenes that she had most objected to so as not to "offend the refined and sensitive spirits such as yourself."[37]

Critical response: In a April 5, 1918, review, *The New York Times* was impressed by "the scenes of actual fighting made by Mr. Griffith at the front in co-operation of the British and French Governments. Sometimes one does not know whether what he is seeing is a real war or screen make-believe. The pictures of hand-to-hand fighting in the trenches, the bursting of shells from the big guns, the demolition of buildings, the scouting trips and raids into enemy trenches are impressively realistic." The review went on to praise the cast, noting that "all of the actors in the play were frequently applauded. Lillian Gish, as the Girl, moved the people in her biggest moments and Dorothy Gish, as the Little Disturber, with her bewitching ways, was applauded many times. Ben Alexander as the Littlest Brother was a child wonderful, and Robert Harron as the Boy, Robert Anderson as Monsieur Cuckoo, George Fawcett as the Village Carpenter and Eugene Pouyet as a Poilu were especially good."[38]

Variety's April 6, 1918, review, while lauding D. W. Griffith for "making his principal love story a fleshless skeleton upon which to hang a large number of brilliant war scenes, in an effort to show the horrors of war at close range," gave a great deal of praise to three of the principals. "Robert Harron as the Young American (the Boy) is the outstanding artist of the picture," the reviewer wrote. "Another role, admirably planted, but which fails to develop to the full strength of its promise is The Little Disturber. Dorothy Gish is The Disturber. Her sister Lillian Gish is the heroine. Both are excellent and wholly equal to the demands of their respective parts."[39]

George Siegmann, as Von Strohm, is not mentioned in either review.

While still finishing *Hearts of the World* in early February, D. W. Griffith decided to use his excess European footage in another war movie, writing a script that featured the kaiser's agents in Germany plotting to use disloyal German Americans to further their cause: *The Hun Within*, released on August 28, 1918, by Famous Players Lasky, directed by Chester Withey. Cast: Dorothy Gish (Beth), George Fawcett (Henry Wagner), Charles K. Gerrard (Karl Wagner), Douglas MacLean (Frank Douglas), Herbert Sutch (Krippen), Max Davidson (Max), Lillian Clark (Leone), Robert Anderson (Krug), Erich von Stroheim (Von Bickel), Adolph Lestina (Beth's father), Kate Bruce (Beth's mother). Plot[40]: The American-born son (Karl Wagner) of a German American father (Henry Wagner) visits Germany before the First World War, attends a German college, and swears allegiance to the German cause. At the start of the war, Karl is sent back to the United States by spymaster Von Bickel with instructions to blow up an America troop transport. His sweetheart Beth is appalled when Karl drinks to the kaiser's health. Henry denounces his son as a traitor, but Karl makes plans with Krug, Von Bickel's agent, to blow up an American transport ship. Although Beth loves Karl, she is drawn to her school friend Frank Douglas, who has joined the United States Secret Service. While Krug plants a bomb on the ship, Karl imprisons Beth. Frank, learning of the plot, fights off the band of spies and rescues Beth. The two throw the bomb off the ship just in time to prevent the explosion, after which Karl and his cohorts are apprehended. Realizing that she loves Frank, Beth marries him.

The backstory: After writing the script for *The Hun Within*, D. W. Griffith assigned his young protégé Chester Withey (1887–1939) to direct the film.[41] Withey started his career as an actor in films in 1913, eventually turning to directing in 1917 with a crime drama *The Bad Boy* starring his friend Robert Harron. Griffith liked the film and would subsequently cast Robert Harron in his star-making role in *Hearts of the World* and give Withey a chance to direct under his tutelage. Von Stroheim was immediately recognizable to audiences as the nasty German spy, so much so that, while taking his fiancée Valerie Germonprez to dinner one evening at the Ship Café in Venice, California, he was pelted with bread rolls by some of his fellow actors,[42] perhaps as a bizarre acknowledgment of his notoriety as the screen's most detestable Hun.

Critical response: Reviews were enthusiastic, with *The New York Times* lauding the film, saying in part:

> It's plot is a plot, not a series of loosely linked episodes arranged for whatever effect they individually may have, and several of its characters are screen personalities that one will remember. Dorothy Gish, as the American girl, will conquer new worlds on motion picture spectators, and George Fawcett's realistically sympathetic portrayal of the German-American father whose loyalty never falters, but who does not throw off the old ties lightly, is bound to breed respect and understanding such as he gains in actual life. Charles Gerrard plays with skill the part of the disloyal son, and Douglas MacLean as the American youth brings the atmosphere of his role into what he does. Not the least among those to be credited with contributions are Chester Withey, the director, and Granville Warwick,[43] the author of the scenario.[44]

In a September 7, 1918, review, *The New York Times Tribune* stated, "*The Hun Within* is one of the most beautifully produced pictures seen

3. "Horrible Hun" Films of 1918

recently and it is hard to mention anyone, excepting Griffith, who could make a picture like it. It is a masterpiece, one of the best pictures shown this season."[45] *The New York Evening Telegram* agreed, declaring in their same-day review that "there are numerous scenes that are genuinely exciting, and there is not a moment when the action drops. Dorothy Gish is most effective, George Fawcett plays with telling effect and force."[46]

With his poisonous portrayals of villainous Huns in *The Unbeliever, Hearts of the World,* and *The Hun Within,* Erich von Stroheim would finally be offered a leading role that would define the term "Horrible Hun" and make him a star character actor: *The Heart of Humanity*, released on December 22, 1918, by Universal Pictures, directed by Allen Holubar. Cast: Dorothy Phillips (Nanette), William Stowell (John Patricia), Robert Anderson (Paul Patricia), Walt Whitman (Father Michael), Margaret Mann (Widow Patricia), Erich von Stroheim (Eric von Eberhard), Lloyd Hughes (Jules Patricia), Frank Braidwood (Maurice Patricia), George Hackathorne (Louis Patricia), Patrick H. O'Malley Jr. (Clancy), William Welsh (Prussian officer), Lieutenant Smith (Canadian officer), Joseph W. Girard (Canadian colonel), Valerie Germonprez (ambulance driver). Plot[47]: The Patricia family—a widowed mother and her five sons, John, Paul, Jules, Maurice, and Louis—lives in a remote Canadian village. All of the boys are in love with Nanette, the niece of Father Michael, but she loves only one of them—eldest son John. One day, John brings home a German friend, Eric von Eberhard. Von Eberhard tries to seduce Nanette but fails. Not long after, John and Nanette are married by Father Michael. The wedding reception is interrupted by a horseman bringing news that war has been declared in Europe; von Eberhard (actually a German lieutenant) leaves to fight for Germany, and the brothers all enlist and leave a month later. Nanette is pregnant, and their son is born while John is fighting in Belgium. Nanette, feeling that she is needed more in Europe than at home, leaves the baby with his grandmother and becomes a Red Cross nurse. In Europe, when starving Belgian children cry out for food, Lieutenant von Eberhard instead empties cans of milk into the mud. One by one, the brothers die in combat; one of the brothers (Paul) is killed by von Eberhard, who grinds his boot in his face as he lies dying. Only John is left, and he is taken prisoner by the Germans. Nanette nurses French and Belgian children in a convent that is captured by the Germans. Von Eberhard and his men pursue her into a Red Cross building, where she is hiding with a crying child. Von Eberhard dismisses his men and then tries to rape her. The crying baby interrupts his attack, so he throws the baby out of a window. He rips off most of her clothing (using his teeth to tear the buttons off her blouse) until she goes berserk and locks herself in the next room. At the same time, John escapes from his captors, reunites with Canadian soldiers, and goes to rescue Nanette. He arrives just in time to kill the lieutenant, but Nanette, delusional, thinks that she is about to be raped and stabs herself. She recovers, and later, accompanied by homeless Belgian children, returns with John to Canada and to their own child. The ghosts of the four brothers appear at the dinner table; they have given their lives for humanity.

The backstory: Directed by Allen Holubar (1890–1923) and starring his wife Dorothy Phillips, *The Heart of Humanity* borrowed much from *Hearts of the World*, including plot elements and actors; aside from von Stroheim, Robert Anderson played Paul Patricia. Von Stroheim's characterization of von Eberhard—sexually suggestive, intellectually lecherous, and gleefully evil—is in direct contrast to George Siegmann's portrayal of brute strength in *Hearts of the World*.[48] D. W. Griffith was so sure that *The Heart of Humanity* would fail at the box office that he made a little bet with movie producer Sol Lesser: Griffith staked $100 that the movie would not gross more than $7,000. The movie proved to be a big hit with audiences, and he lost his bet.[49] Harry Pomeroy, manager of Montreal's 925-seat Holman Theatre, said of the film in a publicity ad: "It rocked Montreal to its foundations! From the time it was first shot on the screen until the conclusion not a soul in the place took their eyes from the screen and not a person left their seats, and when the finish of the picture came they rose from their seats in a body and cheered and cheered until the building shook under the mighty voiced opinion."[50]

Critical response: In a December 22, 1918, review, *The New York Times* characterized some of Holubar's battle panoramas "as among the most comprehensive and vivid ever reproduced on the screen," also delicately noting that "the making of a few of the scenes in which children appear was not very good for the children." The review also singled out Erich von Stroheim, opining that he played "a German villain as convincingly as any actor on the screen."[51]

Encouraged by Universal's Pictures publicity department, the *Ohio State Journal*'s May 28, 1919, issue devoted a full article to von Stroheim's noble birth, enthusing that "Erich Oswald Hans Maria von Stroheim, in Archduke Karl's Austrian regiment, makes his most recent appearance on the screen in *The Heart of Humanity*. This 'reformed'

3. "Horrible Hun" Films of 1918

Austrian 'soldat,' famed for his superb representations of Teutonic culture on the screen, has the most graphic role of his histrionic career.... He was persuaded against his will once again ... to typify the exponent of frightfulness by the argument that he was performing, in effect, a patriotic service in delineating the cruel product of an aristocratic system."[52]

Von Stroheim had finally achieved stardom and would go on to become one of the great directors of the silent era, whose body of work would rank in the same class as Cecil B. DeMille and D. W. Griffith.

While the public loved the "Horrible Hun" films depicting German atrocities, their loathing was specifically directed toward the one man who was the face of Germany: Kaiser Wilhelm II. The upcoming chapter delves into the "Kaiserphobia" movies that depicted Wilhelm in all his evil intentions and bombastic pomposity.

4

"Kaiserphobia" Films of 1918

Dramas and Comedies

By the beginning of 1918, Kaiser Wilhelm II (1859–1941) was the most hated man in America. With his bellicose attitude, tactless public statements, and contemptuous attitude toward Americans, he came to be regarded by the American public as the very epitome of the overbearing Hun.[1] The American public was also deeply suspicious of German Americans, some of whom were unfairly targeted as potential spies and saboteurs.[2] Hollywood filmmakers were quick to capitalize on the growing paranoia and would build on these fears, turning out Kaiser-hating, Kaiser-baiting films, serials, and animated cartoons as well as Huns-in-the-hometown films featuring nefarious German spies and "immigrant traitors."

January kicked off with the exciting 20-part serial *The Eagle's Eye*, produced by Wharton, Inc., highlighting patriotic Americans aiding the Secret Service in ferreting out German plots planned by the kaiser. The serial was based on the actual experiences of William J. Flynn, former chief of the United States Secret Service from 1912 to 1917. Viewing a special showing of the first three episodes at the Biltmore Hotel in New York City, Dr. William T. Hornaday, trustee of the American Defense Society, stated that "Chief Flynn's picture represents the ideal of patriotic propaganda toward which all active American societies had been striving for the past three years."[3] In a May 8, 1918, review, *The Lewiston Evening Herald* hailed the serial as "laying bare the treachery of the Imperial German Government's spies and plots in America."[4] At the same time, Jaxon Film Corporation released their 12-part serial *A Daughter of Uncle Sam* featuring a plucky all–American girl thwarting a German plot to obtain a secret weapon that can see through walls. Both serials played to

4. "Kaiserphobia" Films of 1918

packed theater houses across the United States from January into June of 1918.[5]

January also brought to the screen a movie that featured a real-life survivor of the *Lusitania* vowing revenge on the kaiser and Germany: *Lest We Forget*, released on January 27, 1918, by Metro Pictures, directed by Léonce Perret and co-directed Clifford P. Saum, produced by Rita Jolivet and Count Giuseppe de Cippico. Cast: Rita Jolivet (Rita Heriot), Hamilton Revelle (Harry Winslow), L. Rogers Lytton (Baron von Bergen), Kate Blancke (Madame Heriot), Clifford Saum (Fritz Muller), Emil Roe (Mayor Le Roux), Henry Smith (General Joffre), Gaby Perrier (young mother), bit parts: Texas Cooper, H. P. St. Leger, Ernest Maupain. Plot[6]: Rita Heriot is a French telegrapher who rises to fame as an opera star pre–World War I. She is courted by both wealthy American Harry Winslow and German diplomat Baron von Bergen. At the outbreak of the war, she returns to be with her family in France, where she becomes involved in espionage, is caught and sentenced to death by firing squad on orders of the kaiser. The American hears that she has been killed; in reality, she has survived and escapes to America. While in America, she receives an offer to return to the opera stage in England, and boards the *Lusitania*, despite warning from the German diplomat who has hatched a plot to sink the ship. On board, Rita strangles the diplomat, survives the sinking, and is eventually reunited with her American lover.

The backstory: New York–born actress Rita Jolivet (1884–1971) began her career on the London stage as a young girl in *Much Ado About Nothing*, and then played Juliet in *Romeo and Juliet* under the leadership of producer William Poel, who maintained a company of players performing Shakespearean plays in university towns in Britain. In 1910, she attained leading-lady status in George Alexander's play *The Eccentric Lord Cumberdene*. She made her debut on the New York stage in the role of Marsinah in the first American stage production of *Kismet* in 1911 starring Otis Skinner,[7] attracting the attention of the distinguished American theatrical manager Charles Frohman (1856–1915), with whom she became close friends. She made her American film debut in *The Unafraid* in 1914. Frohman and Jolivet, along with Jolivet's brother-in-law George Ley Vernon,[8] were passengers on the *Lusitania* when it was struck by a German torpedo on the night of May 7, 1915. The three were standing on deck when the torpedo struck the ship. Jolivet was able to find a lifejacket in her cabin while the two men gave their jackets to children; when Jolivet rejoined them, the ship was listing and passengers were falling into the sea. The two men urged Jolivet to jump, and as she did, she heard Frohman's last words, quoting a line from his great theatrical success *Peter Pan*: "Why fear death? It is the most beautiful adventure in life." Her last recollection was a wall of water dividing her from Frohman.[9] Rescued by a nearby ship, she returned to the United States and resumed her career, forming her own production company (with financial backing by Lewis Selznick) and producing and starring in *Lest We Forget* in 1918. She raised tens of thousands of dollars for the war effort, and during the week of April 22, 1918, "it was just one big Liberty Loan drive, for manager George A. McDermott arranged for the personal appearance of Rita Jolivet in conjunction with the forcefully patriotic film play 'Lest We Forget.' She made so strong a plea that $350,250 was subscribed to the loan."[10] The film was a huge financial success.

Critical response varied: In its January 28, 1918, review,[11] *The New York Times* declared the film "an eloquent statement of this country's reason for entering the war," while the January 19 review in *Moving Picture World* found it strong in the lead-up to the sinking "with many thrilling scenes."[12] *Variety*'s February 2, 1918, review trashed the film, sneering that the filmmakers were hypocritical in excluding the word "Lusitania" from the title when it was an obvious attempt to profit from the disaster. *Lest We Forget* "as a 'big picture' is severely disappointing," the review continued, "with no offsets, and that is as it should be, though the reality behind the production is commercialism. As a 'big picture' it is the poorest one from every angle that has ever been turned out over here. Picture people will have several laughs at its shortcomings." The performance of the film's star also met with criticism: "Miss Jolivet was called upon for dramatic work often, but was unequal to it, perhaps through her limited appearance before the screen."[13] In spite of *Variety*'s grousing, the film would perform well across the United States and Canada for nearly two years.

In March of 1918, two movies were presented with equally negative views of the kaiser. The first was a based-on-fact depiction of the kaiser and his court: *My Four Years in Germany*, released March 10, 1918, by Warner Bros., directed by William Nigh and co-directed by Clifford P. Saum. Cast: Halbert Brown (Ambassador James W. Gerard), Willard Dashiell (Sir Edward Goschen), Louis Dean (Kaiser Wilhelm II), Earl Schenck (Crown Prince of Germany), George Ridell (Field Marshall von Hindenburg), Frank Stone (Prince Henry of Prussia), Karl Dane (Chancellor von Bethmann-Hollweg), Fred Hearn (Foreign Minister von Jagow), Percy Standing (Under-Secretary Zimmerman), William

4. "Kaiserphobia" Films of 1918

Bittner (Grand Admiral von Tirpitz), Arthur C. Duvel (Field Marshall von Falkenhayn), Ann Dearing (Aimee Delaporte), A. B. Conkwright (a socialist), William Nigh (socialist). Plot[14]: Through the eyes of America's ambassador to Germany James W. Gerard (1867–1951), the kaiser and his court are introduced through a series of superimpositions comparing each one to an animal. The kaiser is shown riding on a hobbyhorse (controlled by his right hand, as his left hand is useless) while he makes plans to begin World War I. After the brutal conquest of Belgium, German troops are shown slaughtering innocent refugees and tormenting prisoners of war at a camp in Wittenberg. Near the end of the film, one of the German officials boasts that "America won't fight," text that dissolves into newsreel footage of President Wilson and marching American soldiers. Some American troops are seen fighting their way across European battlefields. As he bayonets another German soldier, a young American doughboy turns to his companions and says, "I promised Dad I'd get six."

The backstory: Based on the experiences of U.S. ambassador to Germany James W. Gerard as described in his book (see below), the film was the first nationally syndicated production of the newly formed Warner Bros. (Harry, Albert, Sam, and Jack). Gerard had served as Woodrow Wilson's ambassador to Germany from 1913 through 1917, and his view of the kaiser and his court was sharply critical, based on personal interactions and observations of Wilhelm's erratic behavior. When the German government asked him to leave the country in January of 1917, he was detained until rumors of the German ambassador to America being mistreated were disapproved. He was finally allowed to depart in February of 1917. When he arrived back in the United States, he retired from the diplomatic service and wrote *My Four Years in Germany*,[15] which quickly became a bestseller with the American public. The film version was massively promoted by Warner Bros., which included speaking appearances by Ambassador Gerard throughout the United States. It was a huge hit and profitable: the film cost $50,000 to produce and earned $430,000.[16] Audiences went wild: In New York City, the film opened to applause and cheers at the April premiere; thousands of people were turned away from showings in Indianapolis; and the National Convention of the General Federation of Women's Clubs endorsed the film to their membership as an "ideal example of the work that the motion picture is doing in quickening the patriotic fervor of Americans."[17]

Critical response was unanimously favorable. A March 15 *The New*

The Silents Go to War

York Times review stated: "Another movie exposé of the Kaiser and the workings of German politics reached Broadway last night at the Knickerbocker Theater, where a film version of ex–Ambassador James W. Gerard's book *My Four Years in Germany* was shown for the first time. Mr. Gerard, who figures conspicuously in the story, was among those present, and the audience which packed the house found much to applaud, considerable to hiss, and not a little to cheer. The most interesting part of the film is the treatment of the prisoners at Wittenberg."[18]

In another March 15, 1918, review, *Variety* observed: "*My Four Years in Germany* proports to depict the events in Berlin continuing up to the time the United States declared war on Germany, principally the events in which the American ambassador participated such as his interviews with the Kaiser and other German officials, showing how they systematically double crossed the United States and other nations with whom they were supposed to be on terms of amity."[19] The March 23 issue of *Motion Picture News* noted: "There is no stone left unturned to arouse the audience to a sense that the German manner of conducting war is synonymous with barbarism."[20] *Photoplay*'s June issue declared: "The entire production stands apart from the eagle screaming variety of war films, which are only too common in these martial times."[21]

The film did inspire considerable controversy: included were scenes of brutalities in German prison camps where English prisoners were exposed to Russian prisoners suffering from typhus, which purportedly came from newsreels but actually were faked in a small studio in Grantwood, New Jersey. In Chicago, the head of the city's censor board, Major Metellus Lucullus Funkhouser, ordered these scenes cut; he was overruled by George Creel, head of the Committee on Public Information. Creel requested that Funkhouser step down, and, due to pressure from the city of Chicago, Funkhouser was forced to resign. The scenes were restored by Funkhouser's successor.[22]

Next up: the Kaiser's brutality toward helpless women and children, his delight in the sinking of the *Lusitania*, and various other devious doings were depicted in a melodrama that made a star of its actor/director/producer/writer Rupert Julian:

The Kaiser, the Beast of Berlin, released March 19, 1918, by Universal Jewel. Written, produced, and directed by Rupert Julian. Cast: Rupert Julian (The Kaiser), Elmo Lincoln (Marcas the blacksmith), Nigel De Brulier (Captain von Neigle), Lon Chaney (Chancellor von Bethmann-Hollweg), Harry von Meter (Captain von Hancke), Harry Carter (General von Kluck), Joseph W. Girard (Ambassador Gerard),

4. "Kaiserphobia" Films of 1918

Evil personified by Rupert Julian as Kaiser Wilhelm II plotting world domination in Universal Jewel's 1918 production of *The Kaiser, the Beast of Berlin* (Picture Lux/The Hollywood Archive/Alamy Stock Photo.

Harry Holden (General Joffre), Alfred Allen (General John Pershing), C. E. Anderson (Captain Kovich), W. H. Bainbridge (Colonel Schmiedcke), Henry A. Barrows (General Douglas Haig), F. Beauregard (General von Weddingen), Walter Belasco (Admiral von Pliscott), Betty Carpenter (a bride), Edward Clark (General Erich von Falkenhagen), Ruth Clifford (Gabrielle), Wallace Coburn (General Rüdiger von der Goltz), F. Corcoran (General von Hoetzendorf), Orlo Eastman (President Woodrow Wilson), Mark Fenton (Admiral von Tirpitz), Robert Gordon (Louis Lomenie), Winter Hall (Dr. Von Gressler), Wadsworth Harris (General von Ruesselheim), Georgie Hupp (Little Jean), Ruby Lafayette (Grandmother Marcas), Gretchen Lederer (Bertha von Neigle), Frankie Lee (Hansel), Jack McDonald (King Albert I of Belgium), K. Painter (General Hans von Beseler), Zoe Rae (Gretel), Allan Sears (Captain von Wohlbold), Jay Smith (Field Marshal von Hindenburg), Pedro Sose (General Porfirio Díaz). Plot[23]: Marcas, a mighty blacksmith, lives with his daughter Gabrielle, his son Jean, and old Grandmother Marcas in the town of Louvain, Belgium. Far away in Berlin lives Emperor Wilhelm II, the kaiser of Germany. The kaiser is in a foul mood and hurls numerous insults at his aide Captain von Wohlbold. The captain, able to endure no more, strikes the kaiser and then commits suicide to atone for his disgrace. The power-hungry kaiser soon declares war, announcing his intention to his staff to invade Belgium. Marcas tries to calm the fears of his townspeople, saying that Belgium has signed a treaty of neutrality with Germany, but the kaiser has torn up the treaty, and soon troops march into Louvain. When a soldier tries to rape Gabrielle, Marcas kills the man and throws his body into a burning building to hide his crime. Soon after this, the kaiser orders the *Lusitania* sunk by Captain von Neigle. The kaiser bestows a medal on him, but the captain, haunted by the thoughts of the women and children he drowned, goes mad. The president of the United States declares war on Germany, and troops of soldiers go into battle against Germany. The kaiser is brought the news of the American entrance into the war and is stunned. An end to the war soon comes, after which Allied generals turn the kaiser over to King Albert I of Belgium. Albert appoints Marcas the blacksmith as his jailer.

The backstory: New Zealand–born Rupert Julian (1879–1943) had acted, directed, and starred in a number of movies from 1913 onward, but his role as the kaiser gained him instant recognition, and he later reprised the role in a number of films.[24] The film was a great hit, and Universal Studios, distributor of the film, spared no expense in promoting it. The film's posters generated such hate for the kaiser that in the New York City area, they were pulled down by movie patrons and used for target practice. In La Crosse, Wisconsin, the Majestic Theatre proclaimed in their newspaper advertising that "anyone who resents the message of this picture IS NOT A LOYAL AMERICAN." While there was a quiet boycott by elements of the local Wisconsin German American population, this had no effect on the popularity of the movie, which played to sold-out theaters. Attendance records were shattered in northern Ohio, and Seattle film patrons willingly paid higher-than-average ticket prices to view the movie.[25]

Critical response: *Moving Picture World*'s March 23, 1918, review[26] succinctly noted: "The main intent of the producers, and they have adhered to it admirably, was to give the observer a look at the private and public life of this human monster.... Mr. Julian's personal delineation of the Kaiser is a splendid bit of acting all told."

The March 30, 1918, issue of *Exhibitor's Herald* featured a spectacular review of the film,[27] lauding both the scenario and Rupert Julian's performance:

> Everyone concerned in the production of "The Kaiser the Beast of Berlin" must have a deep sense of satisfaction—a satisfaction which can only be obtained through a worthy task well done. If after viewing this picture the spectator is not filled with loathing and repulsion for everything Hohenzollern it is because the last vestige of decency has dropped from

4. "Kaiserphobia" Films of 1918

his makeup. Rupert Julian's impersonation of "The Beast" wallowing in the blood of the youth of Europe, his insane frenzy of joy jumping with leaps and bounds at the report of such new atrocity committed at his dictate, is a high tribute to that screen artist's ability.

In making "The Kaiser," the producers have accomplished more than the production of a photoplay—they have been of distinct service to the government and the allied cause. Through this the real danger confronting democratic nations of the earth will be presented to the masses in such tangible form as to defy contradiction.

The June *Photoplay* issue[28] said: "THE KAISER is less a photoplay than a dramatic presentation of the crimes of Germany dominated by the Satanic sneer of her leader. It shows the invasion of Belgium, the wreck of the *Lusitania* and the attempted drive towards Paris all guided by a fiend in a royal helmet and spiked moustache who does everything but snort fire. Rupert Julian impersonates this master-villain so successfully that his entrance is greeted with spontaneous hisses."

The third Liberty Bond drive kicked off in April of 1918, lasting three weeks. Hollywood luminaries hit the road on bond-selling tours: "America's Sweetheart" Mary Pickford took in $14 million in bond subscriptions during her swing through New England, Douglas Fairbanks raised over $8 million in the Middle West, fan favorite Marguerite Clark brought in nearly $15 million during her trip from Chicago to New Orleans, and Charlie Chaplin sold over $500,000 in bonds in Atlanta, Georgia. Stars, stars, and more stars jumped on the bond bandwagon to raise funds for the war effort.[29] The cartoon world also contributed to the bond drive, with Paramount-Bray Pictographs coming out with *Liberty Bonds*, featuring the all–American war eagle defeating the kaiser's parrot!

"Huns in the hometown" was given a laughable look in a movie starring one of America's most beloved comediennes in a May 1918 release:

Joan of Plattsburg, released on May 5, 1918, by Goldwyn Pictures Corporation, directed by William Humphrey and George Loane Tucker. Cast: Mabel Normand (Joan), Robert Elliot (Captain Lane), William Frederic (Superintendent Fisher), Joseph W. Smiley (Ingleton), Edward Elkas (Silverstein), John Webb Dillon (Miggs), William Dashiell (Colonel), Edith McAlpin (Mrs. Lane), Isabel Vernon (Mrs. Miggs). Plot[30]: Joan is an earnest little orphan who becomes interested in the drilling of soldiers at an American World War I training camp in Plattsburg near where the orphan asylum is located. One day, while evading the cruel superintendent, she hides in the cellar and reads a story about

The Silents Go to War

Mabel Normand as poor little orphan Joan, slaving away in the dingy orphanage kitchen in the 1918 Goldwyn Pictures production of *Joan of Plattsburg* (Picture Lux/The Hollywood Archive/Alamy Stock Photo).

Joan of Arc and imagines herself as the reincarnation of the warrior maid. Hearing voices in the cellar, she thinks that, like Joan, she can hear voices. The voices are actually German spies plotting to acquire the important invention of a young man named Ingleton, staying at the camp under the guardianship of Captain Lane. When Joan reports the conversation to Captain Lane, with whom she is in love, he refuses to believe her. Later, he realizes the plot is real and, with Joan's help, captures the spies. He sends her to live with his mother, proposing marriage after he returns from the war, and Joan accepts.

The backstory: By 1918, Mabel Normand (1893–1930) was one of the foremost film comediennes in Hollywood and had become famous as the "pie-in-the-face girl" in numerous Mack Sennett Keystone Cop comedies. She was instrumental in giving Charlie Chaplin his start and in 1916 had opened her own company in a tumultuous partnership with Sennett. By 1918, that strained relationship had at come to an end, and Normand signed a $3,500-per-week contract with Samuel Goldwyn

4. "Kaiserphobia" Films of 1918

Pictures.³¹ Goldwyn was able to secure the permission of the United States government to film a number of shots showing student officers in training, and Mabel Normand and her directors were given permission by the Plattsburg commandant to film any routine of the camp that was needed to further the storyline. Normand was not permitted to interact with soldiers in any of the scenes, however. To express thanks, Goldwyn named the picture after the camp.³² In spite of the (limited) cooperation of the government in the making of *Joan of Plattsburg*, the film was ultimately a box office failure, not generating the income or the audiences expected of a Mabel Normand picture.

Critical response: In an unflattering May 9 review,³³ *The New York Times* said, "To expect an actress who has scored her biggest hit in broad farce to illuminate the face of a modern Joan with the divine fire of the Maid of Orleans is to look for a miracle." The May 18 *Exhibitor's Herald* review³⁴ was somewhat kinder, opining that "the story of *Joan of Plattsburg* is not as strong as one might expect, probably due to the fact that it was necessary to revamp it to comply with the government wishes. But Mabel Normand does much to add to its enjoyability, and for Mabel Normand's admirers, it will doubtless prove a good attraction."

May also saw the release of three different animated cartoons: *Doing His Bit* (released by the Educational Film Corporation of America) had popular hobo character Happy Hooligan making audiences laugh by dropping a bomb on the kaiser. *The 75 Mile Gun* (released by Fox Film Corporation) had those two zanies Mutt and Jeff capturing and turning the German super cannon on the kaiser and the crown prince. In stark contrast, *The Sinking of the* Lusitania (released by Jewel Productions) brought home the dark terror of the U-boat lurking beneath the ocean and the terrifying fates of the passengers, including the harrowing closing sequence with a mother struggling to keep her baby above the waves. Animated by distinguished cartoonist Winsor McCay (1869–1934) it was, at 12 minutes long, the longest work of animation ever released, and the first animated documentary.³⁵

June brought two features: one with a farcical look at the kaiser and the other a melodramatic mixture featuring a supposed slacker taking on a hometown Hun spy. The former was *To Hell with the Kaiser!*, released on June 30, 1918, by Screen Classics, Inc., directed by George Irving. Cast³⁶: Lawrence Grant (the kaiser/Robert Graubel), Olive Tell (Alice Monroe), Betty Howe (Ruth Monroe), John Sunderland (Winslow Dodge), Earl Schenck (crown prince), Mabel Wright (empress), Frank Currier (Professor Monroe), Karl Dane (von Bethmann-Hollweg),

The Silents Go to War

Walter P. Lewis (Satan), Henry Carvill (Bismarck), Charles Harley (Count Zeppelin), Emil Hoch (Von Hindenburg), George S. Trimble (Von Tirpitz), Frank Farrington (General Pershing), William J. Gross (councilor), May McAvoy (wounded girl), Maude Hill (mother superior), P. Reybo (Von Mackensen). Plot[37]: The film opens with the death of the kaiser's father Frederick III, and the abuse of his English-born mother immediately thereafter. Terrified of being assassinated, the kaiser hires lookalike actor Robert Graubel to impersonate him at various political functions. The kaiser makes a pact with Satan, whereby he will conquer the world in exchange for his soul. His armies invade France and Belgium, with the crown prince raping convent girls, including American Ruth Monroe, and gunning down protesting nuns. Ruth is the daughter of Professor Monroe, who has perfected a noiseless communications device. When the professor protests his daughter's treatment, he is executed. Ruth's sister Alice vows revenge. While Alice's sweetheart, Winston Dodge, fights with American forces as an aviator, Alice arranges through her friend Robert Graubel to meet the crown prince. Using her father's device, Alice is able to direct Winston and a battalion of planes to bomb the small German village where the kaiser is hiding. Alice then kills the crown prince. Captured by the Allies, the kaiser is dumped into a POW camp, where he commits suicide and wakes up in hell. Satan abdicates his throne, confessing that the kaiser's tortures are far more fiendish than any he has devised.

The backstory: Starring English-born character actor Lawrence Grant (1870–1952), *To Hell with the Kaiser!* was a huge hit; Metro Pictures publicized the picture by distributing thousands of lapel pins all over the country with the title imprinted upon them. The pins were so popular that the Toledo, Ohio Commerce Club had all of their members sporting the pins at their September meeting, and the city held over the picture for more than a week. In Pittsburgh, the theater playing the film was unable to handle the large crowds and moved to a house seating 2,500 for an extended run.[38]

Critical response: *The New York Times* panned the film, writing in its July 1 review[39]:

> Someone ought to write a movie of how this movie was made. It seems to be a sort of composite of the ideas of a number of movie-mad men who cast about in their imaginations for whatever would make a remunerative number of people hiss and ha-ha and try to win the war by cheering, and then dumped all that they found into a scenario. Many Americans would like to see the Crown Prince killed, so they had the deed done. What's easier—on

4. "Kaiserphobia" Films of 1918

the screen? More Americans would like to see the Kaiser captured. So they had that done, too. It was a cinch. And why not put both achievements to the credit of one wonderful American girl? Splendid. Let Alice do it. And she did. Seriously, "To Hell with the Kaiser!" seems a travesty of war and of America's serious purpose in it.

In contrast, *Variety* had a different opinion: their July 5 review highlighted the utter brutality of the Germans in a scene where "nothing is sacred to the invaders, and when the mother superior protests, she is shot dead in the presence of the Crown Prince, who declares he will take the first choice among the girls, and the others may follow suit," and concluded by calling the movie "a wonderfully effective propaganda picture ... is bound to arouse enthusiasm whenever shown."[40]

On the same day, Thomas Ince (well known for his pre-war pacifist production *Civilization*) released a much different film, featuring an unfairly labeled slacker taking on a German spy intent upon stealing a secret formula: *Claws of the Hun*, released on June 30, 1918, by the Thomas H. Ince Corporation, directed by Victor Schertzinger. Cast: Charles Ray (John Stanton), Jane Novak (Virginia Lee), Robert McKim (Alfred Werner), Dorcas Matthews (Muriel Charters), Melbourne MacDowell (Godrey Stanton), Mollie McConnell (Mrs. Godrey Stanton). Plot[41]: When the United States enters World War I, John Stanton wants to enlist, but his sick mother prevents him from going "over there" by telling him that the shock of his leaving would kill her. Frustrated when his friends and his fiancée, Virginia Lee, label him a slacker, John goes on a drinking spree and later is put (to dry out) into a room occupied by Alfred Werner, a German spy in the confidence of the elder Stanton, a munitions manufacturer. When John learns of Werner's plot to secure Godfrey Stanton's formula for a powerful explosive, he foils the plan and rescues his father at the risk of his own life. John's mother, realizing the necessity of defeating the Germans, sends her son off to war with her blessing.

The backstory: Charles Ray (1891–1943) was a Thomas Ince discovery, finding stardom with his boyish, juvenile performances in crowd-pleasers like 1913's *Favorite Son* and his star-making performance in 1915's Civil War historical drama *The Coward*, with *Photo-Play Journal* proclaiming him "Tom Ince's New Wonder-Boy."[42] Additionally, Ince and director Victor Schertzinger[43] composed a song especially for the film titled "I'm Giving You to Uncle Sam," which became a big hit with audiences around the country.

Critical response: *The New York Times* lauded the film, commenting

The Silents Go to War

in a July 1 review that *The Claws of the Hun* is "a melodrama in which an American manufacturer of munitions and his son are brought into conflict with German secret service agents. The play has more real plot, with better developed suspense, than most productions of its kind."[44]

A trio of short films released around the same time took a slapstick look at the kaiser: comedian Harold Lloyd plays an American doughboy who mistreats the kaiser in *Kicking the Germ Out of Germany*, and *The Geezer of Berlin* has the kaiser dropped by airplane into a bakery, pelted with pies, and shoved into an oven.[45] Comedian Larry Semon, master of extravagant gags, joined in the fun with his wildly inventive comedy *Huns and Hyphens*, culminating with a hair-raising chase of Hun spies across New York City.[46]

August brought a film involving conflicting loyalties of German Americans toward the war: *Me und Gott*, released on August 18 1918, by Romayne Super-Film Company, directed by Wyndham Gittens. Cast: Paul Weigel (the kaiser), Frank Brownlee (August Weber), Jim Welch (Chancellor von Hollweg), Fred Bond (Herman Weber), Nigel De Brulier (the pacifist), Jack McCredie (Irish), Gertrude De Vere (the daughter), Robert Dunbar (the father), Betty Burbank (Hilda), Josephine Crowell (Nanette), Adeline M. Alvord (the mother), Ray Eberle (Fifine). Plot[47]: August Weber is a former Prussian officer who served under the kaiser and Chancellor von Hollweg. He now runs a delicatessen store in Hoboken, New Jersey. His son Herman is an electrician, and when America enters the war against Germany, August plans to use Herman to help the Prussian cause by destroying munitions plants. Herman has allied himself with pacifists and is not ready to take strong measures against his country. But, when he sees his chums going to war, he tries to enlist in the United States Army, but is rejected because of a weak heart. His father plans that Herman nearly blows up a plant in the belief that he is helping the American cause, but Herman discovers the old man's perfidy and proves himself to the country that has given him a chance to prove that he is a loyal American.

The backstory: *Me und Gott* was the first picture released by the newly founded Romayne-Super Film Company, owned by Henry Y. Romayne, who decided to produce five- and six-reel features for independent release. He chose Barbados-born writer/director Wyndham Gettins (1885–1967) as the director of the film. Gettins chose Betty Burbank as the company's first leading actress, with Josephine Crowell playing supporting roles.[48] For the cameo role of the kaiser, actor Paul Weigel, born in Saxony and bearing a great likeness to Wilhelm II, was

4. "Kaiserphobia" Films of 1918

selected. English-born actor/singer Nigel De Brulier (1877–1948), who played the pacifist, had actually worked as a butler in a wealthy private household in Colorado in 1900 before attaining success on the American stage.

Critical response: *Motion Picture News* gave the film a positive review, noting in the September 7 issue that "this is the story of a conflicted young man of German parentage who realizes his destiny and stands up for his country!" The review also mentioned the acting of Frank Brownlee and Fred Bond as August and Herman Weber, respectively.[49]

On August 23, 1918, a directive came down from the Wilson administration that gave the film industry the recognition it had long craved for its contributions to the war effort: the War Industries Board, headed by financier Bernard Baruch (1870–1965), declared motion pictures an "essential industry" as a medium recognized by the United States government as necessary to the life of the nation.[50] The grateful picture industry would respond in kind, coming out with hit films that included, in addition to one showing mob justice dispensed to disloyal German Americans, a pair of patriotic comedies.

September saw the release of a film involving a true-life German counterintelligence spy starring as himself: *The Prussian Cur*, released on September 1, 1918, by Fox Film Corporation, directed by Raoul Walsh. Cast: Miriam Cooper (Rosie O'Grady), Sidney Mason (Dick Gregory), Captain Horst von der Goltz (Otto Goltz), Leonora Stewart (Lillian O'Grady), James Marcus (Patrick O'Grady), Pat O'Malley (Jimmie O'Grady), William McEwen (Count Johann von Bernstorff), William W. Black (Wolff von Eidel), Ralph C. Faulkner (Woodrow Wilson), Walter M. Lawrence (Wilhelm II), James Hathaway (Field Marshal von Hindenburg), P. C. Hartigan (Admiral von Tirpitz), John E. Franklin (Ambassador James W. Gerard), John W. Harbon (U.S. congressman). Plot[51]: The kaiser has plans to conquer the world while all the other nations are engaged in peaceful pursuits. The Germans enter France, and their U-boats work like sharks in the sea, and after many insults the RMS *Lusitania* is sunk, causing the United States to enter the war. Before Count Bernstorff leaves the country, he establishes a spy system headed by Otto Goltz. Under his orders, German agents burn factories, wreck trains, stir up labor troubles, and interfere with American war work. Goltz marries a young American woman and brutally drives her to her death. Her sister finds her dying and takes her home to die. Their young brother Patrick tracks Goltz to a small western town, where Goltz

The Silents Go to War

is running a nest of bomb-making spies. One of the spies tries to enlist a loyal German American in sabotage, but is rebuffed and arrested. Dick Gregory, an American soldier, sees Goltz on the street dressed in an officer's uniform on a day when a confidential order was given that no officer was to wear one. Dick follows him and has him arrested, as well as the rest of the spies. Goltz is freed from jail by a rioting group of pro–German sympathizers, but a squadron of hooded horsemen, commanded by Dick, sweeps into the mob and captures the sympathizers, who are made to swear allegiance to the American flag before being hauled off to jail. Eventually, Goltz is overtaken by Patrick and is killed. Meanwhile, American forces are pouring into France so fast that the kaiser sees his dream of world conquest crumbling and dies like a rat.

The backstory: German counterintelligence agent Horst von der Goltz[52] wrote a book titled *My Adventures as a German Secret Agent* in 1917, published in the United States by R. M. McBride & Co., which quickly became a best-seller. Sensing a golden propaganda opportunity, the Committee on Public Information had von der Goltz (basically playing himself) appear in William Fox's production of *The Prussian Cur* in 1918. Fox spared no expense in promoting the film in the trade papers, using an editorial cartoon concept to turn out an iconic image of a muscular, club-wielding Uncle Sam going after a cowering kaiser stepping on the bodies of his innocent Belgian victims.[53] Raoul Walsh, who directed the film, called it his "rottenest picture" ever for its anti–German sentiment, while his wife Miriam Cooper (who played Rosie O'Grady) called it the worst film in which she had ever appeared.[54] The film, which advocated mob violence, came out soon after President Wilson expressed to the nation that mob rule should cease. Contrary to the opinions of the director, leading lady, or even the president, the public loved the film, which did "Extra Big" business in theaters nationwide in October.[55]

Critical response: In her September 1, 1918, review for *The Los Angeles Times*, columnist Grace Kingsley said that *The Prussian Cur* had "an absorbing story thread that runs throughout." She continued: "With those who like their war news sugar-coated with fiction this picture is bound to make a smashing hit."[56] The *Moving Picture World*'s September 7, 1918, review by Walter K. Hill called the film "another picture created to foment the proper determination in the hearts of the Allies to 'Treat 'Em Rough' in the crucial test between democracy and military autocracy."[57] *The Richmond Palladium* called *The Prussian Cur* "a war drama of unusual strength,"[58] and *Exhibitor's Herald and Motography*

4. "Kaiserphobia" Films of 1918

enthused in an October 15, 1918, review, reflecting that, "unlike many propaganda pictures which are supposed to stir an audience to great indignation and enthusiasm, this picture really fulfills its mission, and registers all the recorded facts of the great World War in such a way that it adds fuel to the fine art of protest this country is making to *The Prussian Cur* and all that he represents."[59]

Homefront war fervor was running high in mid–September, and nobody embodied the virtues of feminine patriotism more than "America's Sweetheart" Mary Pickford: *Johanna Enlists*, released on September 15, 1918, by Mary Pickford Film Corporation/Famous Players-Lasky Corporation, Artcraft Pictures Corporation, directed by William Desmond Taylor. Cast: Mary Pickford (Johanna Renssaller), Anne Schaefer (Ma Renssaller), Fred Huntley (Pa Renssaller), Monte Blue (Private Vibbard), Douglas MacLean (Captain Archie van Renssaller), Emory Johnson (Lt. Frank Le Roy). Plot[60]: Johanna Renssaller is an uncouth, freckled country lass who works from dawn until late at night caring for her siblings and livestock on her father's Pennsylvania farm. Her only love affairs were with the hired man and a "beautiful brakeman" on the railroad. The hired man proved to be married, and the brakeman proved impossible. She prays for a beau ... and then one day a whole regiment of soldiers camp out on her father's land and she is overrun by men. Everyone from Lieutenant Emory down to Private Vibbard is charmed by the girl, as is Captain van Renssaller (although he won't admit it). Johanna takes milk baths, tries Isadora Duncan–style calisthenics, bakes pies for the men, and finally falls in love with Captain van Renssaller. She tells the men how much she hates the kaiser and wants America to win. When the captain realizes that she comes from good, solid Dutch stock, just like he does, he decides to marry her when the regiment packs up and heads for the next town. Johanna rides off proudly at the head of the officer staff at his side.

The backstory: By 1918, Mary Pickford was one of the major forces in the movie industry. In 1916, she signed a contract with movie mogul Adolph Zukor of Famous Players–Lasky (later called Paramount Pictures) for a salary of $10,000 a week as well as full authority over productions of the films in which she starred. In addition, her compensation was half of a film's profits plus a guarantee of $1,040,000, making her the first actress in film history to sign a million-dollar contract. She also became vice president of Pickford Film Corporation, a division of Paramount.[61] She produced *Johanna Enlists*; chose the director, William Desmond Taylor (1872–1922); hired powerhouse pioneer

The Silents Go to War

female screenwriter Frances Marion (1888–1973) as her own personal scenarist and good friend Charles Rosher (1885–1974) as her cinematographer; and selected the cast. Filming took place on location at Camp Kearney, near San Diego, California, with the participation of the U.S. Army 143rd Regiment of Field Artillery.[62] As usual, the film was a big hit with Pickford's legions of fans.

Critical response: *Variety*'s September 13, 1918, review gushed: "Seen at private showing the latest Mary Pickford feature, *Johanna Enlists* (Artcraft), is as attractive, refreshing and original a picture as one would care to see.... The comedy situations derived are delightful.... It is not the plot which makes the film interesting, but the charm of Mary Pickford, the delicate vein of comedy which runs through it all, and the excellent support from everyone concerned. Outside of the principals the soldiers shown are the actual members, now gone across, of the regiment to which Miss Pickford is a godmother."[63] *Moving Picture World*'s September 14 review[64] concurred; their reviewer Louis Reeves Harrison commented: "The regimental action and encampment near the house of Johanna of the story is real and is cleverly incorporated in the movement of the play at every stage of development. This realism, some humorous sub-titles and Miss Pickford's artistic interpretation constitute the main values, but they are winning enough to please almost any American film audience." *The Los Angeles Times* September 16 review[65] specifically gave a hearty endorsement to the charms of Mary Pickford: "Does anybody in pictures give us better, sweeter, more wholesome and natural comedy than Mary Pickford? And how does she manage to look forever like 14? And what does she do to her lovely face to make it so ugly when she wills? All these things are secrets of her wonderful art, and we would like to know."

On September 27, 1918, the Fourth Liberty Loan bond drive kicked off, with Hollywood stars including Mabel Normand, Douglas Fairbanks, Mary Pickford (smashing a bottle of California wine over a replica of a tank), Sessue Hayakawa, Corinne Griffith, Norma Talmadge, Mae Murray, Marguerite Clark, Charles Ray, and Alla Nazimova, joined by cowboy stars William S. Hart and William Farnum plus comedians Charlie Chaplin and Fatty Arbuckle, all participating in short skits during the coast-to-coast drive urging fans to support bond buying. Each of these stars also made short films[66] that were shown at theaters throughout the bond drive, as well as having their appeals syndicated by newspapers in cities across the United States.[67]

Fans were treated to more Mutt and Jeff cartoon mayhem in the

4. "Kaiserphobia" Films of 1918

fall from Fox Films: in *The Kaiser's New Dentist*, the boys set up shop in Berlin to attract the kaiser, kidnap him, and set out for America. In *Our Four Days in Germany*, Mutt and Jeff force the crown prince to take them to the kaiser, where they take the place of his chefs and turn his military dinner into a pie-throwing disaster![68]

Meanwhile, film fans were asking: why hasn't Charlie Chaplin enlisted? Charlie's answer:

Shoulder Arms, released on October 20, 1918, by First National Pictures, directed, written, and produced by Charlie Chaplin. Cast: Charlie Chaplin (Charlie, the Doughboy), Edna Purviance (French girl), Sydney Chaplin (the sergeant, Charlie's comrade/the kaiser), Jack Wilson (German crown prince), Henry Bergman (fat German sergeant/Field Marshal von Hindenburg/bartender), Albert Austin (American officer/ clean-shaven German soldier/bearded German soldier), Tom Wilson (dumb German wood-cutter), John Rand (U.S. soldier), J. Parks Jones (U.S. soldier), Loyal Underwood (small German officer), W. J. Allen (motorcyclist), L. A. Blaisdell (motorcyclist), C. L. Dice (motorcyclist), G. A. Godfrey (motorcyclist). Plot[69]: Charlie is recruited to the "awkward squad." He undergoes training in boot camp and is sent to the front line in France. He encounters all the privations of trench life—snipers,

Charlie Chaplin gets ready to go "over the top" in his 1918 hit *Shoulder Arms*, produced, written, and directed by Chaplin for First National Films (Photo 12/Alamy Stock Photo).

The Silents Go to War

flood, food rations, solitude, lice, and other vermin. He meets a French girl, whom he subsequently rescues from German troops. After assuming a series of disguises, he manages to hijack the German kaiser along with the crown prince and Field Marshal von Hindenburg and is fêted with a ticker-tape parade in New York City ... but then wakes up from his dream, still in the "awkward squad."

The backstory: Although Charlie Chaplin was known and loved worldwide for his films featuring his "Little Tramp" persona, the fact that he (as a British citizen) did not answer his country's call to arms in 1914 did not sit well with many people. For the British, any man of military age who did not join up and remained out of uniform was considered a coward and received white feathers; Chaplin received not only white feathers but also threatening letters and public attacks in newspapers questioning his courage,[70] with a smear campaign spearheaded by Lord Northcliffe, editor of Britain's influential newspaper *The Daily Mail*. The French press joined in, featuring a cartoon depicting The Tramp wearing a German helmet instead of his usual bowler hat.[71] Although he participated in many of the Liberty Loan bond drives, made a one-reeler called *The Bond* to boost bond buying, and had raised tens of thousands of dollars for the war effort, the fact remained that he was a very, very wealthy man, having signed a contract in 1917 with First National Films that guaranteed him $1 million per year. The film public was less than pleased, and in 1918, when the United States signed a treaty with Great Britain that permitted the drafting of British residents in America, Chaplin knew that he had to act. He had registered for the draft in 1917 and was rejected by British army doctors as being underweight and unfit for service, but he still had a cloud of doubt regarding his patriotism hanging over him. The answer was *Shoulder Arms*.[72] Originally conceived as a much longer picture, Chaplin deleted scenes and instead presented a three-reel film filled with clever sight gags, including Charlie heroically "going over the top" into battle ... and the ladder collapses! Later in the film, he disguises himself as a tree to infiltrate German lines. Instead of depicting the Germans as cruel and vicious, he lampoons them as bumblers, making them very human.[73] His ability to find humor and humanity in the grim realities of war made the picture a resounding success, with audiences (including servicemen and their families) flocking to see the movie. At the Star Theater in Elgin, Illinois, not only was the box office record shattered, but six doors were torn from their hinges, seven lobby frames were trampled to bits, a ticket box was crushed beyond repair, six policemen were

4. "Kaiserphobia" Films of 1918

badly bruised by the enthusiastic crowds, and a cast iron effigy of Charlie Chaplin was battered to pieces.[74]

Critical response: *Shoulder Arms* was acclaimed as a masterpiece, with the October 21, 1918, *New York Times* review[75] applauding:

> "The fool's funny," was the chuckling observation of one of those who saw Charlie Chaplin's new film, *Shoulder Arms*, at the Strand yesterday—and, apparently, that's what everybody felt. There have been learned discussions as to whether Chaplin's comedy is low or high, artistic or crude, but no one can deny that when he impersonates a screen foll he is funny. Many of those who go to find fault with him remain to laugh. They may still find fault, but they will keep on laughing.

Variety's review on the same day[76] agreed, saying:

> Chaplin wrote and directed the story. His camouflage as a small tree, during which he runs through a wood is one of the best and most original pieces of comedy ever put on the screen. There is some slapstick, laughably worked in, also pie-throwing with limburger cheese substituted. That occurs in the trenches. The trenches are good production bits. There is fun also in the dug-out, with the water, and a floating candle burning one of the boy's toes.

November brought two films. One asks the question: What do you do if you find out you're the illegitimate son of the kaiser? *Kaiser's Finish*, released on November 2, 1918, by Warner Bros. Pictures, directed by John Joseph Harvey and distributed by Warner Bros. Pictures. Cast: Earl Schenck (Robert Busch/crown prince), Claire Whitney (Emily Busch), Percy Standing (Richard Busch), Louis Dean (the kaiser), John Sunderland (Lieutenant Patin), Fred G. Hearn (Carl Von Strumpf), Charles T. Parr (Lewis Keene), Philip Van Loan (a Blue Devil pilot), Billie Wagner (a little French girl), Vic De Linsky (the butler). Plot[77]: In pre–World War I Germany, Kaiser Wilhelm fathers a number of illegitimate children and sends them to various parts of the world to be reared by his loyal agents. Under the guardianship of Dr. Carl Von Strumpf, one of these children, Robert Busch, grows up believing that he is the son of wealthy German American Richard Busch, but in reality Strumpf and Busch are servants of the kaiser. When the United States declares war on Germany, Robert expresses his earnest desire to enlist in the American army, much to the delight of his patriotic sister Emily. Before he can do so, however, Strumpf tells Robert the secret of his parentage, believing that the young man now will be eager to fight for Germany's cause. Robert feigns enthusiasm but secretly offers his services to the United States government as an American agent, and with the passport provided him by the Pan-German League, he goes to Germany, impersonates his look-alike brother the crown prince, kills him, kills the kaiser, and blows up the entire palace, thus sacrificing his life for the principles of democracy.

The backstory: After the success of their first film hit *My Four Years in Germany*, which came out in March of 1918, the Warner Bros. (Albert, Jack, Harry, and Sam) decided to produce a picture with an intriguing premise: What if the kaiser sires an illegitimate son who's the exact double of his legitimate son the crown prince? And what if that son turns out to be an American secret agent willing to sacrifice his life for the American cause of democracy? The brothers decided to have Earl Schenck reprise his role of the evil crown prince (having played him in both *My Four Years in Germany* and *To Hell with the Kaiser!*) but this time also playing his noble American twin brother, with notable results: the film turned out to be a runaway hit. When it opened for a run in Baltimore, crowds destroyed the lobby in their eagerness to get into the theater and streets were jammed with people trying to get in just behind them. A December report from the Washington, D.C., area noted that the film was "playing to phenomenal business in every house in which it has been booked."[78]

Critical response: In his early review for *Moving Picture World* dated October 19, 1918,[79] film critic Edward Weitzel enthused: "The result is a picture in which there is always something doing and it should prove to be a popular hit. It hits straight at the mark and hits home. There is nothing subtle about its propaganda." He went on to note that "acting honors go to Earl Schenck in the dual role of Robert Busch and the Crown Prince. Claire Whitey, Percy Standing and Louis Dean have the other leading parts."

The other November film takes a last, grim look at German treatment toward helpless French civilians: *The Road Through the Dark*, released on November 4, 1918, by Selznick Pictures, directed by Edmund Mortimer. Cast: Clara Kimball Young (Gabrielle Jardee), Jack Holt (Duke Karl), Henry Woodward (John Morgan), Elinor Fair (Marie-Louise), Bobby Connelly (Georges), John Stepping (Antoine Jardee), Lillian Leighton (Louise Jardee), Edward Kimball (Father Alphonse), Elmo Lincoln (Private Schultz), Eugenie Besserer (Aunt Julie). Plot[80]: Gabrielle Jardee, daughter of a conservative Parisian family, is in love with an America, John Morgan, of whom her parents disapprove. She is sent away from Paris to a small village, where her aunt lives with her sister and little brother. The war comes and the Germans enter the town. They shoot down men, outrage young girls, and kill women and children, including Gabrielle's young brother Georges. In order to

4. "Kaiserphobia" Films of 1918

help her country, she becomes the mistress of the German commandant, Duke Karl, goes to Berlin with him, and lives openly with him for three years. By means of a code that John understands she supplies the French government with valuable information. In Berlin, Karl discovers her rifling through his desk and she kills him in the struggle that ensues. She makes her escape to Paris, where she meets John, who offers her the love she thought she had lost.

The backstory: Clara Kimball Young (1890–1960) came from a family of actors and made her stage debut at the age of three. She toured in her parents' theater company, eventually marrying fellow actor James Young. In 1912, after sending a photograph to Vitagraph studios, she and her husband were offered yearly contracts with Vitagraph, and she quickly became one of the most popular leading ladies of the studio, usually playing virginal young women. She was signed to a contract by movie mogul Lewis J. Selznick, and together they formed the Clara Kimball Young Film Corporation.[81] This movie, the first of four in their brief collaboration, turned her into a (noble) patriotic sexpot[82] and elicited excellent reviews from both her public and film critics.

Critical response: *Variety*'s review on December 20, 1918,[83] was positive, but raised one potential issue:

> As a photoplay production, from the standpoint of acting, direction and atmospheric detail, it ranks with the best. The only doubt as to its success is how the general picture patrons will regard such a theme. Do they demand their heroines be delivered to the hero for the "clinch" as undefiled, or will they regard the circumstances as extenuating and accept her as a martyr to a sacred cause?

Moving Picture World's December 21 review[84] by Edward Weitzel concurred:

> When Maud Radford Warren wrote "The Road Through the Dark" she built her plot on a situation that is bound to arouse a difference of opinion as to whether its use is justified by the author. No one will deny its dramatic value. In order to help her country, by spying on the enemy, a young French girl becomes the mistress of a German officer, goes to Berlin with him and lives openly with him for three years. At the end of that time, he discovers her rifling his desk and she kills him in the struggle that ensues. Produced by Clara Kimball Young and her own company and released on the Select program, the picture has been adequately directed by Edmund Mortimer and given the benefit of a thoroughly competent cast. Its construction brings out the points of the story clearly and with dramatic effect.
>
> Kathryn Stuart made the scenario. She has introduced one incident that will not be accepted by loyal Americans. No one who has followed the

history of the German war lords in the present conflict is going to believe that His Highness, Duke Karl of Strellitz, was instructed by his superiors to stop all killing and unnecessary violence in the town he had captured where his soldiers are shown shooting down defenseless men and women and outraging young girls. The sooner this misleading incident is cut, the better for the picture.

According to the scenario, when the Duke receives this communication he tells the young French girl, who has just seen her aunt and little brother murdered and her young sister attacked by a brute of a Hun, that he has been instructed not to spare anyone in the village, but that she can save them all at the price of her honor. Gabrielle consents, and for three years conceals her loathing of him so skillfully that the duke never suspects his victim is not deeply in love with him. After killing the Duke Gabrielle escapes across the border and joins her American lover, with whom she has kept up a correspondence in code that betrayed valuable secrets to the Allies.

Clara Kimball Young plays Gabrielle with her usual artistic grasp and dramatic strength. Jack Holt, as the duke, is fully entitled to his position as leading support. The other characters are played by Henry Woodward as John Morgan, Eleanor Fair as Marie Louise, Bobby Connolly as Georges, John Stepping as Antoine Jardee, Lillian Leighton as Louise Jardee, Elmo Lincoln as Private Schultz, Edward M. Kimball as Father Alphonse, and Eugenie Besserer as Aunt Julie. Arthur Edeson was the photographer.

Vitrol toward the kaiser and all that he represented would continue unabated up through the end of 1918, including in a series of documentaries produced by the U.S. Army Signal Corps in conjunction with the CPI's Division of Films. These documentaries would represent American men of all races and creeds fighting for democracy and will be profiled in the next chapter.

5

Documentaries of 1918

Under the aegis of the Committee on Public Information (CPI) the United States Signal Corps in 1918 produced a number of documentaries made specifically to influence and support American participation in World War I.¹ The CPI films were shown in theaters decorated with flags, bunting, and patriotic paintings. Opening nights were often turned into war rallies, with invitations issued to prominent men and women in each community, as well as government officials and members of visiting war missions.²

In addition to the feature film documentaries, the CPI's Division of Films (under the directorship of Charles Hart) was also responsible for a weekly newsreel titled *The Official War Review*. Each weekly newsreel was edited from a combination of footage supplied by the Army Signal Corps and the French, British, and Italian film services. Although the Red Cross was the original conduit for screening French, British, and United States Signal Corps war footage through its own film production unit at the American Relief Clearing House in Paris, the CPI eventually reached an agreement with the Red Cross and persuaded them to turn over all of the film activities to the CPI film division. The next step was gaining control of foreign war films being shown in the United States.

Charles Hart nosed out the fact that Captain George Baynes, who controlled not only the British war pictures but the *Italian Film Journal* as well, had a lucrative deal with the Kineto Company, a laboratory responsible for printing his war films. It turned out that Baynes had sold the rights to his films to Kineto. The CPI immediately contacted Kineto's president, who, after a little persuasion and an appeal to his patriotism, gave the CPI control of all British and Italian war pictures in the United States.³

The French, under Edmond Ratisbonne, head of the French Pictorial Service, were the last holdouts. With the Red Cross out of the picture and British and Italian pictures now under the control of the CPI, Hart offered Ratisbonne the following agreement:

95

The Silents Go to War

It is our opinion that the Official French War Pictures can be shown to much better advantage through this Official War Review than under your present arrangement. We realize the importance of the financial returns you are receiving at the present from the News Weeklies and will arrange to pay you $400 a week during the life of this agreement for the exclusive rights to the weekly French pictures in the United States. The amount of footage to be devoted to the French pictures under this proposed agreement would be determined by the interest of the pictures. However, we will agree that a minimum of 100 feet of French pictures will be used in each issue.[4]

The French agreed, and Hart now had control of all war films in the United States. To distribute *The Official War Review*, he sold the rights to the Pathé Company, largest of the newsreel organizations. Under the contract terms, Pathé agreed to return 80 percent of the proceeds to the Division of Films.

Hart would start to assemble a production staff: Jane Stannard Johnson, former advertising and publicity manager for Paramount Pictures, was lured away to work for the CPI; from the Pathé newsreel organization, he hired experienced film editor H. C. Hoagland and his assistant Marie Ginoris. For cameramen, he hired veteran cameramen Albert Richard, Joseph Rucker, and Robert Donahue. From the Signal Corps came two cinematographers, Lieutenant Edwin F. Weigle and Lieutenant W. H. Durborough.[5]

In order to maintain good relations with the film industry, Hart established an advisory committee composed of the editors of the three leading industry trade magazines: Leslie Mason of the *Exhibitor's Trade Review*, James Hoff of *Moving Picture World*, and William Johnston from *Moving Picture News*.[6] In addition, Hart had the Scenario Department within the Division of Films offer a tempting deal to encourage private film companies to make films for the government. Hart authorized Scenario Department head Rufus Steele to offer private companies a completed script plus government permits, as well as the commercial rights to each picture. This not only saved the CPI the expense of producing films but guaranteed that Scenario Department productions would be widely distributed through commercial channels. This would allow private producers the opportunity not only to recoup their production expenses but also to make a profit. By the end of the war, 18 one-reel pictures were completed through this joint production plan. Films included two by the Pathé Company: *Solving the Farm Problem in the Nation* (mobilizing the United States Boy's Working Reserve Corps) and *Feeding the Fighter* (focusing on the work of the army quartermaster

5. Documentaries of 1918

and U.S. Food Administration). Universal films contributed *Reclaiming the Soldier's Duds* (showing the conservation efforts of the army quartermaster) and *The American Indian Gets into the War* (patriotic activities of American Indians). From Paramount-Bray came four films: *Keep 'Em Singing and Nothing Can Lick 'Em* (explaining the importance of vocal music in the military), *I'll Help Every Willing Worker Find a Job* (a film about the U.S. Employment Service), *A Girl's a Man for A' That and A' That* (highlighting women's war work), and *I Run the Biggest Life Insurance Company on Earth* (a film about the government's War Risk Bureau).[7] Chicago's Black film company, Ebony Films, contributed a patriotic spy spoof *Spying the Spy* with a bumbling Black detective hot on the trail of what he thinks is a German spy.[8] On the delicate subject of sex hygiene for soldiers, the Commission on Training Camp Activities (in cooperation with the CPI) produced *Fit to Fight* about the dangers of venereal disease. Written and directed by Army Lieutenant Edward H. Griffith with graphic photographs of lesions caused by venereal disease, the film was initially shown to U.S. soldiers but was released to the general public after the end of the war.[9]

Lastly, Hart turned his attention to the Signal Corps in France. Although the Corps Photographic Section had begun to produce an ongoing stream of filmed material for the CPI, there were often long delays in getting the footage to the CPI back in the United States. So, in May of 1918, Hart sent E. B. Hatrick, the CPI's film representative in France, on a tour of the facilities of the Signal Corps. Hatrick determined that what the Signal Corps needed most was a capable, no-nonsense film editor who could eliminate inferior material. He also made the recommendation that the Signal Corps separate its efforts to shoot a military history of the war from attempts to provide material for CPI propaganda films. By placing a CPI liaison with the Signal Corps Intelligence Section, Hatrick felt that the Division of Films could not only speed up the censorship process but obtain the best film material available. His suggestions were adopted by the Signal Corps; CPI film editor H. C. Hoagland became the liaison within the Signal Corps Intelligence Section, and for the rest of the war he funneled footage directly through James Kearney, the CPI director in France, eliminating the need to send film via registered mail or through a diplomatic pouch.[10]

The first documentary produced was *Pershing's Crusaders*, released on May 21, 1918. The early part of the film details the grueling process that whipped raw recruits into a clean, efficient fighting machine. The second part of the film was comprised of footage gleaned from previous

The Silents Go to War

wartime newsreels, augmented by actual footage shot in France. There was also a prologue, featuring President Woodrow Wilson speaking before the United States Congress, and the film ended with an image of an animated American flag overshadowing the emblem of the kaiser.[11]

The backstory: George Creel recruited journalist Walter Niebuhr (1890–1946)[12] to become the associate director of the CPI's Division of Film, giving him the job of producing America's first war documentaries. Niebuhr's opening shot of General John J. Pershing mounted on horseback, leading his troops, with a hazy image of medieval crusaders in the background, became the basis for the iconic poster used to publicize the picture, which became an instant hit with the public. The movie had its initial premiere on April 29, 1918, in Cincinnati, and the first official screening on May 21, 1918, in New York City played to sell-out crowds. The film would be shown in 24 cities around the nation. In each city, theaters would have the resident organist provide musical accompaniment for the film, usually patriotic songs.

Critical response: *The Milwaukee Journal*'s May 24, 1918, review[13] hailed *Pershing's Crusaders*, saying "as a pictorial record of how the war came to America and what America did to prepare for her share in the world conflict, the work cannot be excelled. It emblazons before its audience a picture of soldiery in the making so comprehensive and of such magnitude as to give a conception of our progress that is to be gained in no other way." *Variety*'s May 31, 1918, review[14] enthused: "One is impressed by the general excellence of the photography, which may be due to the fact that most of the scenes are taken in the open air."

The CPI would face congressional scrutiny for its expansion into feature films during hearings from June 11 through June 14, 1918, centering on the fact that their films, produced with government funding, were being sold for profit. Representative J. Swagar Sherley of Kentucky (1871–1941), chairman of the Appropriations Committee, asked George Creel to explain why this profit-making venture could not be turned over to the private film industry. Creel answered that films like *Pershing's Crusaders* did not really make a profit, since all income received was used to defray CPI production costs and to underwrite free film distribution at home and abroad. Nonetheless, the committee cut the CPI's government funding by 40 percent, and also included a provision that banned salary payments to any CPI employees of draft age, which affected between 15 and 20 men, forcing the CPI to cut back on some of its activities.[15]

Now came an attack on Creel and the CPI from an old foe: on June 19, 1918, at hearings on the motion picture war tax that was before the

5. Documentaries of 1918

House Ways and Means Committee, Patrick A. Powers, the treasurer of Universal Films, accused the CPI of giving the Hearst-Pathé Newsreel organization a complete monopoly of Signal Corps films in the United States. He also claimed that the government treated Hearst-Pathé with special deference because of the large number of employees who worked for the Division of Film.[16]

For Powers, the attack was personal: he had been appointed to the industry-based American Cinema Commission, but when the CPI created the Foreign Film Service, Powers was not asked to be part of the group. In addition, Powers was involved in an acrimonious dispute with Raymond B. Fosdick, the head of the War Department's Committee on Training Camp Activities. Fosdick and Powers had developed conflicting plans for showing films at military installations. That prompted Fosdick to write to President Wilson to complain about Power's "prima donna temperament." Creel was called in to mediate and eventually sided with Fosdick, causing more bad blood between Creel and Powers.[17]

Powers had a plan to explode his charges before the Ways and Means Committee. Universal Studios had shot a film, *The Yanks Are Coming*, at the Dayton-Wright airplane factory. Universal announced that *The Yanks Are Coming* would be shown at the Broadway Theater in New York City on June 23, 1918, knowing full well that government agents would seize the film, since Universal had not secured from the CPI the required permits to shoot the film at the airplane factory. On the night of the premiere, Universal had a sign hung in the lobby that read, "*The Yanks Are Coming* Stopped by Hearst Committee." With the theater sold out, Universal's attorney James M. Sheen walked to the front of the screen and announced that the film could not be shown because of Hearst's influence within the CPI. *The New York Times* gave the story front-page coverage, with a headline blaring "War Film Stopped, Hearst Influence on Creel Blamed."[18] In addition, Universal's publicity man Robert H. Cochrane held a press conference where he passed out a list of Hearst-CPI employees who were supposedly responsible for blocking the film.[19]

The CPI responded with its own press conference: Charles Hart contended that no one on the CPI payroll was still a Hearst employee, and that none of the so-called "Hearstlings" was in a position to influence the committee's decision as to whether or not to release *The Yanks Are Coming*. On June 25, 1918, George Creel gave the press an official statement[20] on the conflict between the CPI and Universal, which essentially said that Universal planned to exploit the film only for its own profit. The War Department under Secretary of War Newton D. Baker backed Creel's position, and appointed Major Nicholas Biddle, chief of the Army Intelligence Service in New York, to mediate the conflict between Powers and Creel. *The Yanks Are Coming* was never publicly released. The only people who ever saw the movie were the employees of the Dayton-Wright airplane factory, and the War Department later donated a print of the film to the Bureau of Aircraft Production in Washington, D.C. Universal never presented convincing evidence of Hearst influence, and the controversy dissipated a short time after the end of the hearings.

On July 30, 1918, the CPI released its second United States official war picture: *America's Answer to the Hun*, which covers the transfer of American manpower and materiel across the Atlantic, culminating in the first major engagement of American forces at the Battle of Château-Thierry in July of 1918. The film[21] starts with the caption: "The time has come when it is America's high privilege to spend her blood upon the fields of battle already hallowed by the sacrifice of her Allies' stalwart sons." American shipping has increased by "more than two million tons," with cargo vessels crossing the Atlantic under escort and unloading troops and equipment in France. American engineers construct ports to unload equipment, food, and supplies in France. Locomotives are assembled (Austrian prisoners of war help in the work) and cars and lorries full of supplies made in America are unloaded. The troops move forward on foot and by train to their base villages, and from their trenches launch an attack through the woods. The wounded are loaded onto a hospital train bound for a base hospital. Nearby, trainee pilots are taught to fly French-built Nieuport 17 and 27 fighters, along with veterans of the volunteer Escadrille Lafayette, now part of the elite 94th "Hat in the Ring" Pursuit Squadron, which include French-born Raoul Lufbery and Americans Douglas Campbell and Alan Winslow. In the battle zone, shells for 75 mm and 155 mm guns are moved into position in preparation for battle. American troops are shown eating in the trenches. The French commander, General Passaga, presents the Croix de Guerre to Colonel George Henry Shelton, Major John H. Douane, and Chaplain John B. de Valles of the U.S. 104th Infantry Regiment on April 25, 1918. On May 15, more guns—400 mm railway guns of the 53rd Artillery Corps—are moved into position. French, British, and American troops, including some wounded, talk together near Château-Thierry. As the initial bombardment opens up on May 31, trucks and columns of troops move up.[22] General John J. Pershing is

5. *Documentaries of 1918*

seen addressing his staff, and there is a shot of President Wilson making a speech. American troops are seen marching through Paris on July 4, 1918. The film ends with a brief mention of Britain: "So long as Britannia rules the waves, democracy is safe."

The backstory: Made as a means to show both the scope and detail of how America has prepared for the war, as well as the close relationship between American and French forces, the film, one hour and 20 minutes long, premiered at George M. Cohan's Theatre in New York City on July 30, 1918. Before the film, sailors from the Pelham Bay Naval Training Station sang "The Star-Spangled Banner," and a musical prelude composed by Hugo Riesenfeld[23] introduced the film. During the intermission, CPI chairman George Creel addressed the audience, explaining the purpose of the film and urging Americans "over here" to make supreme and unselfish efforts of their own on the other side.[24] The film was released to theaters across the United States and was enthusiastically received by the public.

Critical response: *The New York Times* headlined their review page on July 30, 1918, with the caption: "'America's Answer' Stirs War Spirit; Vivid Pictures Of All Our Forces At Work In France Cheered At Cohan Theatre. Creel Makes An Appeal Patriotic Music And Setting Add To Effectiveness Of Supplement To 'Pershing's Crusaders.'" The review[25] was magisterial, declaring in part:

> "America's Answer" was shown on the screen of the George M. Cohan Theater last night, first in flaming words symbolizing the spirit of the nation at war and then in the physical forces of men and munitions and the vast constructions that make the answer the practical, powerful thing it is on the fields of France. The purpose of the motion picture is to set before Americans here what Americans over there are doing and to bring the war as a living, familiar fact home to those who are fighting it on this side of the Atlantic, so that they may more actively realize their part in it. For accomplishing this purpose "America's Answer" is competent. It accomplished it last night with those who went to the Cohan Theatre. Not a man and not a woman in the crowd that filled the seats failed to feel the pull of the war, the urging of its influence, the sense of participation in it. It was not only that the music, tableau and almost every scene of the film brought forth cheers, but that the war seemed actually to come close in its full meaning for everyday life and to explain itself in many of the practical details that are needed for the stimulation of those who buy bonds and save food and spend their energies in a thousand occupations imperatively essential.

In the closing months of the war, the CPI turned out four two-reel films for the public: *If Your Soldier's Hit, Our Wings of Victory, Our*

The Silents Go to War

Horses of War, and *Making the Nation Fit*. These films were not released until after the war ended, and two other films, *The Storm of Steel* and *The Bath of Bullets*, made at the same time were never released to the public.²⁶

The CPI produced two last documentaries, shot at the end of the war.

The first one was *Our Colored Fighters*, a two-reel film released in late November of 1918 showcasing the heroics of Black soldiers in France, most notably the 369th New York Infantry Regiment (93rd Division) of the United States Army, known as the "Harlem Hellfighters." Running a little over 20 minutes, it was released through the Downing Film Company based in New York primarily for viewing by Black audiences; the film would later be released to Black theaters around the country.²⁷

The backstory: On September 16, 1918, George Creel announced that the Committee on Public Information had appointed Ralph W. Tyler, former auditor of the Navy Department and distinguished writer for the *Columbus Evening Dispatch*, as "the first colored man to be named as a regularly-commissioned war correspondent, to specialize on the conditions surrounding the colored troops in France and to make daily reports of the activities and engagements in which colored

The gallant 369th Regiment, known as "The Harlem Hellfighters," returning home in February 1919. The entire regiment received the French Croix de Guerre citation for bravery (American Photo Archive/Alamy Stock Photo).

5. Documentaries of 1918

soldiers are prominent. He will be on the staff of General Pershing, commander-in-chief of the American Expeditionary Forces overseas." In the three months that Ralph Tyler was in France, he would send back graphic dispatches of the important contributions of Black soldiers serving in American units under direct command of the French army, many of which were published in CPI publications that were circulated throughout the country.[28] One of the best-known units was the "Harlem Hellfighters," with the entire unit receiving the French Croix de Guerre for bravery against German troops, who (respectfully) gave them the nickname "Höllenkämpfer" (Hellfighters).[29]

Critical review: In the December 7, 1918, issue, the *Cleveland Advocate*[30] noted: "'Our Colored Fighters' is a two reel picture illustrating graphically the important part the Negro troops have taken in the World War. It pictorializes the enlistment and training of the colored soldiers in the cantonments and also shows them in action in some of the most thrilling combat overseas."

The third (and final) United States war picture was released by the CPI on November 18, 1918: *Under Four Flags*, which documented the American offensive in France. As a contribution to the Allied war effort, the film has scenes of the Italian Army fighting against the Austrians in the Alps, as well as footage of French and British soldiers fighting on the western front. Running at two hours, the film also showed French refugees fleeing from the Germans, enemy submarine attacks, the victorious battle of Château-Thierry, Field Marshal Haig on the British front, the Battle of Saint-Mihiel, and the review of U.S. and French troops by General Pershing.

The backstory: The armistice, declared on November 11, 1918, just as the film was being assembled by writer Kenneth C. Beaton of the CPI, rendered it useless as propaganda. To give it some value, however, quick shots of New Yorkers celebrating the war's end were inserted in the final reel, and the titles changed to make it a summary of the last days of the war.[31] The film, with 1,820 bookings in American theaters, grossed about $64,000, which did not live up to the expectations of the CPI Film Division. The movie premiered in New York City at both the Rialto and Rivoli Theatres at the end of November 1918.[32]

Critical reviews: The November 18, 1918, review[33] in *The New York Times* extolled the film:

> To say that Under Four Flags is a work of art, is first of all, to say that the United States Signal Corps and allied camera men, who took the pictures, performed their task exceptionally well. The response of the spectators was

spontaneous. Emotions mounted to a climax as the pictures were unrolled in dramatic sequence. The man in the street must see Under Four Flags to know what it is, both as a war review and as a picture. As for the music, by a skillful arrangement of both patriotic and popular airs and by the threading through it of significant motifs, it has been made to enhance the picture at every point.

The Great War ended on the 11th hour of the 11th day of the 11th month of 1918, and within 24 hours, the Committee on Public Information ended its activities. On November 14, 1918, the government announced the discontinuation of "the volunteer censorship agreement," and on the very next day the CPI issued a formal statement announcing an end to the censorship of cables, mail, and films.[34]

While the signing of the armistice ended the war, the American public's appetite for war propaganda films took time to fade, and there were five films released in 1919 (highlighted in the next chapter) that served as a reminder of the still-potent hatred of the Huns and Kaiser Wilhelm II.[35]

6

Postwar Films of 1919

January 1919: Germany was in complete turmoil. The populace was drained after four years of war. The kaiser had abdicated, people were rioting in the streets due to food shortages brought on by the war, and there was no cohesive leadership. The Marxist Spartacus League, with the newly formed Communist Party of Germany and the Independent Social Democratic Party, began mass demonstrations and labor strikes. The German Workers Party (*Deutsche Arbeiterpartei*, DAP), predecessor of the Nazi Party, was formed and joined in the strikes.

At the same time, President Woodrow Wilson of the United States was in France to attend the Paris Peace Conference in Versailles, which opened on January 18 with delegates from 27 nations attending. Germany was punished mercilessly for prosecuting the war and perpetrating war crimes on civilians: they were required to pay $269 billion gold marks—the equivalent of $37 billion—in reparations.[1]

Wilson pushed for a League of Nations, designed to solve international conflicts through diplomacy, and on January 25, the league was founded in the palace of Versailles in Paris, France, with 42 nations becoming founding members. When Wilson returned to the United States with the hope that the houses of Congress will ratify the agreement, it was defeated by an isolationist Congress that refused to ratify the league's agenda with its vague language and legal loopholes regarding America's sovereignty.[2] The United States would turn inward; Europe could solve its own problems in the future.

The American movie-going public welcomed peace, and the opportunity to throw off the years of patriotic film fervor. Still, antipathy and bitterness toward wartime German behavior was slow to fade, and Hollywood would release six postwar 1919 propaganda films (one comedy and five dramas) that reflected these negative feelings, starting with the January 1 release of *The Great Victory* or *The Great Victory, Wilson or the Kaiser? The Fall of the Hohenzollerns*, released by Metro Pictures, directed by Charles Miller. Cast: Creighton Hale (Conrad Le

The Silents Go to War

Brett), Florence Billings (Vilma Le Brett), Edward Connelly (Paul Le Brett), Helen Ferguson (Amy Gordon), Frank Currier (William Gordon), Frederick Truesdell (Woodrow Wilson), Henry Kolker (Kaiser Wilhelm II), Joseph Kilgour (General Von Bissing), Margaret McWade (Nurse Edith Cavell), Earl Schenck (Crown Prince), Henry Carvill (Count von Bismarck), Florence Short (Elaine), Baby Ivy Ward (Elaine's child), Andy Clark (François), James A. Furey (priest), Fred R. Stanton (Sergeant Gross), Leo Delaney (Frederick III), Fanny Cogan (Empress Victoria), Emil Hoch (General von Hindenburg), Charles Edwards (Rev. Joseph Wilson), May Allen (Mrs. Joseph Wilson), Karl Dane (Von Bethmann-Hollweg), Carl De Mel (Count von Moltke). Plot[3]: A young French Alsatian man is forced to enlist in the German army on the outbreak of the war. Appalled by the atrocities committed by his fellow soldiers, including the rape and murder of his sister, the desecration of churches, and the murder of babies, he manages to escape and makes his way to America. He falls in love with and marries an American nurse, and by special permission of President Wilson, enlists in the American army, goes back to Alsace, and avenges the death of his sister at the hands of a German lieutenant.

The backstory: *The Great Victory* was originally shot prior to the armistice as a 10-reel picture. Postwar editing cut it down to five reels, with scenes contrasting the birth of Woodrow Wilson and the imperialistic kaiser. The film details the kaiser's desire to rule the world, the rape of Belgium (led by the crown prince, played by Earl Schenck, reprising this role for the third time[4]), the shooting by the Germans of nurse Edith Cavell (1865–1916), and other atrocities that prompt President Wilson to bring America into the war to defeat the Germans. The last scenes in the film, added to maintain audience interest, show Woodrow Wilson sailing for France to attend the peace conference. Shown nationwide, the film was a modest success with audiences, whose interest in war films had begun to taper off.[5]

Critical response: Writing for the January 4, 1919, issue of *Moving Picture World*, critic Walter K. Hill thought the picture would keep Americans focused on "the fiends who ran riot among their decent and respectable neighbors." He was also thankful that there was no attempt to envision the future, and thought that "for the immediate present, it was a very good exhibitor's prospect."[6]

Early January also saw a step forward for the film industry: the formation of Hollywood's *American Society of Cinematographers*, established to advance the science and art of cinematography.

6. Postwar Films of 1919

Founding members included: Eugene Gaudio (1886–1920), special effects wizard for the 1916 fantasy/adventure *20,000 Leagues Under the Sea*[7]; Robert Newhard (1884–1945), Thomas Ince's choice for his 1916 production of *Civilization*; Charles G. Rosher (1885–1974), Mary Pickford's photographer for her 1918 comedy *Johanna Enlists*; Fred LeRoy Granville (1896–1932), lensman for 1918's *The Heart of Humanity*; Victor Milner (1893–1972), distinguished photographer of Presidents Theodore Roosevelt and Woodrow Wilson; and Phil Rosen (1888–1951), master photographer of silent vamp star Theda Bara.

On February 5, director D. W. Griffith and actors/producers Charlie Chaplin, Mary Pickford, and Douglas Fairbanks launched their own movie studio, United Artists. The premise of the studio was to allow actors and directors to control their own interests, rather than being dependent upon commercial studios. When studio heads heard about the upstart studio, Richard A. Rowland, head of Metro Studios,

Henry B. Walthall (left) as Michael Lanyard (a.k.a. "The Lone Wolf"), jewel thief/British spy, menaced by Lon Chaney (center) as jewel thief/Hun assassin Karl Eckstrom in Paramount Pictures' 1919 production of *The False Faces* (the actor at right is unidentified) (World History Archive/Alamy Stock Photo).

The Silents Go to War

was heard to laughingly remark that "the inmates are taking over the asylum!"

Later in the month, a film premiered that served as a bravura showcase for the "Man of a Thousand Faces," character actor Lon Chaney, portraying an evil Hun assassin pitted against the famous English gentleman thief known as "The Lone Wolf":

The False Faces, released on February 16, 1919, by Paramount Pictures, directed by Irvin Willat and produced by Thomas Ince.[8] Cast: Henry B. Walthall (Michael Lanyard, a.k.a. the Lone Wolf), Mary Anderson (Cecelia Brooke), Lon Chaney (Karl Eckstrom), Milton Ross (Ralph Crane), Thornton Edwards (Lieutenant Thackery), William Bowman (Captain Osborne), Garry McGarry (submarine lieutenant), Ernest Pasque (Blensop). Plot[9]: During World War I, Michael Lanyard, a former jewel thief known as "The Lone Wolf," is assigned to cross no man's land to steal a cylinder with important information and bring it to Allied intelligence headquarters on the British side. Once there, British intelligence officer Captain Osborne sends him on a mission to the United States, crossing the Atlantic by ship. German agents are out to stop him, however, headed by the dreaded Hun assassin Karl Eckstrom. Eckstrom, a former jewel thief himself, hates Lanyard, and has had his sister and her child murdered in occupied Belgium. On the ship, Lanyard meets Cecilia Brooke, who gives him a secret message. Eckstrom is able to signal a German submarine in the area and has the boat torpedoed. Lanyard is picked up by the drunken U-boat commander, who was responsible for sinking the *Lusitania*. The commander is haunted by the faces of those his vessel has drowned, surrounding and imploring him for air. Lanyard is able to fool the crew into believing that he is actually Eckstrom and manages to destroy the sub as it heads for a secret base off Martha's Vineyard in the United States. He heads for New York City, where he discovers that Cecilia, who also survived, is being held by Eckstrom and the Germans in a secret headquarters there. Lanyard breaks in and fights Eckstrom to rescue Cecilia, tricking Eckstrom's own men into shooting Eckstrom moments before they are seized by the American Secret Service. Lanyard realizes that he loves Cecilia, learning that a man he thought was her sweetheart was actually her brother, also a spy.

The backstory: Thomas Ince included a number of motifs from his 1916 film *Civilization*, most tellingly the use of the submarine commander's guilt over his sinking of the *Lusitania*. Ince chose young director Irvin Willat (1890–1976) to direct, and cast the slight Henry B.

6. Postwar Films of 1919

Walthall (1878–1936, one of the stars of D. W. Griffith's seminal 1915 hit *Birth of a Nation*), as Michael Lanyard and soon-to-be-horror superstar Lon Chaney as the villainous Eckstrom. The picture would receive excellent reviews, with Chaney and Walthall both receiving good notices for their performances.

Critical response: In a February 17, 1919, review,[10] *The New York Times* gave the film a positive review:

> Whereas other melodramas make some effort to create the temporary illusion of possibility and consistency, THE FALSE FACES soars through its own high course of fights, feats and thrills, regardless of all laws, human and divine. Thomas H. Ince, who produced the photoplay, and Irvin V. Willat, who directed it, seem to have set out to make No Man's Land look tame compared to the New York battlefront, and they have done so.

Moving Picture World's February 22, 1919, write-up[11] noted:

> [The film] is derived from one of the best stories of its kind. It is also one of the best released by Paramount-Artcraft.... *The False Faces* will hold closely the attention of any audience.... With all this masterly handling of incident, there is lacking at moments that dramatic quality which leads up to a crisis. This is compensated for in a measure by the fine impersonation of Walthall, whose native ability and admirable training enable him to make effective use of his opportunities. He is capably supported by Lon Chaney as "Eckstrom," and practically all the men in the cast, but Mary Anderson seldom rises to the gravity of her role.

Wid's Film Daily, in a February 27, 1919, review, lauded the film:

> It's a sure 'nuff thriller from beginning to end, with a mystery plot that introduces a succession of surprises and a lot of situations that will get any crowd by reason of their novelty and dramatic strength.... Lon Chaney is the personification of villainy as Eckstrom.

March brought a movie featuring twin sisters (and their mother) suffering atrocities at the hands of heinous Huns in Belgium: *The Unpardonable Sin*, released on March 2, 1919, by Blanche Sweet Productions, Harry Garson Productions, directed by Marshall Neilan. Cast: Blanche Sweet (dual role of Alice Parcot/Dimny Parcot), Edwin Stevens (Stephen Parcot), Mary Alden (Mrs. Parcot), Matt Moore (Nol Windsor), Wesley Barry (George Washington Sticker), Wallace Beery (Colonel Klemm), Bull Montana (The Brute), Bobby Connelly[12] (boy scout), Dick Curtis (uncredited), John De Lacey (uncredited). Plot[13]: The gentle, passive Alice Parcot and her mother are caught in Belgium when the war breaks out and are raped by German soldiers. In the meantime,

The Silents Go to War

Alice's twin sister, the adventurous Dimny, living with her ailing father in the United States, decides to go to Belgium to search for her mother and sister. While walking down the street toward the passport office, Dimny faints. She is found by a caring boy scout and medical student Nol Windsor, who take Dimny to the medical student's home. It turns out that Nol is going over to Belgium for the Commission for Relief in Belgium. The next day, accompanied by the boy scout, Dimny and Nol apply for passports at the same time. Dimny is refused a passport because she is single, so they agree to marry in name only to facilitate their travel. Arriving in Belgium, they meet the evil Colonel Klemm, the German officer who raped Dimny's sister and mother. Klemm mistakes Dimny for her sister, but they outwit Klemm, find Alice and her mother, and embark on a breakneck race to the Dutch border, eventually escaping Klemm's clutches. Nol and Dimny have grown to love each other and find happiness together and marry.

The backstory: Coming at a time when Americans were trying to heal from the recently ended war and not wanting to be haunted by the past behavior of their former enemy, the film generated considerable controversy among film critics, but not among audiences. Based on a novel written by respected author Rupert Hughes,[14] the film was a huge hit, breaking box office records in Detroit, with police having to hold back massive crowds.[15] Star Blanche Sweet, a rival to screen stars Lillian Gish and Mary Pickford, had originally worked for D. W. Griffith, but lost the plum role of Elsie Stoneman in Griffith's 1914 epic *Birth of a Nation* to Gish. Shortly afterward, Sweet parted ways with Griffith and joined Paramount Productions, eventually forming her own production company along with her friend, producer Harry Gerson. During the production, Sweet started a love affair with director Marshall Neilan, which eventually resulted in Neilan's divorce from actress Gertrude Bambrick on charges of adultery. Sweet married Neilan in 1922 and divorced him in 1929 ... also on charges of adultery.[16]

Critical response: In a March 3, 1919, review,[17] *The New York Times* was scathing: "Whatever may be the propriety of stirring up the memory of German atrocities in Belgium, certainly a photoplay without the character of greatness, presented for public entertainment after the war is over, is not the proper medium." The *New York Tribune* review, written by columnist Virginia Tracy on August 3, 1919,[18] concurred: "We have a reasonable case against the picture in that it partakes lavishly of the book's faults and scarcely at all of its extraordinary virtues."

6. Postwar Films of 1919

Mid–March also saw the release of *The Homesteader*, the first feature-length "race"[19] film, written, produced and directed by Oscar Micheaux (1884–1951) starring pioneering African American actress Evelyn Preer (1896–1932). Adapted from Micheaux's own novel, the film premiered to a packed 8,000-seat Black theater in Chicago. While the film was embraced by Black filmgoers, white audiences would not watch race pictures, an aversion compounded by the fact that the film has a brief mention of the taboo topic of abortion.[20]

April films trended toward romantic love stories: *The Exquisite Little Thief* (girl thief plots sensational robbery, foiled by handsome male

Mack Sennett's 1919 comedy extravaganza *Yankee Doodle in Berlin*, featuring the Keystone Cops: (from left) Bert Roach (Field Marshal von Hindenburg, seated), unidentified actor, Malcolm St. Clair (Crown Prince Freddy, seated), Ben Turpin (Prussian guardsman, standing behind Freddy), Ford Sterling (the kaiser, standing), two unidentified Keystone Cops, and Joseph Belmont (Admiral von Tirpitz, seated). One of Mack Sennett's "Bathing Beauties" is on the near right. Female impersonator Bothwell Browne is Captain Bob White (disguised as an exotic dancer) and Marie Prevost (the Belgian girl) is seated on the floor (Mack Sennett Comedies).

The Silents Go to War

fellow thief), *Modern Husbands* (philandering husband versus philandering wife), and *The Delicious Little Devil* (showgirl impersonates star, lands millionaire, played by soon-to-be-star Rudolph Valentino).

May saw two very different hit films: D. W. Griffith's *Broken Blossoms*, an interracial love story (opium-smoking Chinese man loves abused London waif), and Marshall Neilan's charming comedy *Daddy Long Legs* (orphan girl is educated by older mysterious benefactor, falls in love with him).

June brought a movie that took a last rollicking slapstick look at the kaiser and his court: *Yankee Doodle in Berlin*, released on June 29, 1919, by Mack Sennett Comedies, directed by F. Richard Jones. Cast: Bothwell Browne (Captain Bob White), Ford Sterling (the kaiser), Malcom St. Clair (the crown prince), Bert Roach (von Hindenburg), Charles Murray (Irish POW soldier), Marie Prevost (Belgian girl), Chester Conklin (officer of the Death's Head Hussars), Heinie Conklin (Prussian Guard drill leader), Eva Thatcher (the kaiserin), Joseph Belmont (Von Tirpitz), Phyllis Haver (uncredited), James Finlayson (commander's officer, uncredited). Plot[21]: Captain Bob White, an American aviator behind enemy lines, is tasked with stealing an important map from the members of the German High Command, including the kaiser himself. With the aid of a girl who is a Belgian slave laborer, Captain Bob disguises himself as an exotic Balinese dancer and proceeds to seduce the entire German court, including the kaiser and the crown prince. The kaiser is in hot pursuit of the "dancer," to the disgust of the kaiserin, who beats up on the kaiser. Eventually exposed as a man, Captain Bob still manages to steal the map (with help from an Irish POW, who knocks out a German officer) and, assisted by the Belgian girl, makes his escape across enemy lines.

The backstory: Producer Mack Sennett (1880–1960), dubbed the King of Hollywood's *Fun Factory*, opened Keystone Studios in 1912, and originated slapstick comedic routines including pie-throwing and hair-raising car chases, especially in the *Keystone Cops* series. Sennett used his entire corps of comedians to play the kaiser and his court; to play Captain Bob White, Sennett hired the most famous cross-dresser in Europe, vaudeville star Bothwell Browne (1877–1947), noted for his/her seductive routines and flair for comedy. Sennett sold the distribution rights to producer Sol Lesser (1890–1980), who proceeded to publicize the picture with various road-show companies using Sennett's famous "Bathing Beauties," clad in scanty bathing suits. The film did approximately $10,000 a week in every big city where the movie played.

6. Postwar Films of 1919

The Beauties drew huge crowds, also drawing charges of indecent exposure in Atlanta, Georgia.[22]

Critical response: *Moving Picture World*'s July 4, 1919, review[23] called the film "a laugh riot, with many of the Keystone's resident comics (Bert Roach, Chester Conklin, Heine Conklin) featured as slapstick Huns." The February 5, 1920, *Watertown Daily News Times* review[24] gushed: "*Yankee Doodle in Berlin* is the funniest, jazziest, shimmiest, most daring, astounding, laugh-producing and breath-taking comedy ever produced by that past-master of film fun makers!"

July brought a reminder of the real-life heroism and trauma endured by American soldiers under German fire in *The Lost Battalion*, released on July 2, 1919, by W. H. Productions Company and directed by Burton L. King. Cast: Major General Robert Alexander (himself), Lieutenant Colonel Charles W. Whittlesey (himself), Major George McMurtry (himself), Captain William J. Cullen (himself), Lieutenant Arthur F. McKeogh (himself), Lieutenant Augustus Kaiser (himself), Private Abraham Krotoshinsky (himself), Helen Ferguson (the stenographer), Marion Coakley (Nancy Brystal), Mrs. Stuart Robson (the landlady), Blanche Davenport (the mother), Lt. Jordan (himself), Bessie Learn (the girl next door), Sidney D'Albrook (the burglar), Gaston Glass (Harry Merwin), Jack McLean (the kicker), William H. Tooker (German American father, uncredited), Stephen Grattan (tong member, uncredited), J. A. King (tong member). Plot[25]: The men of the 308th Infantry Regiment, part of Major General Robert Alexander's 77th Infantry Division, have been drafted from diverse ethnic, economic, and social groups in New York City. Two men are from rival Chinatown tongs;[26] another is a burglar; one is a wealthy merchant's son in love with his father's stenographer, who dreams of becoming a great movie actress; another is a private in love with the merchant's ward; and finally there is "the Kicker," who finds fault with everything. After training in Camp Yaphank in the United States and in France, the 554 men advance under the command of Lieutenant Colonel Charles W. Whittlesey advance into the Argonne Forest to help break down the German forces. Cut off from French and American forces and surrounded by the enemy, the battalion, nicknamed "The Lost Battalion," withstands six days without food or water. Carrier pigeons carrying communications to Allied headquarters are all shot down by the Germans. When the German commander asks for their surrender, Whittlesey replies, "Tell them to go to hell!" One carrier pigeon, Cher Ami,[27] gravely wounded, is able to get through, and the battalion is rescued with 197 men killed in action, including the two Chinese tong rivals and the burglar, all of whom die bravely. After their rescue, the survivors are given a parade in New York City and are reunited with their families and sweethearts.

The backstory: When the independent production company MacManus Corporation was formed in 1918, it was basically used as a conduit by the New York Motion Picture Association, the Keystone Film Company, and Triangle Film Corporation to re-release their older movies.[28] In 1919, Edward A. MacManus, head of the company, decided to produce his own movie and selected the true-life exploits of the "Lost Battalion" with the idea of a using a fictitious story as a framing device for the actual battle in the Argonne Forest. He chose Burton L. King (1877–1944) to direct after King had a scored a hit with renowned magician Harry Houdini's 1918 serial success *The Master Mystery*. As part of the fictional story, writer Charles A. Logue inserted Chinese stereotypes as "tong" members; in reality, the two Chinese members of the Lost Battalion were Pvt. Henry Chinn (1889–1918), who was killed in action in the Argonne, and Sgt. Sing Lau Kee (1896–1967), who survived. Both were honored with the Distinguished Service Cross, the first Chinese Americans ever to receive a combat medal in United States history. Although the picture was shown to a jury of 100 selected important Americans for endorsement and received a good review from *The New York Times*, it was not a box office hit, as the American public showed little enthusiasm for the postwar film.[29]

Critical response: *The New York Times* gave the film a respectful review in their July 3, 1919, article[30]:

> Major General Robert Alexander, U.S.A. was the host last night for a reception and entertainment for the survivors of the Lost Battalion, the unit of the Seventy-seventh Division which under his command penetrated the Forest of the Argonne and held out for six days in one of the most spectacular defenses of the war. The entertainment, given at the ballroom of the Ritz-Carlton, included the first showing of the screen reproduction of the "Lost Battalion" and was the first re-enactment of a history-making battle of this war. The picture was reproduced by Edward A. MacManus, under the personal supervision of General Alexander. The United States Signal Corps collaborated in the photoplay, making it possible to show the public the original maps and documents used by the staff officers of our army during the fighting. Lieut. Col. Whittlesey, commanding the six companies which were trapped, companies A, C, D, F, G and K, was one of the "stars" who acted in the picture. With the pictures showing the actual fighting and hardships the boys went through in France there was a story. It began in September, 1917, when the division came into being. Into the recruiting

6. Postwar Films of 1919

offices came men from every walk of life. There was much gold and much dross—thieves, Chinamen, and bankers who used their influence and succeeded in getting their sons "K.P.'s." Because 50 percent of our ancestors were women, there was love in the story—love of society maidens and stenographers. Each had a service star close to their hearts, and after fevered knitting and anxious waiting they all shared in the honor and glory of the victory. The picture seemed to please the many notables present, with the thrills and smiles and tears of a retold story. Of course there was no villain and all were heroes from the 26th of September, when the Yanks climbed over the top and penetrated the German lines. The 308th, under the command of Major McKinney, was shown fighting their way forward and finally succeeding in liberating the surrounded Lost Battalion.

Tragically, Congressional Medal of Honor winner Lieutenant Colonel Charles Whittlesey committed suicide by drowning on November 26, 1921, unable to bear the horrific memories of the events in the Argonne Forest. He was considered a traumatized battle casualty of World War I.

July also brought the release of two crowd-pleasing Western films, *The Wilderness Trail* and *Wagon Tracks*, while August saw audiences mesmerized by *The Miracle Man*, with Lon Chaney playing a contortionist named "The Frog" who finds redemption in faith healing!

A newspaper ad for the 1919 Paramount film *Behind the Door* (caution: something nasty lurks behind the door!) (Matteo Omied/Alamy Stock Photo).

The Silents Go to War

The autumn had film-lovers spellbound by Sessue Hayakawa's exotic turn as *The Dragon Painter*, Gloria Swanson's erotic spoiled socialite/seductress in Cecil B. DeMille's production of *Male and Female*, and Erich von Stroheim's sensational directorial debut of *Blind Husbands* (neglectful husband, unhappy wife, plus predatory officer—played by von Stroheim).

The final "atrocity" movie—drenched in blood—came out at the end of 1919: *Behind the Door*, released on December 14, 1919, by Paramount Pictures, directed by Irvin Willat and produced by Thomas Ince. Cast: Hobart Bosworth (Oscar Krug), Jane Novak (Alice Morse), Wallace Beery (Lieutenant Brandt), James Gordon (Bill Tavish), Dick Wayne (McQuestion), J. P. Lockney (Matthew Morse), Gibson Gowland (Gideon Blank), Otto Hoffman (Mark Arnold), Tom Ashton (fishing boy). Plot[31]: The film is told in flashback. In 1925, former sailor Oscar Krug enters an abandoned taxidermy shop that he once owned in a small coastal town in Maine and is lost in memory. Before the start of World War I, Krug had been a sailor in the United States Navy. When news arrives that the United States has entered the war, the townspeople, who regard Krug with deep suspicion for his German American parentage (his father was an American sea captain who married a German girl), question his patriotism. Krug gets into a mass fistfight, led by the group's leader, Bill Tavish. When the two men fight to an eventual standstill, they shake hands, swear friendship, and go off to enlist in the navy. Krug has been secretly courting the much younger Alice Morse, daughter of the town banker. Just before Krug takes command as captain of the navy ship *Perth*, he and Alice are married in secret. When Alice's father learns about the marriage, he throws Alice out of the house. Alice stows away as a nursing assistant on the *Perth*, and only when they are out to sea does she reveal her presence to Krug. Krug's ship is sunk by German U-boat 98, commanded by Lieutenant Brandt. All hands are lost, except for Krug and Alice, who manage to cling to a lifeboat. The U-boat surfaces, and Brandt rescues Alice, laughing as he and his crew leave Krug to drown in the sea. Krug vows to the grinning Brandt that if he ever catches him, he will skin him alive. Rescued by an American ship, Krug is given command of another ship, with Bill Tavish as his loyal first officer. One night, the ship destroys a German U-boat, which turns out to be U-98. Krug dives into the sea to rescue Brandt, to the confusion of Tavish and the rest of the crew. Krug takes him to his cabin, plying him with brandy and getting him drunk. Brandt, who doesn't remember Krug, brags to him about how he raped Alice and then gave her to his

6. Postwar Films of 1919

crew. Krug then reveals himself and binds Brandt behind a closet door. When Krug's officers, led by Tavish, enter the cabin, they are horrified to find that Krug, with his taxidermy skills, has skinned Brandt alive.

In the final scene set in the film's present, Krug collapses at his old worktable and dies. His spirit is greeted by that of Alice, and the two are united again in death.

The backstory: Producer Thomas Ince and director Irvin Willat used the San Pedro Harbor for the scenes featuring Krug's ship and Brandt's U-boat. Willat enlisted the assistance of Lt. John Cook of the United States Navy Submarine Service in San Pedro as a technical advisor for the picture, leveraging his expertise to turn an American submarine into a U-boat to be featured in the production. Star Hobart Bosworth (1867–1943) was known for appearing in action/adventure movies and had already played Captain Wolf Larsen in the 1913 movie adaptation of Jack London's epic tale *The Sea Wolf*. At the age of 52, Bosworth did all his own stunt work on *Behind the Door*, including leaping 30 feet from a battleship into the ocean.[32] Audiences flocked to see the picture, which had cost $84,660 to produce. It grossed $289,039 at the box office.[33]

Critical response: *Exhibitor's Herald* in a December 14, 1919, review commented: "One Paramount special that is special: Too bad they're not all in this class."[34] Writing for the January 1920 issue of *Motion Picture Classic*, critic Frederic James Smith extolled the acting skills of Hobart Bosworth: "Hobart Bosworth is decidedly strong in this role, over-playing but occasionally a role that would be maudlin in most other hands."[35] *Photoplay* in a March 20, 1920, review proclaimed that "it took courage to make such a picture as this, for it is a 'he-picture,' no pap for puking infants."[36]

The year 1919 would close out with *Out Yonder* (New England girl is romanced by wealthy boy, solves mystery of death of boy's father), *The Wicked Darling* (Lon Chaney stars as an evil pickpocket), *When the Clouds Roll By* (a Douglas Fairbanks comedy produced by the upstart United Artists), and the Harold Lloyd comedy *From Hand to Mouth*.

The 1920s beckoned, and the film industry would enter a new era. Films that channeled Prohibition, speakeasies, flappers, women's rights, and Mickey Mouse brought new actors and directors to the screen. The new decade also saw films that looked at the legacy of World War I through the lens of the rise of the antiwar movie, described in the next chapter.

7

Antiwar and War Trauma Films of 1921–1930

It was the 1920s, better known as the "Roaring 20s": women were granted the right to vote, economic growth soared, Prohibition[1] took hold, and America danced into the Jazz Age. After all, hadn't America been through enough in the First World War? Hadn't the nation sent 2,100,000 men to fight alongside allies France and England? Wasn't it enough that 117,000 men died on the fields of France, and 224,000 soldiers returned home wounded? Why should Americans care about the fracturing of European society when they had been dragged into a war not of their making? America gradually became an isolationist country; Americans were sick of war and sick of conflict.

But the damage caused—physical and mental—by the First World War remained for many years to come. Hollywood would try to take the public's mind off the damage caused by the "Great War" with a new era of movies: daring social melodramas, historical epics, romantic comedies, and crowd-pleasing Westerns.

By 1920, there were more than 20,000 movie theaters operating in the United States. Movie audiences were so large that major studios build bigger and better luxurious "picture palaces" in Hollywood and New York City to accommodate thousands of patrons, as well as space for orchestras to play music to accompany projected films.[2]

In 1921, Hollywood had not contemplated making a war-related picture, since current wisdom indicated that the public was weary of the subject and preferred lighter fare. That would change with a sweeping antiwar epic that would catapult both a young director and a little-known actor into the front ranks of stardom: *The Four Horseman of the Apocalypse*, released on March 6, 1921, by Metro Pictures, directed by Rex Ingram.[3] Cast: Pomeroy Cannon (Madariaga), Josef Swickard (Marcelo Desnoyers), Bridgetta Clark (Doña Luisa), Rudolph Valentino (Julio Desnoyers), Virginia Warwick (Chichí), Alan Hale

7. Antiwar and War Trauma Films of 1921–1930

Rudolph Valentino is Argentinian/French playboy Julio Desnoyers, about to dance the tango with an unidentified actress. His drunken grandfather Madariaga (Pomeroy Cannon) looks on with approval. Released in 1921 by Metro Pictures, *The Four Horsemen of the Apocalypse* made Valentino a household name (United Archives GmbH/Alamy Stock Photo).

(Karl von Hartrott), Mabel Van Buren (Elena), Stuart Holmes (Otto von Hartrott), John St. Polis (Etienne Laurier), Alice Terry (Marguerite Laurier), Mark Fenton (Senator Lacour), Derk Ghent (René Lacour), Nigel de Brulier (Tchernoff), Bowditch M. Turner (Argensola), Edward Connelly (lodge keeper), Wallace Beery (Lieutenant Colonel von Richthosen), Harry Northrup (the general), Arthur Hoyt (Lieutenant Schnitz). Plot[4]: Madariaga, a harsh but popular Argentine landowner, has two sons-in-law: one is a German named Karl Hartrott, whom he dislikes, and the other is a Frenchman named Marcelo Desnoyers, whose family he favors. Julio, son of Marcelo, grows up to be elegant and spoiled, while one of Karl's rejected sons, Otto, is trained to be a Prussian soldier. One night, Julio accompanies his grandfather on a tour of seedy dives in Buenos Aires. At one of the dives, Julio takes a woman away from her partner and dances a provocative tango. The man attacks him, and Julio strikes him and knocks him out. His grandfather watches the action approvingly and then slides to the floor, drunk. Julio's dance

The Silents Go to War

partner laughs at the drunken old man, but Julio picks him up and takes him home. Not long after, Madariaga dies, and his estate is divided up between the two families: the extended family breaks up, with one half returning to Germany and the other half to France.

In Paris, Julio is a would-be artist and tango-dancing sensation at local tea dances. In his apartment block lives a mysterious Russian named Tchernoff, who has visions of impending disaster for the world, warning that the Four Horsemen of the Apocalypse—War, Death, Hunger, and Disease—will soon invade a sleeping world and trample on mankind. Julio falls in love with Marguerite Laurier, the unhappy and much younger wife of a French lawyer. The affair is discovered, but Marguerite's kind husband Etienne agrees to a divorce. Before that happens, the Great War starts in 1914 and lives are changed forever.

Marguerite becomes a nurse in the town of Lourdes; Etienne becomes a decorated officer and is blinded in battle. He winds up in the hospital where Marguerite is working, and she cares for him. Julio, who follows Marguerite, sees her caring for her blinded husband and, ashamed of his wastrel life, enlists in the French army.

In the meantime, the German army overruns Marcelo Desnoyers' castle in the Marne Valley during the First Battle of the Marne. Marcelo is forced to host a German general and his staff in the castle. One of his German nephews is part of the staff and tries to protect him, but Marcelo is arrested after a melee involving a German officer's assault on a young French woman. Marcelo is about to be executed, but his life is saved when the French army counterattacks; his nephew dies during the attack and the castle is destroyed.

Four years later in 1918, Julio is still alive and renowned for his bravery in the trenches. During a final mission in no man's land, Julio encounters his last surviving cousin, Otto. The two young men recognize each other, but before they can say anything, both are killed by a shell. Back in Paris, Marguerite considers abandoning the blind Etienne, but Julio's ghost guides her to continue her care for him.

After the war ends, Marcelo and his family travel to the battlefields to visit Julio's grave. There, they encounter Julio's grieving friend Tchernoff, and when Marcelo asks him, "Did you know my son?" Tchernoff lifts his arms, forming the shape of a cross with his body, and says, "I knew them all!" He then points to the sky and shows Marcelo the vision of the Four Horsemen riding away into the clouds, and tells him that peace has come, but that "the Four Horsemen will still ravage

7. Antiwar and War Trauma Films of 1921–1930

humanity—stirring unrest in the world—until all hatred is dead and only love reigns in the heart of mankind."

The backstory: In 1919, screenwriter June Mathis (1887–1927) became head of the scenario department for Metro Pictures, making her the fourth most powerful female executive in movie history, behind superstars/actresses/producers Mary Pickford, Norma Talmadge, and Mabel Normand. Richard Rowland, the head of Metro Pictures, had become interested in the best-selling antiwar novel *The Four Horsemen of the Apocalypse* written by Spanish author/newspaper man/political agitator/adventurer Vicente Blasco Ibáñez (1867–1928) and assigned Mathis to craft a screenplay from the unwieldy novel. Rowland offered Ibáñez $75,000 for the rights to the novel with an advance of $20,000 against 10 percent of the book royalties. Ibáñez accepted, making him a wealthy man for the rest of his life.[5] Next, Rowland asked Mathis for suggestions for a director and a star. She chose up-and-coming Rex Ingram as director and an unknown young actor named Rudolph Valentino (1895–1926), who would become a screen sex symbol as the smoldering Julio, dancing an erotic tango at the beginning of the film. For authenticity, Ingram hired both French and German ex-officers to assist him on set. The assistant director, Curt Rehfeld, was German and took vicious delight in training the extras and cast to goose-step, causing major fights between the French and Germans. To further complicate matters, Mathis in all probability had romantic feelings toward both Valentino and Ingram, both of whom were involved with other actresses, and neither of whom reciprocated her affections.

Metro Pictures decided to market the film as a nationwide high-art event, forming the Four Horseman Exhibition Corporation and sending more than 100 road companies to screen the film around America. The screenings had local orchestras playing the musical score, as well as hometown actors recruited to perform spoken prologues to the movie. The music was composed by Louis F. Gottschalk (1864–1934) with well-known conductor/composer Hugo Riesenfeld leading the orchestra at the movie's Los Angeles, California premiere.[6] With its extended scenes of the devastated French countryside, the stunning sequence of the four horsemen riding across the red-tinted sky, plus a personalized story of love and loss, the film was hailed by critics as a serious antiwar film. The film officially opened on March 6, 1921, at the New York Lyric Theatre and was a blockbuster success, eventually making $4 million for Metro.[7]

Critical response: Reviews were lavish in their praise for the movie,

The Silents Go to War

its direction, and its new star. *Variety*, in a February 18, 1921,[8] review, declared:

> For this young director, hardly more than a boy in years, must be accorded a place alongside Griffith. His production is to the picture of today what "The Birth of a Nation" was. For a clear understanding of its artistic and pictorial superiority, comparison with the best of its predecessors becomes necessary. Therefore, be it said that "The Four Horsemen" is the equal of everything that was great in "Intolerance," "Cabiria," "Passion," "Hearts of the World" and "The Birth of a Nation."

The New York Times review on March 7, 1921,[9] raved:

> Many of its scenes are the result of fine photography, and better still, fine cinematography. Rex Ingram, the director of the production, is among those who believe the principles of painting and sculpture should be applied to motion pictures, and scenes in The Four Horsemen are concrete illustrations of what the application of these principles means.

The review went on to compliment the acting:

> The characters used primarily to give color to the picture—South American natives, Spanish, French and German specimens—are all strikingly individualized, and those who have the more extensive roles not only look their parts but act them intelligently, especially Rudolph Valentino as the young Julio, Joseph Swickard as old Don Marcelo, Alice Terry as Marguerite, Alan Hale as Karl von Hartrott and Nigel De Brulier as Tchernoff, the Russian mystic.

The review also remarked on the contributions of June Mathis:

> June Mathis, who made the scenario, has followed the main trend and thought of the novel. All things considered, she has done a difficult job well ... when all is said about The Four Horseman, however, the central fact remains that it is an exceptionally well done adaptation of a novel, and an extraordinary motion picture work to boot.

Writing in his March 10, 1921,[10] review for the *Los Angeles Times*, movie critic Edwin Schallert enthused that the scenes in Argentina and Paris "positively take you to those places," and the film overall bore the stamp of "excellent work."

Playwright Robert E. Sherwood, reviewing the movie for *Life* magazine's March 24, 1921, issue,[11] wrote: "'The Four Horseman of the Apocalypse' is a living, breathing answer to those who still refuse to take motion pictures seriously. Its production lifts the silent drama to an artistic plane that it has never touched before."

There were a few critics who found the film occasionally static

7. Antiwar and War Trauma Films of 1921–1930

and a bit overlong and its depiction of Germans somewhat one-sided. Equally disturbing was the eerie sense at the end of the movie that another war loomed. But there was one thing that the critics (and the public) agreed upon: Valentino was a new kind of star. There had been romantic leading men before him, but never had there been a star with such erotic appeal, and 1921 was a banner year for Valentino: his other pictures included the April premiere of *The Sheik* (Valentino as an amorous Arab chieftain), July's *The Conquering Power* (Valentino acting in a modernized adaptation of the French novel *The Miser* by Honoré de Balzac), and September's *Camille* (a modernized version of the famous Dumas novel updated to 1920s Paris, with Valentino as the French lover of the doomed Camille, played by Alla Nazimova).

While 1921 Hollywood would congratulate itself for bringing a critically acclaimed picture on the horrors of war to an appreciative audience, film fare in 1922 and 1923 would wander across the globe with a selection of racy melodramas set in Europe (including Erich von Stroheim's erotic *Foolish Wives*), across history (Douglas Fairbanks romping through Sherwood Forest as *Robin Hood* and Rex Ingram's French Revolution epic *Scaramouche*), a first-ever documentary (*Nanook of the North*), and a couple of fast-paced slapstick comedies (Buster Keaton being chased by the entire Los Angeles police in *Cops* and Harold Lloyd scaling the side of a building in the jaw-dropping *Safety Last*). Warner Bros. introduced their new leading man: heroic dog Rin Tin Tin[12] starring in the action-adventure *Where the North Begins*.

In 1923, an unusual film would debut on the screen—a modern-day cowboy film featuring a traumatized First World War veteran, starring a major cowboy star who had experienced trench warfare: *Shootin' for Love*, released on June 28, 1923, by Universal Pictures, directed by Edward Sedgwick. Cast: Hoot Gibson (Duke Travis), Laura La Plante (Mary Randolph), Alfred Allen (Jim Travis), William Welsh (Bill Randolph), William Steele (Dan Hobson), Arthur Mackley (Sheriff Bludsoe), W. T. McCulley (Sandy), Kansas Moehring (Tex Carson). Plot[13]: Returning young veteran Duke Travis renews his friendship with pretty Mary Randolph, the daughter of a neighboring rancher, on a train bound for their California hometown. On arrival, they find that their respective fathers are fighting over water rights. Duke has been shell-shocked, as evidenced by his aversion to guns and loud noises. When villainous Dan Hobson taunts Duke over his unwillingness to engage in a fight with him, the local citizenry (and his father) declare him a coward and mock him. Hobson decides to blow up a dam to flood both ranches, but Duke

The Silents Go to War

overcomes his condition in time to fight Hobson (shooting a pistol out of his hand) and save the ranches and his girl from a potential flood. His reputation restored, Duke and Mary make plans to marry.

The backstory: By 1923, "Hoot" Gibson (1892–1962) was a major cowboy star, second only to film legend Tom Mix as a box office draw. Acquiring the nickname "Hoot" for hunting owls in caves as a child, he became an all-around rodeo champion in 1912,[14] and was then cast by director Jack Conway in his first feature Western, *His Only Son*, in a supporting role. When the United States entered the war in 1917, Gibson became a non-commissioned officer in the newly created Army Tank Corps and served in France with the American Expeditionary Force. After returning from service, Gibson resumed his career in Westerns, and as the demand for cowboy films increased, he became a huge star for Universal Pictures. Normally using slapstick and comedy in his films, he kept it to a minimum in *Shootin' For Love*, instead tapping into his experiences from World War I. His fans nationwide loved the film, which became a big hit.

Critical response: In the July 1923 issue,[15] *Moving Picture World* called the picture "a wonderful mix of comedy and drama, involving a range war, a romance and a World War I veteran, played by engaging cowboy star Hoot Gibson."

The year 1924 brought a film that would attempt to explore both the physical and psychological damage experienced by a returning First World War veteran: *The Enchanted Cottage*, released on March 24, 1924, by Inspiration Pictures, directed by John S. Robertson and produced by Richard Barthelmess. Cast: Richard Barthelmess (Oliver Bashforth), May McAvoy (Laura Pennington), Ida Waterman (Mrs. Smallwood), Alfred Hickman (Rupert Smallwood), Florence Short (Ethel Bashforth), Marion Coakley (Beatrice Vaughn), Holmes Herbert (Major Hillgrove), Ethel Wright (Mrs. Minnett), Harry Allen (Riggs). Plot[16]: Oliver Bashforth has been badly wounded and traumatized during the war. Bent and crippled, he is embittered and alienated. He stares into a mirror and sees the physical and psychological wreck that the war has made of him. When he finds out that his fiancée can't stand the sight of him and becomes engaged to another man, he hides himself away in a country cottage. His family is concerned for him and his bossy older sister Ethel announces that she will come and be his housekeeper and look after him. Bashforth can't bear his sister's interference and sends her packing. Wanting his family to leave him alone, Bashforth has an idea. He has become friendly with a homely, sweet-natured young woman

7. Antiwar and War Trauma Films of 1921–1930

"Who would want me?" asks physically and mentally damaged First World War veteran Oliver Bashforth (Richard Barthelmess). May McAvoy (Laura Pennington) is his plain but compassionate housekeeper in 1924's *The Enchanted Cottage*, produced by Barthelmess for his company Inspiration Pictures and distributed by Associated Film International (Pictorial Press, Ltd/Alamy Stock Photo).

named Laura Pennington, and proposes marriage. She asks him why he does not marry some pretty girl that he knows, and he answers "a hideous casualty for the rest of my life—a nice husband for a pretty girl!" Despite the callousness of the remark, she agrees to marry him. The cottage's housekeeper, Mrs. Minnett, tells Bashforth that the cottage was once known as Honeymoon Cottage and implies that it is haunted by the benign spirits of past lovers. On their wedding night, magic happens; they see each other as they imagine themselves: Oliver straight and handsome, Laura graceful and charming. They have become beautiful, at least in each other's eyes. They tell their friend Major Hillgrove (himself blinded in the war), and he, with a deep compassion for two lonely souls, believes them. Their growing friendship and mutual admiration grows and becomes love, manifested by the inner beauty in each of them. When Bashforth's family arrives, though, they see only a disfigured cripple and a homely young woman. Bashforth tries to convince them that a magical alteration has occurred, but they think he is mad. They leave the couple alone, but Oliver and Laura come to the conclusion that perhaps they are deluded, but they are happy to be so. The cottage and its benign spirits have worked a spell, and they have fallen in love. Oliver has lost his postwar bitterness, and he and Laura look forward to the possibility of having a child.

The backstory: By 1924, Richard Barthelmess (1895–1963) was a major star in Hollywood, having catapulted to stardom in two D. W. Griffith films: *Broken Blossoms* (1919) and *Way Down East* (1920). A shrewd young businessman, Barthelmess had formed his own production company, Inspiration Pictures, along with film producers Charles Duell and Henry King, starring in their 1921 hit movie *Tol'able David*. A strong supporter of disabled veterans of the First World War, Barthelmess had spoken out at various Hollywood functions in favor of a bill supporting veterans rights and benefits, which was passed by the United States government in 1921.[17] Having seen the play *The Enchanted Cottage* (which focused on a bitter and disabled young veteran) during its run on Broadway in 1923, he decided to buy the play as a vehicle for his company with himself as the star. To aid in preparation for his role, Barthelmess spoke with veterans who were members of the DAV (Disabled Veterans of the World War), while Holmes Herbert, who played the blind Major Hillgrove, visited the New York Institute for the Blind to research the everyday habits and activities of visually impaired men and women.[18] When the film opened on March 24, 1924, it received excellent reviews, but female fans of Barthelmess, who were used to him playing less complicated roles, were disappointed in the film and stayed away, although Barthelmess considered it his "greatest motion picture."[19]

Critical response: The *Film Daily* review[20] of April 11, 1924, called the film "by far the best thing Barthelmess, Robertson and Miss McAvoy

7. Antiwar and War Trauma Films of 1921–1930

have ever done and this is the first picture in months to bring tears to the eye of a hardened reviewer."

Variety's April 16, 1924,[21] critique of the film opined: "This picture is far too advanced and too artistic for the screen. It is one of those things certain to be above the heads of all but a few of the regulars at picture theaters.... Richard Barthelemess plays the war cripple whose life has been ruined, and the performance he gives is decidedly clever, but despite this, the picture in reality belongs to Miss McAvoy, who practically walks away with the production as the ugly duckling."

Photoplay's May 1924 issue[22] lauded the film for its "tender love story, of a love so supreme that the shackles of gross reality fall away."

Writing for the June 1924 issue of *The Educational Screen*,[23] reviewer Marguerite Orndorff remarked: "There was a danger of such a result in filming this whimsy of Pinero's, but the direction of John S. Robertson, and the outstanding portrayals of Miss McAvoy and Richard Barthelmess have in large measure preserved its delicacy."

In a retrospective review dated January 18, 1926,[24] *New York Times* columnist Mordaunt Hall felt that, "due to the modern magic of the camera, resourceful direction and thoroughly competent acting, Sir Arthur Wing Pinero's fantasy is much more satisfying on the screen than it was on the stage ... in this weird effort, Richard Barthelmess gives a good performance in the difficult, gloomy role of a maimed, shell-shocked officer, perpetually conscious of his wrecked form and distorted face.... It is a production infinitely superior to anything in which Bartlemess has appeared since *Tol'able David*."

On November 19, 1924, Hollywood was shocked by the unexpected death of director Thomas Ince (known for his 1916 pacifist movie *Civilization*) after a night of partying on William Randolph Heart's yacht. Speculation was rife that Ince might have been involved in questionable behavior during the champagne-fueled party, although the actual cause of death was heart failure.

In September of 1925, a gentle movie exploring the fate of a traumatized blind veteran opened: *The Dark Angel*, released on September 27, 1925, directed by George Fitzmaurice. Cast: Ronald Colman (Captain Alan Trent), Vilma Bánky (Kitty Vane), Wyndham Standing (Gerald Shannon), Frank Elliott (Lord Beaumont), Charles Willis Lane (Sir Hubert Vane), Helen Jerome Eddy (Miss Bottles), Florence Turner (Roma), Lassie Lou Ahern (little flower girl).

Plot[25]: During the First World War, Captain Alan Trent, while on leave in England with his fiancée Kitty Trent, is suddenly recalled to the front before being able to get a marriage license. Alan and Kitty spend a "night of love" at a country inn "without benefit of clergy," and he sets off. At the front, things go badly for Alan, who is blinded and becomes a prisoner of war after being captured by the Germans. He is reported dead, and his friend, Captain Gerald Shannon, discreetly woos Kitty, seeking to soothe her grief with his gentle love. After the war, however, Gerald discovers that Alan is still alive, living in a remote corner of England, pulled out of his suicidal tendencies by the kindness of village children, becoming an author of children's stories for a living. Loyal to his former comrade-in-arms, Gerald informs Kitty of Alan's reappearance. She goes to him, but Alan conceals his blindness and tells Kitty that he no longer cares for her. She sees through his deception and vows to take care of him, and they are reunited.

The backstory: French-born director George Fitzmaurice (1885–1940) had already worked with rising star Ronald Colman (1891–1958) on two other features: 1924's *Tarnish* and 1925's *A Thief in Paradise*. He was also well acquainted with Colman's military service in World War I: a member of the London Scottish Regiment, Colman was sent to France at the outbreak of the war and was seriously wounded by shrapnel in his ankle at the Battle of Messines in 1914, which gave him a limp that he would attempt to hide for the rest of his career.[26] Beautiful Hungarian-born Vilma Bánky (1901–1991), appearing in her first American film, was later teamed with Colman in a series of love stories, most notably 1926's *The Winning of Barbara Worth*.

Critical response: *The New York Times* review by Mordaunt Hall on October 12, 1925,[27] was lavish in praise of the film:

> While viewing the beautiful screen conception of "The Dark Angel" the play which was launched under the pseudonym of H. B. Trevelyan, one cannot help being stirred by the gentle charm of the love story and also the echoes of the World War: now and again one is carried back to the days when the lads were in khaki, stormed at by shell and machine gun, dragging themselves through the slithering mud of Flanders; when voices were lifted in little French estaminets to the tuneful airs of "Madelon," "Over There," and "Tipperary," and then, because the hero of the film is blinded, one recalls the courage of those men who faced a life-long night with a smile. This is by all means the best picture George Fitzmaurice has to his credit. There is no repetition of action, the narrative being unfolded with admirable skill. When Mr. Fitzmaurice has an idea he pictures it with sincerity but does not shout about it. Frances Marion adapted the story, and she also deserves much praise, for, although the ending is changed, it has been accomplished with a certain subtlety which will not offend those who saw the play. Vilma

7. Antiwar and War Trauma Films of 1921–1930

Banky, the Hungarian actress who was engaged by Samuel Goldwyn while he was in Budapest, is a young person of rare beauty, a girl who might be American or English, with soft, fair hair, a slightly retrousse nose and lovely blue eyes which have the suggestion of a slant. Her acting is sincere and earnest, and her tears seem very real. She is so exquisite that one is not in the least bit surprised that she is never forgotten by Alan Hilary Trent when as a blinded war hero, he settles down to dictating boys' stories. The narrative tells of Trent leaving Kitty Vane before they could be married. He loses his sight in battle and is recorded among the missing. Kitty and Trent's friend, Gerald Shannon, believe that he has been killed. The girl at first refuses to listen to Gerald's proposal of marriage, ever hoping that Hilary may be found. Finally on the day she is to be married to Gerald she learns from him that Trent has hidden himself in a house not far away from where they are. Kitty's whole being goes back to the days when she last saw Trent and she changes her bridal attire for a suit and goes forth to find the man for whom she has waited so many years. Mr. Fitzmaurice pictures the scene of

Bull (Tom O'Brien, second from left) and Slim (Karl Dane, middle) watch best buddy Jim (John Gilbert, right) receive a fervent embrace from French farmgirl Melisande (Renée Adorée) as they march into battle in 1925's *The Big Parade*, released by Metro-Goldwyn-Mayer Studios (Entertainment Pictures/Alamy Stock Photo).

The Silents Go to War

Slim (Karl Dane, left), Jim (John Gilbert, middle), and Bull (Tom O'Brien) wait to go into battle in 1925's *The Big Parade*, released by Metro-Goldwyn-Mayer Pictures (Photo 12/Alamy Stock Photo).

the meeting of Hilary and Kitty in a most convincing way. Hilary pretends that he has forgotten her, and knowing every foot of the room and where his things are placed, he makes Kitty think that he sees as well as she does. Ronald Colman, who acts Trent, is most sympathetic and capable. A strong man might well be excused for weeping at some of the scenes in this delightful romance, especially when Trent decides to end it all and changes his mind through the cheerful note of a youngster's voice. Wyndham Standing gives a natural and easy performance as Gerald, the honorable friend who sacrifices his own happiness on the day he is to be married to Kitty.

In contrast to *The Dark Angel*'s genteel delicacy in dealing with a blinded veteran, movie audiences received a brutal, realistic portrayal of war (including shell-shocked and maimed soldiers) in King Vidor's gritty depiction of American doughboys in the antiwar *The Big Parade*, released on November 5, 1925, by Metro-Goldwyn-Mayer, directed by King Vidor. Cast: John Gilbert (James Apperson), Reneé Adorée (Melisande), Hobart Bosworth (Mr. Apperson), Claire McDowell (Mrs. Apperson), Claire Adams (Justyn Reed), Robert Ober (Harry Apperson), Tom O'Brien (Bull), Karl Dane (Slim), Rosita Marstini (Melisande's mother), Harry Crocker (soldier), Julanne Johnston (Justine Devereux), Kathleen Key (Miss Apperson), Carl Voss (German officer), George

7. Antiwar and War Trauma Films of 1921–1930

Beranger (German soldier), Frank Currier (soldier), Dan Mason (soldier). Plot[28]: In the United States in 1917, James "Jim" Apperson's idleness (in contrast to his hard-working brother) incurs the wrath of his wealthy businessman father. Then America enters the First World War. Jim informs his worried mother that he has no intention of enlisting, and his father threatens to kick him out of the house if he does not join up. When he runs into his patriotic friends at a send-off parade, however, he is persuaded to enlist, making his father very proud.

During training, Jim becomes friends with Southern construction worker Slim and Bronx bartender Bull. Their unit ships out to France, where they are billeted at a farm in the village of Champillon in the Marne. All three men are attracted to Melisande, whose mother owns the farm. She fights off all their advances, but gradually warms to Jim, bonding at first over chewing gum. They eventually fall in love, despite not being able to speak each other's language. One day, however, Jim receives a letter and a photograph from his girlfriend Justyn, telling him that the local newspaper has published news of their engagement. When Melisande sees the picture, she instinctively realizes the situation and runs off in tears. Before Jim can decide what to do, his unit is ordered to the front. Melisande hears the commotion and runs back, just in time for the lovers to embrace and kiss.

The Americans march toward the front and are strafed by an enemy fighter pilot called "Flying Fritzie" before the plane is shot down by American artillery fire. The unit is sent into battle against the Germans in Belleau Wood, advancing against snipers and machine guns in the woods, then more machine guns, artillery, and poison gas in the open fields. Jim, Slim, and Bull make it to a shellhole and settle down to wait for orders.

That night, orders come down for one man to go out and eliminate a troublesome German mortar crew; the men engage in a spitting contest for the opportunity, and Slim wins. He succeeds but is spotted and mortally wounded on the way back. After listening to Slim's agonized pleas for help, Jim begins railing against the strain and pain of war, disobeys orders and goes to his rescue, followed by Bull, who is shot and killed. By the time Jim reaches Slim, he is already dead. Jim is then shot in the leg, but when a German comes to finish him off, Jim shoots and wounds him. The German starts crawling back to his line, but Jim catches up to him in another shell hole; face to face, Jim cannot bring himself to finish off the German with his bayonet. Instead, in a gesture of pity, he gives the dying soldier a cigarette. Just then, the

The Silents Go to War

Americans attack again and Jim is taken away to a makeshift hospital. From another soldier, he learns that Champillon has changed hands four times. Sick with worry about Melisande, Jim sneaks out of the hospital and hitches a ride to Champillon. When he arrives at the farmhouse, he finds it damaged and empty; Melisande and her mother have joined a stream of refugees trudging to safety in the rear. Jim collapses in pain and is carried off in an ambulance by retreating soldiers.

After the war ends, Jim goes home to America. Before he arrives at the family house, his mother overhears Justyn and Jim's brother Harry discussing what to do; in Jim's absence, they have fallen in love. When Jim appears, he is suffering from shell shock and his left leg has been amputated above the knee. Later, a weary and dispirited Jim tells his mother about Melisande, and she tells him to go back and find her. Months later, Melisande and her mother are working on the farm when Melisande spots a limping figure coming toward her; screaming "Jimmee!" she hurls herself into his arms.

The backstory: King Vidor (1894–1982) had been working for nearly a decade, directing a series of short films for Universal Studios focusing on the rehabilitation of juvenile offenders, and had even had his own small studio, "Vidor Village," which went bankrupt in 1922. At that point, Vidor offered his services to the top industry executives, and Louis B. Mayer (of the recently merged Metro-Goldwyn-Mayer studio) engaged him to direct the nearly 40-year-old stage actress Laurette Taylor (playing an 18-year-old girl) in *Peg O' My Heart* (1922), which became a huge hit, as did her next Vidor-directed vehicle *Happiness* (1922). Vidor scored another hit in *Wild Oranges* (1924).[29] Growing frustrated at directing frothy films, he told MGM's head of production Irving Thalberg (1899–1936) that he wanted to take on bigger subjects about the three pillars that built America: "war, wheat and steel." Thalberg agreed on "war" and hired playwright Laurence Stallings (1894–1968), already hailed for his Broadway First World War play *What Price Glory*, to co-write a screenplay showing the war through the eyes of an average American soldier. Stallings, himself a Marine veteran who had lost a leg at Belleau Wood, crafted a blunt, honest look at the war. Next came the casting of the "Everyman" soldier, and Thalberg suggested John Gilbert (1897–1936).[30] Gilbert had just scored a big hit as the dashing Prince Danilo in the August release of *The Merry Widow*. Vidor, who had directed Gilbert in *His Hour* and *Wife of the Centaur* (both in 1924), was not thrilled with Thalberg's choice, as Gilbert was known as "The Great Lover" for his romantic roles. Vidor was wrong; once production

7. Antiwar and War Trauma Films of 1921–1930

started, Gilbert proved to be sensitive to the nuances of Vidor's direction, as well as adding his own touches to the role of the young soldier Jim Apperson. For the role of the farm girl Melisande, Vidor cast French-born actress Renée Adorée (1898–1933),[31] who had come to Hollywood from the New York stage in 1920 and had worked with John Gilbert in three other films. Her understanding of the minute details of domestic French farm life proved invaluable to the production and were incorporated throughout the film. The charming gum-chewing scene between Gilbert and Adorée was real—Gilbert really did teach her to chew gum.

In order to film the graphic battle scenes as authentically as possible, Vidor spoke with and employed many extras who had been in the war; the picture's art director, James Basevi, had been an artillery officer in the British Army, and Tom O'Brien, who played Bull, was also a combat veteran. Vidor brought his own touch to the battle sequence of Belleau Wood (shot in Elysian Park, Los Angeles): he choreographed the soldiers' movements marching into battle to the beat of a metronome, using a base drum to beat out the rhythm and set the soldiers' pace. As they advance through the forest, first one, and then another soldier is hit by sniper fire, and another, and then another. The effect is chilling.[32] In a pivotal scene, after Jim's buddies are in mortal danger, Jim begins railing against the futility of war, yelling, "Waiting! Orders! Mud! Stinking Stiffs! What the hell do we get out of this war anyway!" Vidor allowed Gilbert to improvise the scene, as well as a scene involving Jim—shot in the leg, traumatized, and enraged by the death of his friends—coming face to face with a wounded German soldier. Instead of finishing him off with a bayonet thrust to the throat, he takes pity on him and puts a cigarette in his mouth, just before the German dies.[33]

The Big Parade was one of the greatest hit movies of the 1920s. Budgeted at $382,000, it earned $4,990,000 in the United States and $1,141,000 in Europe during its initial release, with MGM eventually recording a profit of $3,400,000, its biggest in the silent era. It played in some of the larger cities in the United States for a year or more, giving John Gilbert superstar status and making Renée Adorée a major star.[34]

Critical response: Reviews were laudatory. *The New York Times*, in a November 20, 1925, review,[35] said:

> An eloquent pictorial epic of the World War was presented last night at the Astor Theatre before a sophisticated gathering that was intermittently stirred to laughter and tears. This powerful photodrama is entitled "The Big Parade," having been converted to the screen from a story by Laurence

The Silents Go to War

Stallings, co-author of "What Price Glory," and directed by King Vidor. It is a subject so compelling and realistic that one feels impelled to approach a review of it with all the respect it deserves, for as a motion picture it is something beyond the fondest dreams of most people. The thunderous belching of guns follows on the heels of a delightful romance between a Yankee doughboy and a fascinating French farm girl. It is the natural comedy that came to the American troops in France, men who landed in a foreign country without the slightest idea of the lingo. The incidents have been painted skillfully, from the blowing of the whistles as the signal that America has entered the war to the skirmishing attack in the forest. And even in a large shell hole the three pals find something to joke about. There are incidents in the film which obviously come from experience, as they are totally different from the usual jumble of war scenes in films. It is because of the realism that the details ring true and it grips the spectator. Just as the scenes are perfect as human imagination and intelligence could produce them, so the acting is flawless throughout. Nothing could be more true to life than the actions and the expressions of the three buddies in khaki. They are just ordinary citizens, one the son of a millionaire, another a rivetter and the third a bartender. John Gilbert enacts the part of the hero, Jim Apperson, the scion of a wealthy family. Tom O'Brien figures as Bull, the jovial Irishman who served drinks across a bar, and Karl Dane is seen as Slim, the fearless rivetter. Renee Adoree impersonates farm girl Melisande, the bewitching French girl, who falls in love with Jim, her affection being surely and certainly reciprocated by that young gentleman, although he had left a sweetheart in America. There comes the time when the call of battle tears Jim away from Melisande. There is a big parade—a parade of lorries filled with American doughboys bound for the fighting lines. Melisande clings to the vehicle carrying her Jim, until she falls in the street, pressing a shoe he has given to her to her bosom. The battle scenes excel anything that has been pictured on the screen, and Mr. Vidor and his assistants have ever seen fit to have the atmospheric effects as true as possible. This is a pictorial effort of which the screen can well boast. It carries one from America to France, then back to America and finally to France again. And one feels as if a lot has happened in a single evening.

Writing for *Life* magazine's December 1925 issue,[36] Robert Sherwood said:

> I could not detect a single flaw in "The Big Parade," not one error of taste or of authenticity, and it isn't as if I didn't watch for these defects, for I have seen too many movies which pictured the war in terms of Liberty Loan propaganda. "The Big Parade" is eminently right. There are no heroic Red Cross nurses in No Man's Land, no scenes wherein the doughboys dash over the top carrying the American flag.

Carl Sandburg, reviewing *The Big Parade* for the December 29, 1925, issue[37] of the *Chicago Daily News*, praised the film as a grand

7. Antiwar and War Trauma Films of 1921–1930

cinematographic achievement: "'The Big Parade' tells more about the war than any one picture, and probably more than all other war pictures put together. And, oh! It's something to talk about—the last half of this picture—and something to sit speechless and think about."

The film won the *Photoplay* magazine medal for best film of the year 1925, with the medal being the first significant annual movie award prior to the establishment of the Oscars.[38] The only critical response came from England, where newspapers disliked the movie since it had implied that the United States had won the war single-handedly.[39]

On August 23, 1926, the movie world was devastated by the sudden death of Rudolph Valentino from a ruptured appendix and peritonitis. Fans mourned, as tens of thousands paid tribute at his open coffin in New York City and 100,000 mourners lined the streets outside the church where funeral services were held. Valentino's body traveled by train to Hollywood, where he was laid to rest after another funeral service attended by stars, directors, producers, and grieving fans.[40]

Playing upon the success of *The Big Parade*'s appeal depicting war on the ground, the August 1927 movie *Wings*[41]—a romantic action/war film starring Richard Arlen, Clara Bow, and Buddy Rogers—saluted heroic knights of the air. Its realistic aviation sequences featuring stunt work performed by actual pilots of the United States Army Air Corps, brief (male and female) nudity, and a climactic air-battle finale made it a sensation with both the critics and the public.

Hot on the heels of *Wings* came a film that owed a great deal to one of the most famous "slacking" cases of the First World War: *The Patent Leather Kid*, released on August 16, 1927, by First National Pictures, directed by Alfred Santell. Cast: Richard Barthelmess (the Patent Leather Kid), Molly O'Day (Curley Boyle), Lawford Davidson (Lieutenant Hugo Breen), Matthew Betz (Jake Stuke), Arthur Stone (Jimmy "Puffy" Kinch), Ray Turner (Molasses), Hank Mann (Sergeant), Walter James (Officer Riley), Lucien Prival (German officer), Nigel De Brulier (French doctor), Fred O'Beck (tank crew), Clifford Salam (tank crew), Henry Murdock (tank crew), Charles Sullivan (tank crew), John Kolb (tank crew), Billy Bletcher (fight fan), Fred Kelsey (fight fan), Lafe McKee (fight fan). Plot[42]: While World War I rages in Europe, a boxer on the Lower East Side of New York shows little affection for his country. The Patent Leather Kid is pictured with natural gifts, a man who can stand up against the best of fighters and bring them down for the count. Yet, his weaknesses are brought out when his girl, Curley, leaves him to entertain the troops in France and the Kid is drafted along

The Silents Go to War

with his stuttering trainer, Puffy, and his cornerman, Molasses. Once entrenched in the war, the Kid is shown as a shaking, slacking spectacle, while Molasses serves heroically with the "Harlem Hellfighters" and Puffy, who would never have dared to put on boxing gloves in the ring, proves to be a man of steel under fire. When Puffy is shot and dies in his arms, the Kid is spurred on to take battlefield chances and reveals his brave nature when he plunges ahead to bomb a German-held church belfry. He participates in a tank battle, is badly injured, and becomes partially paralyzed. Sent to a makeshift hospital, he is recognized by Curley, now a nurse, and is eventually sent back to the United States, where he receives a decoration for bravery. Later, while watching a military parade and seeing the American flag unfurled, he raises his partially paralyzed arm in salute.

The backstory: The idea for *The Patent Leather Kid* was taken from the real-life "slacker" accusations case made against heavyweight champion Jack Dempsey (1895–1983). Although Dempsey had registered for the draft in 1918, he opted instead to work in a shipyard (wearing red patent leather shoes!) for the duration of the war, taking boxing bouts on the side and being paid well. His popularity wilted in 1920 when the news of his alleged draft dodging surfaced in national newspapers, indicating that the United States Army had exempted him on the grounds that he was the sole support of his immediate family.[43] Boxing fans were incensed, and when Dempsey was defeated in 1926 and 1927 by decorated-Marine-turned-boxer Gene Tunney, he was given little sympathy.[44]

After *The Patent Leather Kid* premiered, Dempsey saw the film and wrote to star Richard Barthelmess: "Dear Dick: Just a little note to thank you for letting me see 'The Patent Leather Kid.' It's a wow! You handled yourself like an old-timer, Dick, and it was a genuine pleasure to see a real ring battle on the screen."[45] The film was a rousing success, earning $1.2 million at the box office and Barthelmess an Academy Award nomination as Best Actor for his performance.[46]

Critical response: *The New York Times* praised the film. Writing in his August 16, 1927, review,[47] critic Mordaunt Hall praised the performance of Barthelmess: "Under the direction of Alfred Santell who has already made his mark in the motion picture world, Richard Bartlemess, in a film called *The Patent Leather Kid*, excels any performance he has hitherto given. There is not a single flaw in his acting throughout this long feature."

In a August 17 review,[48] *Variety* agreed:

7. Antiwar and War Trauma Films of 1921–1930

"For Barthlemess, perfect, even if Barthelmess is made to play what is at times a repulsive role, that of a slacker during wartime, and admittedly so.... Barthelmess is such a big portion of this long film, in action and work, that he must come before the picture itself ... probably the reddest red-fire finish any picture ever had. The Patent Leather Kid one, in battle and performing a valiant act for which he is decorated, after all his professed cowardice, is under the care of his sweetie." The review also went on to praise the performance of Molly O'Day as his wise-cracking girlfriend and noted the use of amplifiers in broadcasting synchronized sound from disc recordings to mimic ringside noises during the big fight scenes.[49]

As war films enjoyed a resurgence in popularity, a daring antiwar film premiered, generating considerable controversy due to its love story between a captured German POW and a French farm girl: *Barbed Wire*, released on September 10, 1927, by Famous Players Lasky/Paramount Pictures, directed by Rowland V. Lee. Cast: Pola Negri (Mona Moreau), Clive Brook (Oskar Muller), Claude Gillingwater (Jean Moreau), Einar Hanson (André Joseph Moreau), Clyde Cook (Hans), Gustav von Seyffertitz (Pierre Corlet), Charles Willis Lane (Colonel Duval), Ben Hendricks Jr. (Sargeant Caron). Plot[50]: Marie is a French farm girl living on a prosperous little farm in France with her grandfather and her brother, André, when war is declared against Germany. André immediately volunteers and is sent to the front. Their farm is commandeered by French authorities to serve as a prison camp for captured Germans. Although her grandfather, a veteran of the Franco-Prussian War of 1870, counsels Marie not to judge all Germans harshly, she treats the Germans who are set to work on their farm with disdain, which is only made worse when her brother is reported killed in action. The Germans, including Oskar Muller (a businessman in pre-war Germany) and Hans (a jolly circus acrobat) treat Marie and her grandfather with courtesy and respect. Her grandfather dies from illness and grief. Gradually, Marie begins to look at the German prisoners as human beings, and Oskar eventually tells her that his young sister has been killed during the French bombardment of town on the French-German border. Marie and Oskar gradually fall in love, with Hans as their confidant. Marie's fellow townspeople begin to look at her with suspicion, and when a coarse French soldier tries to rape her, Oskar comes to the rescue and attacks and beats the soldier. When he is arrested for attacking the Frenchman, she speaks up for him at his trial, incurring the wrath of the locals, especially the women, and is

The Silents Go to War

branded a collaborator. Unexpectedly, André returns to the village at the end of the war, having been blinded in battle and cared for by German doctors. The Germans are released and sent back to Germany, and Marie goes with Oskar back to Germany.

The backstory: The film is based on the novel *The Woman of Knockaloe* published in 1923 by Hall Caine (1853–1931), but director and screenwriter Rowland V. Lee (1891–1975) decided to alter the plot, much to the disgust of the author. In the novel, the action took place at the Knockaloe Internment Camp on the Isle of Man; in the film, Lee moved the action to Normandy, France, and used German war veterans as extras to play the German POWs. Most importantly, Lee changed the ending: instead of the two lovers committing suicide after being rejected by both of their countries, Lee allowed them to go to Germany to hopefully make a life together.[51] He cast Paramount's popular leading lady, Polish-born actress Pola Negri (1897–1987), as Marie, and English actor Clive Brook (1887–1974) as Oskar. Ironically, Brook had fought the Germans as a British officer serving in France during the war. Although the film premiered to excellent reviews, audiences in general disliked the film, with audiences in England reacting with an upsurge of anti–German sentiment.[52]

Critical response: The November 1927 issue of *Screenland*[53] gave the film a glowing review, stating that the film

> actually has the nerve to show us a German hero in love with a French heroine. Pola Negri plays the French farmette and Clive Brook, a prisoner working on Pola's farm—if you can call it work. Thanks to Erich Pommer's supervision, or Rowland Lee's direction to Pola and Mr. Brook's acting, or something, Barbed Wire is direct, and simple and powerful and touching.

Similarly, *Motion Picture* notes in its November 1927 issue[54]

> that the picture "clicks" in New York and other key cities with the performance of Pola Negri as the peasant girl the best she has given since she decided to leave Germany to face American cameras. The portrayal of Clive Brook, cast as the German prisoner, is highly lauded, as is the performance of the late Einar Hanson, who in this, his last picture, plays a French soldier who returns sightless.

On October 6, 1927, history was made with the release of the Al Jolson musical *The Jazz Singer*, the first film to introduce audiences to synchronized singing and speaking in a picture, and 1928 became a year of change. With the advent of sound, silent films would slowly begin to experiment and use synchronized sound in movies; some would be

7. Antiwar and War Trauma Films of 1921–1930

hybrids (part sound, part silent), and some films would still remain silent.

An antiwar, sentimental Hollywood take on a German family torn apart by the futility of World War I came to the screen in February of 1928: *Four Sons*, released on February 12, 1928, by Fox Film Corporation, directed by John Ford. Cast: Margaret Mann (Mother Bernle), James Hall (Joseph "Dutch" Bernle), Charles Morton (Johann Bernle), Francis X. Bushman, Jr. (Franz Bernle), George Meeker (Andreas Bernle), June Collyer (Annabelle), Earle Foxe (Major von Stomm), Albert Gran (the postman), Frank Reicher (the schoolmaster), Archduke Leopold of Austria (a captain), Hughie Mack (the innkeeper), August Tollaire (the burgomeister), Robert Parrish (Joseph's son), John Wayne (officer). Plot[55]: Prior to World War I, Mother Bernle and her four grown sons are living a happy, peaceful life in a small Bavarian village. The oldest son, Joseph, yearns to go to America to live, and his mother gives him her savings to realize his dream. Soon afterward, the war begins, and two of the sons, Johann and Franz, go off to battle. Both sons are killed, leaving the youngest son, Andreas, with his mother. Meanwhile Joseph becomes an American citizen and joins the army to fight against Germany. The evil Major Von Stomm comes to Mother Bernle's house one rainy evening to rebuke her for having a son who is a "traitor" and takes the young Andreas away to join his battalion. Andreas is killed in battle, dying in his brother Joseph's arms. After the war, Joseph goes back to his wife, child, and successful restaurant in New York and sends for his mother to come live with him.

The backstory: John Ford (1894–1973) had directed dozens of feature films during the 1920s, with many of his successes coming in the Western genre, including his first major success *The Iron Horse* (1924) earning the Fox Film Corporation over $2 million worldwide against a budget of $280,000.[56] Ford's work on this film was greatly influenced by the fluid camerawork of the great German director F. W. Murnau, with Ford adapting some of Murnau's expressionist visual style to advance the storyline.[57] For the role of Mother Bernle, Margaret Mann, who'd worked for 10 years as a film extra, was selected by Winfield R. Sheehan, the general manager of Fox Films, to act the principal role in the film. His choice paid off: at the New York premiere of *Four Sons*, Mrs. Mann received an enthusiastic response from the appreciative audience, as well as garnering the best reviews by movie critics. For the hissable villain, Earle Fox played the cruel Major Von Stomm as a caricature of the stereotypical German officer made famous by Erich von Stroheim[58]

The Silents Go to War

10 years before in 1918's *The Heart of Humanity*. The film was an enormous success, receiving the *Photoplay* award as the best film of 1928 and earning $1.5 million at the box office.[59]

Critical response: *Variety*'s December 31, 1927, early review[60] praised the picture as "a profoundly moving picture [from a story by I.A.R. Wylie] of family life in Germany during the First World War, giving a sympathetic insight into the effect upon humble people of rural Bavaria of the great struggle."

> The production is magnificent in the amazing effectiveness of its fine realism and in its utter simplicity.
>
> The story is the commonplace history of a widow and her four sons. Joseph goes to America before the war, marries and has his own little delicatessen shop, and a baby is born. Then the war comes. The other three brothers go to the front one by one and are killed. There is no "war stuff," the war tragedy in enacted in the homely cottage of the lone mother.
>
> Margaret Mann's playing of the big role is a miracle of unaffected naturalness. Her Frau Bernle lives from the moment the film starts to its finish. Something of the same effortless simplicity has been communicated to the whole cast. The picture is rich in fascinating characters, such as the pompous but kindly old German letter carrier (Albert Gran) whose agonizing task it is to deliver the casualty notices to Frau Bernle; the Burgomeister of the village (August Tollaire) and the innkeeper (Hughie Mack).

June of 1929 brought a serio-comic antiwar film (part talkie with a synchronized score and sound effects) seen through the eyes of a gender-bending woman in *She Goes to War*, released on June 8, 1929, by Inspiration Pictures, directed by Henry King. Cast: Eleanor Boardman (Joan), John Holland (Tom Pike), Margaret Seddon (Tom's mother), Eulalie Jensen (Matron of Canteen), Edmund Burns (Reggie), Alma Rubens (Rosie the canteen worker), Yola d'Avril (Yvette), Al St. John (Bill). Plot[61]: Small-town social leader Joan Morant, who holds herself aloof from the "common people," is thrilled when wartime activity strikes her community: enlisting the aid of her uncle, a congressman, she obtains an assignment overseas. Although she loves Reggie, a wealthy sheik, Joan plays with the affections of local garage owner Tom Pike, both of whom she meets in France. Tom, transformed by his war experiences, rebuffs Joan's advances, and she seeks out Reggie, who is living his accustomed life of luxury as a supply sergeant. Joan's female companions, including her new friend Rosie, are constantly making great sacrifices and impress upon her the seriousness of purpose in her work, and she resolves to do her part. When Reggie, called to the front,

7. Antiwar and War Trauma Films of 1921–1930

becomes hopelessly drunk, she dons his uniform and replaces him in the ranks, although one of the soldiers, Al, thinks she's a "gay" young man. Joan experiences a new admiration and love for Tom, her commander. Proving her heroism in battle by killing an enemy German soldier, she returns to Tom, worthy of his love.

The backstory: Eleanor Boardman (1898–1991) had become a star in 1923's *Souls for Sale* and had just appeared in the 1928 critically acclaimed film *The Crowd*, which was directed by her husband King Vidor. Both of them, however, had just been indicted for evading income tax payments between 1925 and 1927,[62] so Boardman was desperate to turn attention away from her personal life and back to her public persona as a serious actress. While the film garnered some respectable reviews, it was not a box office success and quietly faded away.

Critical response: The June 8, 1929, review[63] in the *Detroit Free Press* focused on the battlefield scenes, singling out "the images of valiant doughboys battling menacing Huns, their eyes hidden under steel helmets." In the July 1929 issue,[64] *Motion Picture Magazine* gave the film a balanced review:

> The first part-talkie movie of the World War owes none of its entertainment value to the talking sequences. Most of the dialogue and sound is obviously put in afterward and synchronized as best it could be. On one occasion, a roomful of soldiers is supposed to be singing "There is a Happy Land" and not a mouth is open. There is just enough spoken dialogue in the picture to make it possible for the audience to accustom itself either to it or to the sub-titular periods. Talkie-silent controversy aside, however, the picture should not be missed by anybody who's on the lookout for movie thrills. The war scenes showing soldiers advancing in tanks through liquid fire are about the most exciting thing ever seen on the screen. The picture has other virtues, not the least of which is Eleanor Boardman giving a remarkable acting performance. John Holland, a newcomer, is magnificent as Eleanor's leading man. There is moderate good comedy from Al St. John, and there are moments when the old directorial genius of Henry King shines through the dull mechanics of Rupert Hughes' story.

Silent movie output rapidly diminished, although silent films in general were still very popular with European and South American audiences, who could use their own language titles instead of English.

On October 29, 1929, the Wall Street stock market crashed, with investors from all walks of life losing billions of dollars through panic stock trading, triggering a worldwide global economic collapse that spiraled into the Great Depression.[65] Businesses were forced to close, people lost jobs, and the mood of the country was bleak.

The Silents Go to War

Hollywood was not immune: to finance the purchase of movie theaters for ever-growing audiences in the 1920s and the conversion to sound starting in 1927, studios had tripled their debts to $410 million by 1929. With theaters closing and movie attendance down, the studios were forced to drop ticket prices to the public.[66]

The year 1930 proved a turning point for the motion picture industry. Serious issues (crime, poverty, the effects of the Depression on families and American veterans) started to be addressed, and finally, 12 years after the end of the First World War, an American filmmaker would take an unadorned, brutal, unflinching look at the war strictly from the German perspective: *All Quiet on the Western Front*, released on April 30, 1930, by Universal Studios, directed by Lewis Milestone. Cast: Lew Ayres (Paul Bäumer), Louis Wolheim (Stanislaus Katczinsky), John Wray (Himmelstoss), Ben Alexander (Franz Kemmerich), Scott Kolk (Leer), Owen Davis, Jr. (Peter), William Bakewell (Albert Kropp), Russell Gleason (Müller), Richard Alexander (Westhus), Harold Goodwin (Detering),

Paul Baümer (Lew Ayres, left) has just killed a French soldier (unidentified actor) in 1930's *All Quiet on the Western Front*, released in 1930 by Universal Pictures (MOVIESTORE Collection Ltd/Alamy Stock Photo).

7. Antiwar and War Trauma Films of 1921–1930

Slim Summerville (Tjaden), Walter Browne Rogers (Behn), G. Pat Collins (Lieutenant Bertinck), Edmund Breese (Herr Meyer), Beryl Mercer (Frau Bäumer, Paul's mother), Marion Clayton (Anna, Paul's sister), Heinie Conklin (Joseph Hammacher), Bertha Mann (Sister Libertine, nurse), Raymond Griffith (dead French soldier), William Irving (Ginger, the army cook), Yola d'Avril (Suzanne), Edwin Maxwell (Herr Bäumer), Bodil Rosing (mother of hospital patient), Maurice Murphy (soldier), Arthur Gardner (classroom student). Plot[67]: Inspired by the speech of their teacher Professor Kantorek about the glory of serving in the army and "saving the Fatherland," student Paul Bäumer and his friends join the army as the new Second Company. Their romantic delusions are quickly broken during their brief but intensive training under the tyrannical Corporal Himmelstoss, who bluntly tells them, "You're going to be soldiers—and that's *all*." The new soldiers arrive by train at the combat zone, which is in chaos: soldiers everywhere, incoming shells, horse-drawn artillery lobbing outgoing shells, and prolonged rain. When the young soldiers reach their post, they are assigned to a unit of older soldiers, who are not helpful. No food is available, but one of the more experienced soldiers, "Kat" Katczinsky, returns with a slaughtered hog that he has stolen from a field kitchen. In return for a share of the food, the young soldiers "pay" for their dinner with soaps and cigarettes.

The recruits' first trip to the trenches with the veterans is to restring barbed wire; it is harrowing, with Paul's friend Behn being blinded by shrapnel and hysterically running into machine gun fire. They spend several days in a bunker under bombardment, but finally move into the trenches and repulse an enemy attack. They counterattack and take an enemy trench with heavy casualties but have to abandon it. Eventually, they are sent to the field kitchens, where they receive double rations simply because of the number of dead. The boys have a semi-serious discussion about the causes of war, speculating about whether geographical entities offend each other and whether these disagreements involve them.

Soon after, cowardly Corporal Himmelstoss arrives at the front and is promptly ostracized because of his bad reputation. He is forced to go into battle with the Second Company and is immediately killed. The company attacks a cemetery, and Paul stabs a French soldier but finds himself trapped with the dying man for the night. Paul tries to help him throughout the night, bringing him water, but the soldier dies. Paul cries bitterly and begs the dead man to speak so he can be forgiven. When he returns to the German lines, he is comforted by Kat.

The Silents Go to War

When Second Company goes into battle again, Paul is severely wounded and is sent to a Catholic hospital, along with his good friend Albert Kropp. Kropp's leg is amputated, but he isn't told immediately; when he finds out, he sinks into a deep depression. Paul's other friend Franz Kemmerich dies of sepsis, and Paul must inform his mother of her son's death.

Paul is sent home on leave to visit his family. He is shocked at how uninformed the townspeople are about the actual situation, with everyone convinced that a "final push for Paris" is soon to occur. When he visits his old schoolroom where he was originally recruited, he hears the professor giving the same old speech to even younger students. When the professor asks Paul to detail his war experiences, Paul tells the students that war is not the glorious patriotic experience that they have been taught, but instead, it is mud, death, and destruction. He gives them the names of all the former students in his class who have fallen in battle. The professor and his students refuse Paul's explanation and call him a coward.

Disillusioned, Paul returns to the front and comes upon another Second Company filled with disenchanted young recruits before being reunited with Tjaden and Kat. During an arial bombardment, Kat's shin is broken, so Paul carries him back to a field hospital, only to find that a shell splinter has killed him on the way. Paul leaves and goes back on the front line. Soon after, he sees a butterfly just beyond his trench; smiling, he reaches out for the butterfly and is shot by an enemy sniper.

The backstory: Adapted from the classic 1929 novel of the same name by former German soldier Erich Maria Remarque (1898–1970), the movie directed by Lewis Milestone (1895–1980) would emphasize the grim realism and human cost of life, told from the viewpoint of a young, naïve German soldier. Universal's canny head of production, Carl Laemmle Jr., purchased the film rights so as to capitalize on the international success of Remarque's book.[68] After reading the book, Universal co-founder and president Carl Laemmle, Sr., pleaded with Milestone for a "happy ending" to the film. Milestone replied, "I've got your happy ending. We'll let the Germans win the war."[69] For his two leads, Milestone cast brutish-looking actor Louis Wolheim[70] as "Kat," and a then unknown young actor named Lew Ayres (1908–1996)[71] for the role of Paul. Just 22 years old, Ayres's only other role had been opposite Greta Garbo in 1929's *The Kiss*. Milestone originally conceived *All Quiet on the Western Front* as a silent film and filmed both a silent and a talkie version. For authenticity, he recruited German army veterans living in

7. Antiwar and War Trauma Films of 1921–1930

Los Angeles as both players and technical advisors, and around 2,000 extras were used during filming.[72] The "silent" version was a product of the Western Electric Sound System, which included little music in the soundtrack but a great deal of crowd noise and, crucially, the sound of gunfire, all crafted together by Dutch-born composer David Broekman (1899–1958), who worked for Universal during the transitional years from silents to talkies.

The silent version premiered in New York on April 25, 1930, with intertitles and a synchronized music and sound effects track. Audience response was tremendous, eventually earning Universal Studios $1,634,001 in the United States, and $3,000,000 worldwide.[73]

Critical response: *All Quiet on the Western Front* received extensive praise in the United States. Mordaunt Hall, writing for *The New York Times* in his April 30, 1930, review,[74] heaped plaudits on the picture:

> From the pages of Erich Maria Remarque's widely read book of young Germany in the World War "All Quiet on the Western Front," Carl Laemmle's Universal Pictures Corporation has produced a trenchant and imaginative picture, in which the producers adhere with remarkable fidelity to the spirit and events of the original stirring novel. It was presented last night at the Central Theatre before an audience that most of the time was held to silence by its realistic scenes. It is a notable achievement, sincere and earnest, with glimpses that are vivid and graphic. Like the original, it does not mince matters concerning the horrors of battle. It is a vocalized screen offering that is pulsating and harrowing, one in which the fighting flashes are photographed in an amazingly effective fashion.
>
> Lewis Milestone, who has several good films to his credit, was entrusted with the direction of this production. And Mr. Laemmle had the foresight to employ those well-known playwrights, George Abbott and Maxwell Anderson, to make the adaptation and write the dialogue. Some of the scenes are not a little too long, and one might also say that a few members of the cast are not Teutonic in appearance, but this means but little when one considers the picture as a whole, for wherever possible, Mr. Milestone has used his fecund imagination, still clinging loyally to the incidents of the book. In fact, one is just as gripped by witnessing the picture as one was by reading the printed pages, and in most instances it seems as though the very impressions written in ink by Herr Remarque had become animated on the screen.

He lauded the work of Louis Wolheim as Kat and Lew Ayres as Paul, and then singled out silent film comedian Raymond Griffith, praising his performance in a pivotal scene where Paul stabs a French soldier: "Raymond Griffith, the erstwhile comedian who, years before acting in film comedies, lost his voice through shrieking in stage melodramas, gives a marvelous performance as the dying Frenchman. It may be a little too long for one's peace of mind, but that does not detract from Mr. Griffith's sterling performance."[75]

Columnist Irene Thirer, writing for the *New York Daily News*,[76] said:

> It smacks of directorial genius—nothing short of this; sensitive performances by a marvelous cast and the most remarkable camera work which has been performed on either the silent or sound screen, round about the Hollywood studios ... we have praise for everyone concerned with this picture.

Variety[77] lauded the film as a "harrowing, gruesome, morbid tale of war, so compelling in its realism, bigness and repulsiveness."

In other parts of the world, including Italy, France, and Austria, both the silent and sound versions of the film were banned[78]; due to its antiwar and perceived anti–German messages, Adolf Hitler and the Nazi Party opposed the film. When it premiered on December 4, 1931, in Berlin, Nazi Brownshirts under the command of Joseph Goebbels interrupted the viewings by setting off stink bombs, throwing sneezing powder in the air, and releasing white mice in the theaters, eventually forcing projectors to be shut down. They repeatedly yelled out *"Judenfilm!"* ("Jewish Film!"). The Nazi campaign was successful, and the film was outlawed on December 11, 1930. It would not be released again until April 25, 1952, seven years after the defeat of Nazi Germany, when it was shown at the Capital Theater in West Berlin.[79]

Once *The Jazz Singer* was released in 1927, the market for silent movies began to dry up. Although the spread of sound was slower outside of the United States due to the upgrading of sound equipment, both filmmakers and exhibitors all over the world gradually made the change, and the age of the silent movies came to an end.[80] Silent movies faded away, and the era of sound films began.

While some well-known silent actors seamlessly made the transition to sound films as major stars (Ronald Colman, Wallace Beery), others would transition as supporting actors in the 1930s and 1940s (Hobart Bosworth, Henry B. Walthall, Jack Holt, Alla Nazimova, Lawrence Grant, Montagu Love). Some would retire (Norma Talmadge, Mary Pickford, Alice Terry, Clara Kimball Young, Eleanor Boardman), while others (Marie Prevost, John Gilbert) could not make the transition, dying under tragic circumstances.[81] *Lest We Forget* star Rita Jolivet turned her back on films and married Scottish nobleman James Allan, Laird of Ballikinrain Castle, becoming one of Europe's premier

7. Antiwar and War Trauma Films of 1921–1930

party-givers, entertaining kings, queens, and heads of state.[82] Blanche Sweet's career faltered in the sound era, and she eventually became a salesgirl in a Los Angeles department store until her body of work was rediscovered in the 1960s.[83] Helen Ferguson, co-star of 1919's *The Great Victory*, left acting at the start of the sound era and became one of the most powerful and influential publicity/public relations agents during the Golden Age of Hollywood, representing major stars including Henry Fonda, Barbara Stanwyck, and Loretta Young.[84] Evil crown prince look-alike Earl Schenck retired from the screen, moved to Hawaii, and forged a new career as an explorer, ethnologist, and cartologist of Polynesian culture.[85] Stuart Holmes, Rudolph Valentino's nasty German cousin Otto von Hartrott in the mega hit *The Four Horsemen of the Apocalypse*, appeared occasionally in supporting roles during the talking era but gained national and international fame as a renowned sculptor in the 1930s, creating works for three California post offices in 1936 and 1937 as part of the Depression-era Federal Art Project.[86] Slapstick comedienne Mabel Normand would be involved in two Hollywood scandals in the 1920s,[87] dooming her career. She died an early death in 1930. Polish-born Pola Negri would return to Europe, make films that became favorites of Adolf Hitler, and return to the United States to make a comeback in the 1943 comedy hit *Hi Diddle Diddle*.[88] Jane Novak, Hobart Bosworth's leading lady in *Behind the Door*, left acting at the start of the sound era and became the Julia Child of her generation, lecturing on American cuisine in the 1940s and '50s, writing the best-selling *Treasury of Chicken Cooking* in 1974.[89] British-born comic icon Charlie Chaplin would continue making silent films into the 1930s, transition to talking films in the 1940s, and eventually be knighted for his body of work by Queen Elizabeth II. He also received an Honorary Academy Award from the Academy of Motion Picture Arts and Sciences for his contributions to the film industry. Matinee idol Sessue Hayakawa and "Horrible Hun" Eric von Stroheim would experience career renaissances in iconic late-career film roles,[90] while Lillian Gish would cement her status as the "First Lady of America," acting in both movies and television over the next 57 years, receiving numerous acting honors, and becoming a staunch supporter of film preservation.

Many studios put their silent film reels into storage, not to be seen for decades. Other studios deliberately destroyed films because they had negligible continuing value, and some films were "lost" because the nitrate film used in the silent era was extremely unstable and flammable, and eventually were burned up in accidental studio fires.

The Silents Go to War

Which American World War I propaganda films did survive? Which were destroyed or lost? Which films underwent preservation (the physical storage of the film in a climate-controlled vault) and which films were restored to the version most faithful to its initial release to the public? The final chapter answers these questions.

Epilogue
Lost and Found

With the advent of sound, silent films began to fade from the memory of the movie-going public. Writing in the December 4, 2013, issue of *The Atlantic* magazine, digital arts and culture columnist Abby Ohlheiser stated that during the silent era "about 10,919 films were produced, but just 2,749 are still with us in complete form, either as an original American 34 mm version, a foreign release or as a low-quality copy. That is just 25 percent of the silent era available."[1] Shamefully, many silent films fell victim to careless studio fires; others were junked as valueless, and other films were cannibalized for their set pieces that were repurposed for the talkies.

In 1935, New York's Museum of Modern Art began one of the earliest attempts to collect and preserve silent films, obtaining original negatives of the Biograph and Edison companies and the world's largest collection of D. W. Griffith films. The following year, Henri Langlois (1914–1977), pioneering film preservationist and film archivist, co-founded the *Cinémathèque Française*, which has become the largest international film collection in the world.[2] The Library of Congress hosts the National Film Preservation Board, which annually selects 25 U.S. silent films for preservation. The George Eastman House International Museum of Photography and Film (opened in 1949 to collect, preserve, and present the history of photography and film) founded the Louis B. Mayer Film Conservation Center. In 1967, the American Film Institute was founded and works to preserve America's film heritage from the silent years to the present day.

But what happened to the propaganda films of the silent era? Which films died a slow death from studio neglect? Which films perished in studio vault fires? Which films found their way into private collections, both American and European? Which films were saved and restored by the National Film Preservation Board of the Library of Congress, and

Epilogue

which films were saved and restored by European film preservation foundations? Which films received a new lease on life at showings at popular silent film festivals, and finally, which films are now available for a new generation of silent film lovers to own on DVD or view on YouTube? Stories vary.

In 1915, *The Battle Cry of Peace* premiered to a receptive film-going public and remained popular throughout the First World War. After the war, it was stored in the film vaults of Vitagraph Pictures, where it slowly deteriorated due to neglect. Today, it is considered a "lost" film, although the Cinemateket-Svenska Filminstitutet in Stockholm, Sweden, possesses one reel, which is housed in their library, and can be viewed by film scholars upon request.[3] Additionally, fragments of footage of battle scenes survive and are preserved at the George Eastman House.

The pacifist allegorical drama *Civilization* (1916) was restored by the Museum of Modern Art in 2015 with funding provided by the Hollywood Foreign Press Association and the Film Foundation. The source material was a shortened version that was used as the basis from the 1931 version; it was all that survived of the film.[4] On July 16, 2016, the restoration was shown at the Traverse City Film Festival (Traverse City, Michigan) as part of their annual film festival. "Part powerful allegorical drama, part historic curiosity, part trippy triumph," festival literature read, "'Civilization' is unlike anything you have ever seen."[5] The film was also shown at the International Silent Film Festival in Forssa, Finland, on August 29, 2018.

Part pacifist, part pro-war film, 1916's *Shell 43* is a lost film and no longer exists in any studio archives, private collections, or public archives.

Pro-war film *The Fall of a Nation* (1916) was not a commercial or critical success and was the sole film Dixon Studios produced before collapsing in 1921. It was not widely preserved, and no copies are known to exist. All that exists today are a number of stills and the soundtrack by noted operetta composer Victor Herbert, which is held in the possession of the Library of Congress.[6]

Antiwar film *If My Country Should Call* (1916) survives incomplete at the Library of Congress and the National Archives of Canada/Ottawa. Only reels 2, 3, and 5 survive of the original five reels. The incomplete print, along with a number of other silent films, was discovered in the Dawson Film Find of 1978.[7]

The feminist, pro-choice, 1916 antiwar film *War Brides* is a lost

Epilogue

film; aside from some studio stills, the film is untraceable in any of the world's film archives or private collections.

Although 1916's *Joan the Woman* was not a box office success at the time of its release, it remained a favorite film of its director, Cecil B. DeMille. Occasionally shown at film festivals, copies of the film were in less than pristine condition and were missing most of the original color effects. For the restoration, the George Eastman House partnered in collaboration with Haghefilm Digitaal using DeMille's personal nitrate print. The result was the film with its restored color effects, which was given a gala screening in 2019 at Italy's international film festival held at the La Giornate del Cinema Muto. A DVD was available through Movie World for download rental in four parts but was deleted from their silent film listing in 2022.[8]

The propaganda epic *Womanhood, the Glory of the Nation*, the 1917 sequel to director J. Stuart Blackton's 1915 movie *The Battle Cry of Peace*, is listed as a lost film in the American Film Institute catalog of feature films, and as of February 2021, the National Film Preservation Board included this film on its list of lost silent film features.

A print of Mary Pickford's "manhandled heroine" propaganda movie *The Little American* (1917) is housed at the UCLA Film and Television Archive in Los Angeles, California. In addition, the National World War I Museum located in Kansas City, Missouri, features stills from the movie in a display of vintage First World War silent movies. The DVD of the movie was released in 2007 by Jef Films. The film was shown in Encinitas, California, at the La Paloma Theatre on November 7, 2009, as part of the Mary Pickford Film Festival, which ran from November 6 through November 8, 2009. In 2014, it was featured as part of the Museum of Modern Art's "The Great War: A Cinematic Legacy" with showings on August 27, 2014, and August 29, 2014.

The Secret Game (1917) survives complete at the Library of Congress. The image of a Japanese "James Bond" character—sidestepping the typical "yellow peril" image of Asians during the twentieth century—would influence the work of future Asian filmmakers. In 2006, the documentary *The Slanted Screen*, featuring clips from *The Secret Game*, premiered on March 12, 2006, at the New York Film Festival, followed by premieres on March 19, 2006, at the San Francisco International Asian American Film Festival and on April 14, 2007, at the Wisconsin Film Festival. In 2017, *The Secret Game* was released on DVD through RLJ Films Entertainment Home Video Distributor.

The 1918 thriller *Lest We Forget*, featuring true-life *Lusitania* survivor

Epilogue

Rita Jolivet, is preserved at the Library of Congress and Cinémathèque Française. A fragment of the film is also held at the George Eastman House Motion Picture Collection.

My Four Years in Germany, the 1918 box office hit based on the true-life experiences of Ambassador James W. Gerard, is held at the Turner Entertainment Film Library. The film was released on DVD by Grapevine Video in June 2011, and a grainy version can also be seen on YouTube.

The 1918 Germanophobic film *The Kaiser, the Beast of Berlin* is now considered a lost film; no prints or stills of the film are known to exist.

In October of 2019, the National Film Preservation Board included 1918's Huns-in-the-hometown hit *The Claws of the Hun* on its list of lost silent feature films.

The farcical *To Hell with the Kaiser!* (1918) is considered a lost film, and no prints are known to exist. There is a vintage original lobby card (8 × 10 inches) currently on sale on eBay at a cost of $225.

The bias-against-German-Americans 1918 film *Me Und Gott* is a lost film, and no known prints survive.

The espionage propaganda thriller *The Prussian Cur* (1918) starring real-life German spy Captain Horst von der Goltz was most likely destroyed in the 1937 Fox Film Corporation vault fire and is now considered a lost film. Only a few film stills and lobby cards are known to exist.

In the late 1940s and 1950s, Warner Bros. destroyed many of its negatives, including 1918's *Kaiser's Finish*, due to nitrate film decomposition. The film is now considered lost, and no known copies exist.

Star/producer Clara Kimball Young's 1918 French-girl-versus-the-Germans film *The Road Through the Dark* was a success upon its release, but in 1924, Selznick Pictures, which owned the rights to the picture, went out of business when the studio was bought out by Universal Pictures. The film vanished into the vaults of Universal and is presumed to have disintegrated over time through studio neglect.

Comedienne Mabel Normand's 1918 comedy take on a modern-day Joan of Arc, *Joan of Plattsburg*, is a lost film; only original lobby posters survive, and no holdings are listed in film archives.

The wholesome, patriotic 1918 Mary Pickford recruitment picture *Johanna Enlists* survives in several prints, including one at the Library of Congress. The film was released by Alpha Video on August 30, 2016. It received a viewing on June 18, 2023, at the Library of Congress Festival of Film and Sound at the AFI Silver Theatre and Cultural Center in

Epilogue

Silver Spring, Maryland, introduced by film historian Richard Koszarski with live accompaniment by pianist Andrew Simpson.

Charlie Chaplin's iconic 1918 slapstick war propaganda film *Shoulder Arms* is in the public domain and can be seen on YouTube (without a score but with title cards) posted on January 23, 2023. It was released on DVD by Alpha Video on October 22, 2022. A popular staple at silent film festivals, it was shown at the Barbican Theatre silent film festival in London on November 30, 2014; at a showing by the Silent Film Society of Chicago at the Filament Theatre in Chicago on January 29, 2016; at the Ciné Lumière Festival in London on November 10, 2018; and at the AFI Silver Theatre and Cultural Center in Silver Spring, Maryland, on June 3, 2023, accompanied by the Peacherine Ragtime Orchestra.

The Unbeliever (1918) is preserved at the Library of Congress. As a still-surviving feature from the Edison Company's shorts and features, it was released by Kino-Lorber Films on February 22, 2005, as part of a four-disc collection "Edison, The Invention of the Movies: 1891–1918," and features the original piano score plus commentary by film scholars. It was also released by Alpha Video on May 27, 2014.

The Hun Within (1918) is now in the public domain in the United States. A copy is also preserved at the Cinémathèque Française in Paris, France.

The Cross Bearer (1918), the based-on-fact story of the heroic Belgian Cardinal Mercier, was produced and released by World Films. They ceased production in 1921, and only some production stills and lobby cards advertising the film remain.

Director Cecil B. DeMille's original nitrate of his film *Till I Come Back to You* (1918) is preserved in the Cecil B. DeMille Archives at Brigham Young University. A copy of the film is also preserved in the George Eastman House Motion Picture Collection. The film was given a screening on August 12, 2021, at Rome, New York's Capitolfest film festival, with an original new score composed and played by organist David Peckham.[9]

A print of D. W. Griffith's 1918 blockbuster *Hearts of the World* is held by the Cohen Media Group. The rights to the film are now in the public domain. In 1940, a retrospective of Griffith's films, including *Hearts of the World*, was featured at the Museum of Modern Art (MOMA) in New York City, which had begun the task of preserving and disseminating his films. The full restoration of the film was shown at MOMA on August 14, 2014, as part of "The Great War: A Cinematic Legacy." The restoration was financed through funds received from the

Epilogue

Lillian Gish Trust Fund for Film Preservation.[10] In October 2006, the Pordenone Silent Film Weekend hosted by the Brooklyn Academy of Music Rose Cinema in Brooklyn, New York, featured "Treasures from a Chest," a program of lost and found silent films curated by film preservationist Serge Bromberg, which included a showing of *Hearts of the World* on October 19.[11] The University of Chicago hosted a D. W. Griffith retrospective, showing *Hearts of the World* on Sunday, November 14, 2010. In June 2015 the British Film Institute screened *Hearts of the World* in Southbank, London, during its salute to D. W. Griffith, and on December 30, 2018, the film was given a gala holiday viewing at the Town Hall Theater in Wilton, New Hampshire, with a new score composed and accompanied by composer/pianist Jeff Rapsis.[12] DVD releases include the July 2015 release by Reel Vault studios, which features a new custom music score composed and performed on piano by American silent film composer William Perry, and an August 2015 DVD released by The Film Detective studio with musical accompaniment derived from pre-existing recordings.

A copy of the 1918 throw-the-baby-out-the-window propaganda film *The Heart of Humanity* is preserved at the EmCee Film Library in California, the Library of Congress, Library and Archives of Canada, and the George Eastman House Motion Picture Collection. It was shown at the Museum of Modern Art during its August 2014 film series "The Great War: A Cinematic Legacy." The film was released on Grapevine Video on April 2, 2013. The film can also be seen on YouTube.

The 1918 documentaries *Pershing's Crusaders* and *America's Answer to the Hun* are preserved at the National Archives in College Park, Maryland. Stills and posters from *Under Four Flags* and *Our Colored Fighters* may be found in the Still Holdings Department of the National Archives, but neither film survives intact.[13]

The rollicking, rowdy 1919 comedy *Yankee Doodle in Berlin* is preserved at the Library of Congress. In addition, copies are also held by the Museum of Modern Art, BFI Film and Television, Cinémathèque Royale de Belgique, and the Academy Film Archive in Beverly Hills, California. In 1975, the film was featured in the compilation DVD "The Moving Picture Boys in the Great War" narrated by Lowell Thomas. It was the winner of the Gold Medal at the 1975 Chicago Film Festival. It was released as a single DVD by Alpha Video on July 31, 2012. The film is also available on YouTube. It was given a showing on August 30, 2018, at the International Silent Film Festival in Forssa, Finland.

The 1919 movie *The Great Victory* or *The Great Victory, Wilson or*

Epilogue

the Kaiser? *The Fall of the Hohenzollerns* is preserved in the Performing Arts Database of the Library of Congress.

The Unpardonable Sin (1919) falls into the category of a lost film, although a small segment of the film did surface during the Dawson Film Find (see note 7).

The action film sensation *The False Faces* (1919) survives at the George Eastman House and the Turner Film Library and can be seen on YouTube. Unfortunately, this early film, a rarity in star Lon Chaney's filmography, has never been restored. In 2009, Classic Video Streams released a DVD of the movie titled "The Actors: Rare Films of Lon Chaney Sr.," and in 2015, Alpha Video released a DVD of the movie with commentary by the actor's son Lon Chaney, Jr., on his father's performance.

The fact-based 1919 film *The Lost Battalion* is preserved at the Library of Congress. It was first released on DVD on May 4, 2021, by Alpha Video, with a tinted and scored version released on October 22, 2022, by Grapevine Video. The film is also available for viewing on YouTube.

The anti–German propaganda film *Behind the Door* (1919) has been preserved at the Library of Congress and the Gosfilmofond Russian State Archives. In 2016, the San Francisco Film Festival, working with the Library of Congress and Gosfilmofond, created a more fully restored print of the film. The original color tinting scheme was also restored, based on analysis of the original printing rolls.[14] It premiered on June 3, 2016, at the Castro Theatre, with live musical accompaniment by pianist Stephen Horne and an introduction by movie critic Leonard Maltin. It was then screened on March 27, 2017, at the British Film Institute in Southbank, London, with introductory remarks by film restorer Robert Byrne and British Film National Archives silent film curator Bryony Dixon. Live accompaniment was provided by pianist Neil Brand. On March 8, 2018, the film was shown as part of the Borderlands Film Festival in Hereford, UK, with piano accompaniment by Stephen Horne. The International Silent Film Festival, held in Forssa, Finland, presented a screening of the film on August 29, 2018. A Blu-ray DVD was released on April 18, 2017, by Flicker Alley studio. An unrestored version of the film is available on YouTube.

The hugely popular 1921 antiwar epic *The Four Horsemen of the Apocalypse* is preserved in the United States National Film Registry at the Library of Congress. The film is in the public domain and is available for free download on the Internet Archive. A favorite at silent

Epilogue

film festivals, it was shown on February 23, 2002, at the Kansas City Film Festival with organ accompaniment by Marvin Faulwell. In 2005, the San Francisco Silent Film Festival hosted a festive screening, with noted film critic Leonard Maltin introducing the film; accompaniment was provided by organist Dennis James on the festival's Wurlitzer organ. The film had another showing at the 2014 festival, this time accompanied by the Mont Alto Motion Picture Orchestra.[15] And in 2018, in honor of Dublin-born director Rex Ingram, *The Four Horsemen of the Apocalypse* had two showings (March 18 and March 19) at the St. Patrick's Silent Film Festival in Dublin, Ireland. A new film score especially commissioned for the performances was debuted by Barry Adamson, Matthew Nolan, Seán Mac Erlaine, Adrian Crowley, and Kevin Murphy. A DVD of the film was released by Alpha Video on August 25, 2020.

Shootin' for Love (1923) featuring cowboy star Hoot Gibson as a Western shell-shocked veteran is a lost film; no existing footage or copies of the film exist.

A modest box office success when it first premiered, 1924's *The Enchanted Cottage* is preserved at the United States National Film Registry at the Library of Congress and can be seen on YouTube. In October of 2014, a remastered DVD of the film (with a new score by David Knudtson) was released by Grapevine Video. Alpha Video also released a DVD of the film in June of 2020.

A print of 1925's *The Dark Angel*, a gentle but compelling look at the plight of a blinded First World War veteran, was thought to be a lost film, but has recently been located in a film archive.[16]

Considered one of the greatest films made for its depiction of warfare and the trauma endured by World War I soldiers, 1925's *The Big Parade* was selected in 1992 for preservation in the United States National Film Registry by the Library of Congress. The film was re-issued in 1931 with a soundtrack consisting of composer William Axt's original score. When the film was released on video in the late 1980s as part of the MGM and British television Thames Silents project, silent film composer Carl Davis[17] created a new orchestral score for the film. The original 35 mm negative was eventually discovered intact in MGM's film vault and has been the source for many theatrical showings as well as DVD and Blu-ray editions, with the Davis score featured on these later editions.[18] The 2013 DVD and Blu-ray Warner Home Video release of *The Big Parade* features the most complete print of the movie, with audio commentary by historian Jeffrey Vance. A perennial favorite

Epilogue

at film festivals, *The Big Parade* received a special screening on March 8, 1987, at Radio City Music Hall, with Davis conducting his score played by the American Symphony Orchestra. In 2005, the film was presented at the annual San Francisco Silent Film Festival with live music played by Chris Elliot; the 2008 Kansas City Silent Film Festival showed the film on February 23, 2008, with period music played by organist Marvin Faulwell and percussionist Bob Keckeisen. The International Film Festival, held in Forssa, Finland, hosted a viewing on August 28, 2018. The British Film Institute presented *The Big Parade* on February 2, 2020, with music of the era played by Neil Brand (regular silent film accompanist at London's National Film Theatre) and an introduction by silent film author Dr. Michael Hammond, author of *The Great War in Hollywood Memory: 1918–1939* (New York: SUNY Press, 2019). On November 11, 2023, 105 years after the of the end First World War, *The Big Parade* was shown at the Yorkshire Film Festival in commemoration of the end of the conflict, with an improvised live musical score performed by pianist Jonny Best[19] (founding artistic director of the festival) and his frequent collaborator percussionist Trevor Bartlett.

Barbed Wire (1927) is preserved at the Belgian Cinémathèque in Brussels and at the George Eastman House in the United States. On April 18, 2017, it was shown by the Chicago Film Society and Film Studies Center at the Music Box Theatre with piano accompaniment by house organist Dennis Scott. The film was described in the program as "a spiritual precursor to 'All Quiet on the Western Front,' a quiet anti-war film beautifully photographed by frequent John Ford collaborator Bert Glennon."[20] The film was released by Grapevine Video on October 2, 2012, with a new musical score composed by Christopher Congdon. It can also be viewed on YouTube.

A copy of the boxer-slacker-turned-hero 1927 film *The Patent Leather Kid* is held by the Library of Congress, and a 16 mm print exists at the Wisconsin Center for Film and Theater Research. It was shown at the Museum of Modern Art on Friday, August 29 and Sunday, August 31, 2014, as part of "The Great War: A Cinematic Legacy," which ran from August 4 through September 21, 2014. The film was released on DVD by Zeus Film Archives in 2022, and a version has also been posted on YouTube.

One of the few surviving films made by director John Ford between 1917 and 1928, *Four Sons* (1928), was preserved in The Academy Film Archives[21] in 1999. It was shown at the Museum of Modern Art on Tuesday, August 19 and Wednesday, August 20, 2014, as part of "The

Epilogue

Great War: A Cinematic Legacy," which ran from August 4 through September 21, 2014. The movie is part of the "Ford at Fox: The Collection," 21 discs encompassing 24 of John Ford's films from 1920 through 1952 issued by Twentieth Century–Fox on December 4, 2007. The film is available for purchase to download on personal computers through iTunes, Google Play, Microsoft, and Amazon.

The gender-bending, half-silent/half-sound *She Goes to War* (1929) was a box office failure and slowly faded away within a few months of its initial release. In 1939, with war in Europe looming again, the picture was re-released by United Artists. All of the title cards were removed, and a considerable portion of crucial character development was eliminated, although the original score was retained. Cut from its original length of 87 minutes to 58 minutes, the film, touted as "a tribute to the women who went to war," was a resounding flop.[22] On March 25, 2014, a DVD of the 58-minute version was released by Alpha Video, and is also available for purchase on Amazon. A YouTube version of the 58-minute version, which contains the original score and some sound sequences, is dedicated to co-star Al St. John and was posted on April 5, 2012.

All Quiet on the Western Front (1930) is considered one of the greatest antiwar films, and in 1991 it was selected and preserved by the United States Library of Congress National Film Registry for both preservation and restoration.

In 2006, the actual restoration of the film (both the silent and the sound versions) took place at the Library of Congress's laboratory, which was located in Dayton, Ohio. Technicians worked with a nearly intact master print found in the Universal vaults, filling in scratches and resynching sound effects, producing a new print that made it possible to see a full frame in its entirety. This was considered especially important, since the sense of space is a key element in the film. The visualization of large patterns of movement—parades, horses galloping across the foreground, troops marching in choreographic drill, trucks churning across the ground—are counter to the small-scale shots of frightened, numb soldiers caught in web of war.

Part of the challenge of restoring the film was recovering footage that had been cut early in the film. The library's technicians did find one of these segments in a Universal print distributed in Europe in 1930. Most prints distributed in the United States showed a man picking up a loaf of bread smeared with blood, cutting off the section, and eating it. In the European version, he then breaks off the neck of a cognac bottle

Epilogue

and hands around the sharp-edged "cup" to his friends—perhaps an analogy to the Last Supper.[23]

The restored silent version was shown, on August 3, 2009, at the prestigious New York Film Forum. Writing for *The New York Post*, contemporary film critic Lou Limerick held the opinion that the silent version was far superior to the music-less talkie version, as did the Film Forum's curator Bruce Goldstein, who said, "It's longer, with more shots, more fluid camera movements, smoother acting transitions, more character details ... putting what is already a camera legend in a fresh, more complete light."[24] The San Francisco Silent Film Festival hosted the restoration on May 28, 2015, with a new music score played by the Mont Alto Motion Picture Orchestra, and on July 9, 2021, the Colorado-based Chautauqua Silent Film Series held a screening, again with musical accompaniment by the Mont Alto Motion Picture Orchestra.

On September 28, 2011, the TCM (Turner Classic Movies) channel presented the restored silent version on their weekly "Silent Sundays" film series, with commentary by TCM's noted host/film historian Robert Osborne.[25] The film has become a staple on TCM and is shown annually.

A number of DVDs of the film have been issued over the years, but the gold standard is Universal's 2012 "100th Anniversary Collector's Series" set, digitally remastered on DVD and Blu-ray, which includes both the silent and sound versions. In addition, *All Quiet on the Western Front* can be rented from most movie sites including the Google Play Store, Apple TV, and Amazon instant video. Ninety-two years after the original movie premiered to wide acclaim in the United States, Germany produced their own 2022 version, which was released on Netflix (with subtitles); the film received positive reviews in the American and British press and won four Academy Awards (including Best International Feature Film) at the 2023 Academy Awards in Hollywood, California. It was widely panned by the German press in numerous reviews.[26]

In 1930, the klieg lights went out forever on the silent film era. American First World War propaganda films became passé and out of date and were consigned to the back corners of studio vaults.

Fortunately, and through the efforts of organizations both in the United States and Europe dedicated to the preservation and restoration of silent films, a small number of these once-famous propaganda films now have new life: at silent film festival viewings, on DVD or Blu-ray, or, for those who want a free peek at old curiosities, on YouTube.

Epilogue

Audiences today can still experience all of the excitement, gore, glamor, and controversy that these films generated among appreciative filmgoers well over a century ago. They stand as testament to the artistry of long-forgotten actors and actresses who once graced the silent screen, and as a vital part of American pictorial history that should not be forgotten.

Chapter Notes

Introduction

1. Alfred D. Godley, *Herodotus: The Persian Wars, Books 3–4* (Cambridge: Harvard University Press, 1921), 38–41.
2. Paul Cartledge, *Thermopylae: The Battle That Changed the World* (London: Vintage, 2007), 146, 215, 224.
3. Charles Freeman, *The Greek Achievement: The Foundation of the Western World* (New York: Viking Press, 1999), 241–242.
4. Anthony Everitt, *Augustus: The Life of Rome's First Emperor* (New York: Random House, 2007), 208, 209.
5. Esther Cohen, "The Propaganda of Saints in the Middle Ages," *Journal of Communications* 31, no. 4 (December 1981): 22, 23, 24.
6. Leonie Frieda, *Catherine de Medici, Renaissance Queen of France* (London: Weidenfeld & Nicolson, 2003), 111, 259.
7. Michael Foot and Isaac Kamnick, *The Thomas Paine Reader* (New York: Penguin Classics, 1987), 11. Phillip S. Foner, *The Complete Writings of Thomas Paine, Vol. 2* (New York: Citadel Press, 1945), 48.
8. Claude Gandelman, "'Patri-Arse': Revolution as Anality in the Scatological Caricatures of the Reformation and the French Revolution," *American Imago* 53, no. 1 (Spring 1996): 7–24.
9. Wayne Hanley, *The Genesis of Napoleonic Propaganda, 1796–1799* (New York: Columbia University Press, 2005), 141–158.
10. Claude Markowitz, *A History of Modern India, 1480–1959* (London: Anthem Press, 2004), 197.
11. Claire C. Summers, "The Indian Rebellion of 1857," *Tenor of Our Times* 4, no. 6 (Spring 2015). William Russell, "European Politics," *Blackwood's Edinburgh Magazine* (January–June 1857): 132.
12. "The South African Concentration Camps," *Manchester Guardian*, June 19, 1901, 1.

Chapter 1

1. By 1914, the United States had strained diplomatic relations with Mexico due to the ongoing Mexican Revolution. The government of Mexico had been usurped by Victoriano Huerta (1854–1916) in 1913, with the United States supporting the government of Venustiano Carranza (1859–1920). On April 19, 1914, nine unarmed American sailors were arrested by the Mexican government for mistakenly entering off-limits areas in the city of Tampico, Mexico. Further, Wilson had been alerted that an arms shipment for Huerta on the German-registered cargo steamer SS *Ypiranga* was due to arrive in port on April 21. The United States had already declared an embargo on arms and ammunitions to Huerta, so the shipment was rerouted to the port of Veracruz. Although the initial landing was blocked, the shipment was eventually discharged at the nearby port of Puerto Mexico, under the control of Huerta. Wilson was so incensed by Huerta's actions that he sent American warships into the port of Veracruz to prevent further shipments from reaching Huerta from Europe. On April 21, a contingent of armed navy sailors and United States Marines totaling

Notes—Chapter 1

3,300 men (with naval bombardment) fought 3,360 Mexican soldiers and hundreds of armed civilians in what became known as the Battle of Veracruz, defeating them and securing the port. Robert E. Quick, "The Tampico Incident," in *An Affair of Honor: Woodrow Wilson and the Occupation of Veracruz* (New York: W.W. Norton, 1967), 1–78.

2. Peter Edidin, "La La Land: The Origins," *The New York Times*, August 21, 2005, section 2, 4.

3. Craig W. Campbell, *Reel America and World War I* (Jefferson, NC: McFarland, 1985), 152–153.

4. One of the most egregious true atrocities was the German sack of the Belgian city of Leuven on August 25, 1914. The German army deliberately burned the Leuven university library, destroying approximately 230,000 books and 950 manuscripts. Civilian houses were leveled and many citizens were shot trying to defend their homes. More than 2,000 buildings were destroyed and approximately 10,000 inhabitants were left homeless.

5. The transatlantic cable was severed by Great Britain on August 4, 1914, effectively cutting off German communications to outside Europe, most significantly the United States. Germany was left with one cable, but that was under British control. Any message sent through it could be read and intercepted by Great Britain before it reached the United States. http://blogs.mbs.ox.ac.uk/innovatingcombat, accessed April 12, 2021.

6. Campbell, *Reel America*, 25–28.

7. *Ibid.*, 226.

8. U-Boat is an anglicized version of the German word *U-Boot*, itself a shortening of the word *Unterseeboot*. The word refers to the military submarines operated by the Germans in World War I.

9. "Emanon" is "no name" spelled backward.

10. Plot description from *Variety*, August 13, 1915, 17.

11. J. Stuart Blackton was one of the first filmmakers to use the technique of stop-motion and drawn animation and is acknowledged as the father of animation. "Blackton, Pioneer in movies, Dies, 66. Ex-Commodore of Atlantic Yacht Club. Here is victim of auto accident. A Founder of Vitagraph, Producer of 'Black Diamond Express.' Began as Marine Artist," *The New York Times*, August 14, 1941, 8.

12. "New York Shelled On 'Movie' Screen: 'The Battle Cry of Peace' Meant to Show The Necessity for Preparedness," *The New York Times*, August 7, 1915, 0.

13. *Variety*, August 13, 1915, 17.

14. *The Fatherland* was a pro–German newspaper founded by George Sylvester Viereck in August 1914. The newspaper's motto was "Fair Play for Germany and Austria-Hungary."

15. George Sylvester Viereck (1884–1962) was a German American poet, writer, and pro–German propagandist. His father, Louis, was born out of wedlock to German actress Edwina Viereck and was reputed to be a son of Kaiser Wilhelm I. Viereck immigrated to the United States in 1897 with his parents. He graduated from the College of the City of New York in 1906, and his poetry, written while still in college, gained him national fame. In 1908, he published the best-selling *Confessions of a Barbarian*, which earned him substantial royalties. Viereck became a committed Germanophile and pacifist and in 1914 founded *The Fatherland* to promote American neutrality and give voice to German support among American citizens.

16. George Sylvester Viereck, *The Fatherland* 4, no. 20 (June 24, 1916).

17. The *Staats-Zeitung*, headquartered in New York City, was founded in 1834 by German American businessmen George Zahm, Stephan Molitor, Conrad Braeker, and Gustave Adolph Heumann and claimed to be the leading German language newspaper in the United States. At the start of World War I, in 1914, the paper extolled the virtues of the kaiser. The journalistic enthusiasm prompted some German Americans living in New York City to appear at the German consul's office to inquire as to whether there was a possibility to be transported back

Notes—Chapter 1

"to the old country" to fight on Germany's side. https://gothamcenter.org/blog/fighting-world-war-one-on-the-streets-of-new-york, accessed April 12, 2021.

18. *Deutsches Journal*, September 12, 1915, section 3, 3.

19. Kevin Brownlow, *The War, the West and the Wilderness* (New York: Alfred A. Knopf, 1979), 33.

20. Campbell, *Reel America*, 33.

21. She plays a model posing nude as artistic inspiration for a young sculptor.

22. Sessue Hayakawa (1886–1973) was born in Japan and immigrated to the United States in the early 1900s. He became a major star and matinee idol with the release of *The Cheat*, directed by Cecil B. DeMille. The original nationality (Japanese) and name (Hishuru Tori) was changed to the Burmese Haka Arakau to reflect that Japan was an ally of the United States, and not an enemy.

23. A sense of personal values grounded in Christian traditions infuses *Civilization*, given Ince's background as an Anglo-Saxon Protestant. Brian Taves, *Thomas Ince: Independent Pioneer* (Lexington: University Press of Kentucky, 2012), 93, 97–98.

24. www.filmfoundation.org/civilization-hfpa, accessed April 12, 2021.

25. Ince's vast production company was situated in the Santa Ynez Canyon along the Pacific Ocean. The company included actors, directors, writers, stunt men (and women), lighting directors, lawyers, doctors, and the occasional (local) Indian chief. Taves, *Thomas Ince*, 97–98.

26. Victor Schertzinger (1888–1941) was an American composer, film director, and producer. His first exposure to the film industry came in 1916 when Thomas Ince asked him to compose the orchestral score for *Civilization*. He went on to compose scores for a number of 1930s musicals, including 1934's *One Night of Love*, which he directed. The score (co-written by Schertzinger, Alfred Newman, Louis Silvers, and Howard Jackson) won the Academy Award for Best Original Score of 1934. His most famous songs "I Remember You" and "Tangerine" were featured in the 1942 movie *The Fleet's In*.

27. "Devoted Deep Study To Role: Idealistic Interpreter Plays Role of Master; Youthful Actor Exercises Special Care in Preparation For Portrayal of Man of Peace in Ince Drama-Is Said to Have Achieved Big Message," *Los Angeles Times*, April 19, 1916.

28. After Woodrow Wilson declared war in April of 1917, *Civilization*, which was still playing in theaters around the country, was withdrawn from distribution and was not seen until years after the end of the war.

29. Henry Christeen Warnack, "DRAMA: Not Daring, Violates Good Taste, Artistic Touch is Absent From Story of War Picture," *Los Angeles Times*, April 18, 1916.

30. "Civilization Is Ince Masterpiece Picturing Christ: Biggest Spectacle in History of Motion Pictures Comes to La Crosse Theater Sunday," *La Crosse Tribune*, October 21, 1916.

31. "Large Audience Is Thrilled By Ince Spectacle," *Fairbanks Daily Times*, September 16, 1916.

32. George Sylvester Viereck, *The Fatherland* 4, no. 20 (June 24, 1916).

33. *New Yorker Staats-Zeitung*, August 8, 1916, 4.

34. *Deutsches Journal*, June 13, 1916, 4.

35. https://lostmediawiki.com/The_Fall_of_a_Nation_(lost_sequel_film_to_%22The_Birth_of_a_Nation%22;_1916), accessed April 13, 2021.

36. The reference to Jael comes from the Old Testament: When Sisera, the general of the Canaanite armies, is defeated in battle by the Hebrew general Barak, he flees the battlefield. He seeks shelter in the tent of a woman named Jael. She gives him food and drink. When he falls asleep, she takes a mallet and drives a tent peg through his temple, helping to assist the Hebrews in their fight against Canaanite oppression. Judges 4:18–22.

37. The idea of having women use sexual favors to obtain information from enemy opponents was not a new concept.

Notes—Chapter 1

The French Queen Catherine de Medici maintained a flying squadron (*escadron volant*) of beautiful ladies-in-waiting to seduce vital information from gullible men to further her political agenda. See Leonie Frieda, "Henry III, King of France," in *Catherine de Medici, Renaissance Queen of France* (London: Weidenfeld & Nicolson, 2003), 326–327.

38. Victor Herbert (1859–1924) was one of the most successful composers from the 1880s to World War I. He began to compose operettas in 1894, but his big successes would start in 1903 with *Babes in Toyland*, followed by *Mlle. Modiste* in 1905, *The Red Mill* in 1906, *Naughty Marietta* in 1910, *Sweethearts* in 1913, and *Eileen* in 1917. His score for *The Fall of a Nation* was one of the first original orchestra scores for a full-length film. The score was thought to be lost but was discovered in the film-score collection of the Library of Congress and recorded in 1987. W. Shirley, "A Bugle Call to Arms for the Nation's Defense! Victor Herbert and his score for *The Fall of a Nation*," *Quarterly Journal of the Library of Congress* XL (1983): 26–27.

39. http://www.columbia.edu/en/cjas/conolly-smith-4.html, accessed April 14, 2021.

40. In 1915, American industrialist Henry Ford (1863–1947) organized, paid for, and launched an amateur peace mission to Europe. He chartered the ocean liner *Oscar II*, which became known as *The Peace Ship*, and invited several prominent peace activists to join him. He hoped to create publicity to prompt belligerent nations to convene a peace conference and mediate an end to World War I. There was infighting between the activists; a majority of delegates signed a resolution that denounced Wilson's policy of preparedness, but a substantial minority refused to sign on the grounds that the resolution was unpatriotic. There was mockery by the press contingent onboard and an outbreak of influenza. The *Oscar II* arrived in Norway on December 18, 1915. Five days later, a physically ill Ford (he was still suffering from influenza) abandoned the mission and returned to the United States. The peace mission was unsuccessful. Steven Watts, "Ford Peace Expedition," in *The People's Tycoon: Henry Ford on the American New Century* (New York City: Alfred A. Knopf, 2005), 228–235.

41. "America Is Invaded Again In The Films; 'The Fall of a Nation' Another Sensational Photoplay Plea for Preparedness. Devised By Thomas Dixon Lively, Interesting and Sometimes Preposterous Picture with Victor Herbert's Music at the Liberty," *The New York Times*, June 7, 1916, 0.

42. *Variety*, June 9, 1916, 23.

43. George Sylvester Viereck, *The Fatherland* 4, no. 20 (June 24, 1916).

44. *Zeitgeist* is defined as a spirit or mood of a particular period in history as shown by the ideas and beliefs of the time.

45. "Hyphens" was a derogatory way to refer to German Americans.

46. *Deutsches Journal*, June 6, 1916, 4.

47. According to legend, the island got its name from a Black fisherman who lived there.

48. Soon after the explosion, suspicion fell on Michael Kristoff, a Slovak immigrant. According to Kristoff, two guards at Black Tom were German agents. It is likely that the bombing involved some techniques developed by German agents working for Ambassador Count Johann Heinrich von Bernstorff (1862–1939) and German naval intelligence officer Franz von Rintelen (1878–1949). Von Rintelen gave Kristoff a cash bribe in exchange for access to the pier. It is believed that Kristoff was responsible for planting and initiating the incendiary devices that led to the explosions. H.R. Baukhage and A.A. Hoehling, "The Black Tom Explosion," *The American Legion Magazine* 77, no. 2 (August 1964): 14.

49. www.lonchaney.org/filmography/82.html, accessed April 9, 2023.

50. By 1916, the United States had been involved in protracted military engagements with Mexico on the United States–Mexico border for years. The height of the conflict came in January of 1916, when revolutionary Pancho Villa

Notes—Chapter 1

(1878–1923) attacked the American border town of Columbia, New Mexico. The raid did not go as planned, and Villa's 500 cavalrymen were defeated by more than 300 United States infantry and cavalry who were stationed in a border fort outside of town. Shortly after the raid, President Wilson ordered General John J. Pershing (1860–1948) to proceed into Mexico to capture or kill Pancho Villa. In May of 1916, the president ordered the National Guard to reinforce the United States army garrison at the border. Although the American forces suffered a defeat at the battle of Carrizal in June, by August an estimated 117,000 volunteer guardsmen were stationed along the border in Texas, New Mexico, Arizona, and California. Eventually, Villa was assassinated in 1923, and after his death, his body was exhumed by an American treasure hunter and soldier-of-fortune named Emil Holmdahl (1883–1963), who beheaded him and sold the head to an unnamed American millionaire. The head is now rumored to be in the possession of Yale University's Skull and Bones Society. Claudio Buttica, "Villa, Pancho (1876–1923)," in *American Myths, Legends and Tall Tales: An Encyclopedia of American Folklore* (Santa Barbara: ABC-CLIO, 2016), 898–1001.

51. For a list of their filmography together, see www.lonchaney.org/filmography/82.html, accessed April 9, 2023.

52. *Moving Picture World*, October 7, 1916, 96.

53. Alla Nazimova (1879–1945) was a distinguished Russian stage actress, and by 1916 was noted for her performances in plays of Henrik Ibsen and Anton Chekov. She performed the role of "Joan" in the critically acclaimed stage version of *War Brides*, which was one of the most successful plays of the 1915 Broadway season.

54. Richard Barthelmess (1895–1963) was a 21-year-old college student when he was cast in the movie *War Brides* at the suggestion of Alla Nazimova. His mother, stage actress Carol Harris, was a close friend of Alla Nazimova, and taught her English when Nazimova first came to the United States in 1905. The role of Arno would help Barthelmess on the road to eventual screen stardom in the 1920s.

55. https://www.thebioscope.net/2009/01/05/warbrides, accessed September 20, 2022.

56. Lewis J. Selznick (1869 or 1870–1933) was born in Lithuania and immigrated to the United States in 1888. He established a successful chain of jewelry stores but left the business in 1913 to become involved in the film industry. He first worked for Universal Film Manufacturing in 1913, but soon left to form his own film organization, the World Film Organization with Chicago mail-order magnate Arthur Spiegel. They soon merged with the Peerless Picture Studios and Shubert Pictures Company. The combined company became very successful, but by 1916, Selznick's personality conflicts with his partners saw him ousted from the firm by the Board of Directors. Selznick then formed his own company, Selznick Pictures. He took with him World Film Organization's biggest star, Clara Kimball Young, and became president and general manager of the newly formed Clara Kimball Young Film Corporation. He then launched the film career of Alla Nazimova in *War Brides*, which became a big success. He was the father of producer David O. Selznick.

57. Two full-page ads in *Motion Picture News* 14, no. 23 (December 2, 1916): 366–367.

58. Full-page ad in *Moving Picture World*, December 21, 1916.

59. Full-page ad in *The Sheboygan Press*, April 20, 1917, 2.

60. https://academiccommons.columbia.edu/doi/10.7916/d8-wsObqz96, accessed November 13, 2021.

61. "Nazimova In Film Of War Brides Play; Makes Success in Her First Appearance as a Movie Star," *The New York Times*, November 13, 1916, 0.

62. *Moving Picture World*, December 21, 1916.

63. https://centuryfilmproject.org/2017/01/14/joan-the-woman-1916, accessed April 11, 2023.

Notes—Chapter 2

64. Handsome and charming Wallace Reid was one of the silent screen's most beloved stars throughout the mid-teens and early 1920s. After being injured performing a dangerous stunt in 1919, he became addicted to morphine and died of an overdose complicated by pneumonia in 1923.

65. H. Rosenthal and J. Warrack, "Farrar, Geraldine," in *The Concise Oxford Dictionary of Opera, 2nd Edition* (Oxford: Oxford University Press, 1979), 161.

66. Similar to stenciling, the Handschiegl process was applied mechanically to manually defined image parts, making it an early applied color process. After a film was shot and edited, for each color applied, a separate print was made. Costly, but with striking results, this became the most widely used form of artificial coloring in motion pictures in the 1920s.

67. Sumiko Higashi, *Cecil B. DeMille and American Culture: The Silent Era* (Berkeley: University of California Press, 2004), 130.

68. https://publishing.cdlib.org/ucpressebooks/view?docId=ft2p300573;chunk.id=0;doc.view=print, accessed August 6, 2023.

69. https://medievalhollywood.ace.fordham.edu/items/show/197, accessed April 20, 2023.

70. *Variety*, December 29, 1916.

71. *Motion Picture News*, January 6, 1917.

72. *Moving Picture World*, January 13, 1917.

Chapter 2

1. Originally a German naval officer in the imperial German navy, Witzke was captured after his ship SMS *Dresden* was sunk by a British warship in the early part of the war. Interned in Chile, he escaped and reached San Francisco in May 1916. There, he reported to Franz von Bopp, the German consul general, who put him in touch with German saboteurs in Mexico City. His sabotage activities, both on the East and West Coasts of the United States, finally led to the emerging United States Military Intelligence Corps to connect him with the Mare Island bombing. After evading American authorities, he was finally arrested at the Mexican border on February 1, 1918. He was convicted by a court martial and sentenced to death, but his sentence was commuted to life imprisonment after the November 1918 armistice. After serving five years in prison, he was pardoned by President Calvin Coolidge and deported to Germany in 1923. Spencer Tucker and Priscilla Mary Roberts, *The Encyclopedia of World War I: A Political, Social and Military History*, 5 vols. (Santa Barbara: ABC-CLIO, 2005), 420–422.

2. The Zimmermann Telegram was a secret communication issued by Arthur Zimmermann, state secretary for foreign affairs of the German empire from November 22, 1916, until his resignation on August 6, 1917. The telegram instructed the German ambassador to Mexico to approach the Mexican government headed by President Venustiano Carranza to join a military alliance with Germany. In return, Germany offered Mexico the return of territories that included Texas, Arizona, and New Mexico. The Mexicans, knowing that the United States would invade Mexico if they came out in favor of the alliance, wisely declined. The telegram was intercepted by British intelligence, and an informal copy was sent to President Woodrow Wilson on February 24, 1917. Wilson waited for direct confirmation from British Foreign Minister Arthur Balfour, and then released the contents of the telegram to the American public on March 1, 1917. Christopher Andrew, *For the President's Eyes Only* (New York: HarperCollins, 1996), 42.

3. *Variety*, April 6, 1917.

4. Larry Wayne Ward, "Flourishes and False Starts," in *The Motion Picture Goes to War: The U.S. Government Film Effort During World War I* (Ann Arbor: UMI Research Press, 1981), 53.

5. https://www.silentstillsfilmarchive.com/womanhood1917.htm, accessed April 26, 2023.

Notes—Chapter 2

6. *The New York Times*, April 2, 1917.
7. *Variety*, April 6, 1917.
8. *New York Dramatic Mirror*, April 7, 1917.
9. *Moving Picture World*, April 21, 1917.
10. Alan Axelrod, "Making of a Muckraker," in *Selling the Great War* (New York: Palgrave Macmillan, 2009), 2–8.
11. A muckraker was any group of American writers identified with pre–World War I reform and exposé writing. They provided detailed, accurate journalistic accounts of the political and economic corruption and social hardships caused by the power of big business in a rapidly industrializing United States. https://www.dictionary.com/browse/muckraking, accessed December 21, 2021.
12. Alan Axelrod, "Muckraker on the Make," in *Selling the Great War* (New York: Palgrave Macmillan, 2009), 24–25.
13. *Ibid.*, 26–27.
14. *Ibid.*, 28.
15. *Ibid.*, 30.
16. George Creel, *Rebel at Large: Recollections of Fifty Crowded Years* (New York: G.P. Putnam's Sons, 1947), 116–117.
17. Axelrod, *Selling the Great War*, 30.
18. *Ibid.*, 31.
19. The Ludlow Massacre was a mass killing perpetrated by anti-strike militia during the Colorado Coalfield War. Soldiers from the Colorado National Guard and private guards employed by the Colorado Fuel and Iron Company (CF&I) attacked a colony of approximately 1,200 striking miners and their families in Ludlow, Colorado, killing 21 men, women, and children on April 20, 1914. John D. Rockefeller, Jr., a part owner of the CF&I, was widely blamed for having orchestrated the massacre.
20. Alan Axelrod, "Too Proud to Fight," in *Selling the Great War* (New York: Palgrave Macmillan, 2009), 36–39.
21. *Ibid.*, 38–39.
22. *Ibid.*, 41–45.
23. *Ibid.*, 47.
24. Quoted from the text of Woodrow Wilson's speech of April 2, 1917, on the front page of *The New York Times* calling the nation to war. The headline read "President Calls For War Declaration, Stronger Navy, New Army Of 500,000 Men, Full Co-Operation With Germany's Foes."
25. Alan Axelrod, "Conjuring the Committee," in *Selling the Great War* (New York: Palgrave Macmillan, 2009), 91.
26. *Ibid.*
27. *Ibid.*
28. *Ibid.*, 93.
29. *Ibid.*
30. *Ibid.*
31. *Ibid.*
32. Alan Axelrod, "Hyphenated America," in *Selling the Great War* (New York: Palgrave Macmillan, 2009), 185.
33. Larry Wayne Ward, "Flourishes and False Starts," in *The Motion Picture Goes to War: The U.S. Government Film Effort During World War I* (Ann Arbor: UMI Research Press, 1981), 86.
34. Alan Axelrod, "Conjuring the Committee," in *Selling the Great War* (New York: Palgrave Macmillan, 2009), 84–89.
35. Lisa Mastrangelo, "World War I, Public Intellectuals and the Four Minute Men: Convergent Ideals of Public Speaking and Civic Participation," *Rhetoric & Public Affairs* 12, no. 4 (2009): 607–633.
36. The Espionage Act of 1917 was passed on June 15, 1917. The act made it a crime to interfere with or attempt to undermine or interfere with the efforts of the United States armed forces during a war, or to in any way assist the war efforts of the nation's enemies. Potential punishments for violation of the Espionage Act ranged from fines of $10,000 and 20 years in prison to the death penalty.
37. The policy, titled "What the Government Asks of the Press," asks that for the protection of military and naval forces and of merchant shipping, secrecy be observed in all matters of advance information of routes and schedules of troop movements; information tending to disclose numbers of troops in the expeditionary forces abroad; information calculated to disclose location of American units or permanent bases or bases

Notes—Chapter 2

abroad; information that would disclose locations of American units or the eventual position of American forces on the front; information tending to disclose an event or actual of embarkation; information on the arrival at any European port of American war vessels, transports or any portion of any expeditionary force; information of the time of departure of merchant ships from American or European ports; information indicating the port of incoming ships from European ports; information as to convoys and to the sighting of friendly or enemy ships; information of the locality, number or identity of vessels belonging to our own navy or to the navies of any country at war with Germany; information of the coast or anti-aircraft defenses of the United States; information of the laying of mines or mine-fields or of any harbor defenses; information of the aircraft and appurtenances used at government aviation schools for experimental tests under military authority; information of all government devices and experiments in war material, except when authorized by the Committee on Public Information; information of secret notices issued to mariners or other confidential instructions issued by the navy or the Department of Commerce relating to lights, lightships, buoys, or other guides to navigation; information as to the number, size, character, or location of ships of the navy ordered laid down at any port or shipyard; information of the train or boat schedules of traveling official missions in transit through the United States; information of the transportation of munitions or of war material, and lastly, that photographs conveying the information as specified above should not be published. George Creel, *How We Advertised America* (New York: Harper & Brothers, 1920), 21–23.

38. Alan Axelrod, "Safe for Democracy," in *Selling the Great War* (New York: Palgrave Macmillan, 2009), 64–71.

39. Liberty Bonds were war bonds sold in the United States to support the Allied cause in World War I. Often sold at bond rallies featuring notable stage and movie stars of the era, the Liberty Bond became a symbol of patriotic duty in the United States and introduced the concept of financial securities to many citizens for the first time.

40. The most famous censorship case in World War I centered around a movie produced and written by Robert Goldstein in 1917. Goldstein was a stockholder in the Epoch Producing Company and decided to produce a movie about the American Revolution called *The Spirit of '76*. A mixture of fact and fiction, the fact-based climax of the movie showed the British and their Indian allies slaughtering and raping helpless American colonialists. When the film was shown in Chicago in the summer of 1917, the censors suppressed this scene, as well as others considered too violent, since England was now a wartime ally. Goldstein removed the offending scenes, but at the November 27 opening at Cline's Auditorium in Los Angeles, the scenes had been restored. The picture was seized by the American Protective League, alleging that German money had financed the production and that the picture interfered with American military recruitment and was anti–British in the extreme. Goldstein was put on trial in March of 1918. The judge in the case, Benjamin J. Bledsoe, declared: "This is no time, whatever may be the excuse, for the exploitation of these things that may have a tendency of sowing dissent among our people, and of creating animosity between us and our allies." Goldstein was sentenced to 10 years in the federal penitentiary and a fine of $5,000. In 1919, Woodrow Wilson commuted the sentence to three years and the fine was remitted. Brownlow, *The War*, 80–82.

41. https://moviessilently.com/2013/03/01/the-little-american-1917-a-silent-film-review, accessed December 10, 2021.

42. Simon Louvish, *Cecil B. DeMille: A Life in Art* (New York: Thomas Dunne, 2007), 90.

43. Eileen Whitfield, *Pickford: The Woman Who Made Hollywood* (Lexington: University Press of Kentucky, 1997), 144–146.

Notes—Chapter 3

44. *Variety*, July 6, 1917, 8.
45. *Motion Picture News* 16, no. 3 (July 21, 1917).
46. Brownlow, *The War*, 134.
47. Craig W. Campbell, "Filmography," in *Reel America and World War I* (Jefferson, NC: McFarland, 1985), 207–208.
48. Campbell, *Reel America*, 231–234.
49. *Ibid.*, 166–168.
50. "Every man, woman and child should see this picture and you will stand by the colors that never bleed Red, White and Blue. NO BATTLE SCENES." Full-page ad in Fredericksburg *Daily Star*, December 29, 1917, 6.
51. Campbell, *Reel America*, 167–169.
52. *Ibid.*, 169.
53. Brownlow, *The War*, 74. *Moving Picture World*, November 24, 1917, 1185.
54. Each brother spelled his name differently by choice. William was originally a successful playwright in New York City in the mid–1900s, eventually following younger brother Cecil to Hollywood, where he also became a director. Scott Eyman, *Empire of Dreams: The Epic Life of Cecil B. DeMille* (New York: Simon & Schuster, 2010), 17.
55. Plot description from *Exhibitors Herald* 5, no. 28 (December 16, 1917).
56. Irene Castle (1893–1969) was one half of the famous ballroom dance team Vernon and Irene Castle, credited with reviving the popularity of modern dancing in the early 1900s. They refined and popularized the foxtrot and were credited with promoting ragtime, jazz rhythms, and African American music for dance. Vernon Castle (English by birth) served with distinction in the British Royal Air Corps during World War I. He was killed in a flying accident in the United States in 1918.
57. Although he looked Asian, Warner Oland (1879–1938) was actually Swedish, but his somewhat Asian appearance typecast him as sinister Chinese/Japanese characters in silent movies. Ironically, his greatest fame came in talking pictures as the clever and resourceful Chinese American Honolulu police detective Lieutenant Charlie Chan in the popular film series of the same name in the 1930s.
58. Craig W. Campbell, "America Enlists," in *Reel America and World War I* (Jefferson, NC: McFarland, 1985), 51.
59. The term "Yellow Peril" denoted underlying anti–Chinese and Japanese sentiment among Americans in the early part of the twentieth century, based on the imagined premise that a wave of Chinese and Japanese immigrants to Hawaii, California, and the Pacific Coast would result in hordes of Asians overpowering and subjugating the white population in these areas. American confusion between Japanese and Chinese coupled with the personal threat of increasing Japanese immigration to the West Coast fueled a distrust of Asians in general.
60. *Exhibitor's Herald* 5, no. 28 (December 16, 1917).
61. *Moving Picture World*, December 15, 1917, 1643.
62. In 1918, Hayakawa formed Haworth Pictures Corporation with a loan of $1 million from his friend William Joseph Connery, whose parents were multimillionaire coal mine owners. Over the next three years, Hayakawa produced 23 films: by 1920 he had earned $2 million and repaid the loan. Dausuke Miyao, *Sessue Hayakawa: Silent Cinema and Transnational Stardom* (Durham: Duke University Press, 2007), 303.

Chapter 3

1. The Boxer Rebellion was an anti-foreign uprising in China in 1900 and was put down by an international force of British, French, Russian, Austrian, Italian, American, Japanese, and German troops.
2. Robert K. Massie, *Dreadnought: Britain, Germany, and the Coming of the Great War* (New York: Random House, 1991), 673–679.
3. Jeff Lipkes, *Rehearsals: The German Army in Belgium, August, 1914* (Leuven: Leuven University Press, 2007), 13. John Horn and Alan Kramer, *Notes on German Atrocities, 1914: A History of Denial* (New

Notes—Chapter 3

Haven: Yale University Press, 2001), 39. Michel Dumoulin, *L'entrée dans le XX Siecle, 1905–1918 (The Beginning of the Century from 1905–1918), Nouvelle Histoire de Belgique* (French ed.) (Brussels: Le Cri Edition, 2010), 131.

4. https://www.imdb.com/title/tt008960/plotsummary?ref_=tt_ov_pl, accessed February 4, 2022.

5. Cardinal Désiré-Joseph Mercier (1851–1926) was a well-known scholar before the invasion of Belgium in 1914, having published numerous works on metaphysics, philosophy, and psychology. Many of his works were translated into English, German, Italian, Polish, and Spanish. After the Germans invaded Belgium, they not only murdered thousands of civilians, but also murdered 13 priests in Mercier's diocese. In response to the atrocities, Mercier issued his Christmas 1914 pastoral letter *Patriotism and Endurance* urging the Belgian people to resist as much as possible against the German invaders. Distributed by hand (because the Germans had cut off all postal service in Belgium), Mercier's unflinching plea to the suffering Belgians earned him severe house arrest by the Germans for the remainder of the war. After the end of the war, Mercier undertook to raise funds to rebuild and restock a new library at Leuven, and during his travels, visited New York City, where he was given a warm welcome. Jan De Volder, *Cardinal Mercier in the First World War: Belgium, Germany and the Catholic Church* (Leuven: Leuven University Press, 2018), 167.

6. *Michigan Film Review*, April 1918.

7. *Hattiesburg American*, April 5, 1918, 7.

8. https://thestreamable.com/movies/till-i-come-back-to-you-1918, accessed February 5, 2022.

9. Although DeMille considered enlisting in World War I, he ultimately decided to stay in Hollywood and make films. He did, however, take a few months off toward the end of 1918 to set up a movie theater for the French front, with Famous Players Lasky donating their films to be shown to Allied soldiers. Scott Eyman, *Empire of Dreams: The Epic Life of Cecil B. DeMille* (New York: Simon & Schuster, 2010), 141.

10. *The New York Times*, August 26, 1918.

11. *Exhibitor's Herald*, September 14, 1918, 33.

12. Arthur Lennig, *Stroheim* (Lexington: University Press of Kentucky, 2000), 5.

13. *Ibid.*, 6.

14. *Ibid.*, 10–11.

15. From the Kriegsarchiv, the Austrian war archive records.

16. Lennig, *Stroheim*, 12–14.

17. That was patently untrue. By the twentieth century Austria was (along with Italy), the most enlightened country in Europe in its political attitude toward Jews, having given them full legal rights and allowing them entrée into all walks of life, including the arts, politics, and the military. Emperor Franz-Joseph had warm feelings for "his Jews," and many Jews rose up through the officers' ranks to attain command positions. Peter C. Appelbaum, *Hapsburg Sons: Jews in the Austro-Hungarian Army 1788–1918* (Boston: Cherry Orchard Books, 2022), 14, 24, 30, 55.

18. Lennig, *Stroheim*, 16–17.

19. *Ibid.*, 19–23.

20. During the filming of *Old Heidelberg*, Stroheim met and married his second wife, a young woman named Mae Jones. A son, Erich von Stroheim, Jr., was born on August 25, 1916. The parents were incompatible and separated shortly after their son was born. They were divorced in July 1919. Shortly afterward, von Stroheim married his third wife, Valerie Germonprez. Their son, Joseph, was born in 1922.

21. *Variety*, October 8, 1915.

22. Lennig, *Stroheim*, 41–43.

23. *Photoplay*, April 1917.

24. Lennig, *Stroheim*, 46.

25. *Ibid.*, 47.

26. *Exhibitors Herald*, March 23, 1918, 23.

27. Lennig, *Stroheim*, 52–53.

28. *The New York Times*, February 12, 1918.

Notes—Chapter 4

29. *Variety*, February 15, 1918.
30. The March 12, 1918, date was a limited release date. General release nationwide was on April 5, 1918.
31. Paolo Usai Cherchi and Eileen Bowser, *The Griffith Project: Films Produced in 1916–1918* (London: British Film Institute, 2005), 157.
32. The leftover footage allowed Griffith to use it in another World War I romance, *The Greatest Thing in Life*, released in December of 1918. Again featuring Lillian Gish and Robert Harron, this picture is little known, but at the time, it inspired tremendous controversy, since it featured an interracial kiss between an American white officer and a dying Black soldier on the battlefield of France. Lillian Gish, with Ann Pinchot, *Lillian Gish: The Movies, Mr. Griffith and Me* (Englewood Cliffs, NJ: Prentice-Hall, 1969), 202.
33. https://silentology.wordpress.com/2018/08/17/thoughts-on-hearts-of-the-world-1918/, accessed September 22, 2022.
34. Robert Harron died in 1920 of an accidental gunshot wound he inflicted on himself in a hotel room in New York City. Some historians have speculated that Harron might have tried suicide after losing the main lead in D. W. Griffith's 1920 movie *Way Down East* to rising star Richard Barthelmess, but that was never proven. https://silentology.wordpress.com/2018/08/17/thoughts-on-hearts-of-the-world-1918/, accessed September 22, 2022.
35. Lennig, *Stroheim*, 48–49.
36. "Many Thousands See Griffith Film," *Moving Picture World*, September 12, 1918, 1912.
37. https://www.focusfeatures.com/article/imagining_war, accessed May 16, 2023.
38. *The New York Times*, April 5, 1918.
39. *Variety*, April 6, 1918.
40. *The New York Times*, August 26, 1918.
41. Lennig, *Stroheim*, 50.
42. Brownlow, *The War*, 142.
43. That's D.W. Griffith writing as Granville Warwick.
44. *The New York Times*, August 26, 1918.
45. *New York Times Tribune*, September 7, 1918.
46. *New York Evening Telegram*, September 7, 1918.
47. Campbell, *Reel America*, 186; Lennig, *Stroheim*, 53–56.
48. Lennig, *Stroheim*, 53.
49. https://moviessilently.com/2014/09/06//the-heart-of-humanity-1918-a-silent-film-review/accessed, September 22, 2022.
50. https://moviessilently.files.wordpress.com/2019/11/4e3c-heart-of-humanity-ad.jpg, accessed September 22, 2022.
51. *The New York Times*, December 22, 1918.
52. *Ohio State Journal*, May 28, 1919.

Chapter 4

1. Due to a traumatic birth, Kaiser Wilhelm II was born with a withered left arm six inches shorter than his right. He was delivered in the breech position; the attending physician forcibly pulled the left arm downward, tearing the brachial plexus. Some historians have strongly suggested that this disability affected his psychological development. John C.G. Rohl, *Young Wilhelm: The Kaiser's Early Life, 1859–1888* (Cambridge: Cambridge University Press, 1998), 17–18.
2. German Americans were considered disloyal if they spoke the German language; German language services in churches were disrupted and German language newspapers were shut down; German American schoolchildren were forced to sign pledges in which they promised not to use any foreign language whatsoever; citizens of German descent were dragged out of their homes at night and forced to kiss the flag or sing the national anthem. The most notorious case of mob violence occurred when German immigrant Robert Prager was lynched in April 1918. He was suspected by his neighbors of stealing dynamite, dragged out

Notes—Chapter 4

of town, stripped, and hanged. Although the case caused outrage among many prominent Americans, the court trying the men responsible found the members of the mob not guilty. https://www.immigrantentrepreneurship.org/entries/herman-americans-during-world-war-1/, accessed September 12, 2022.

3. Campbell, *Reel America*, 95.
4. *The Lewiston Evening Journal*, May 8, 1918.
5. Campbell, *Reel America*, 170–171.
6. https://11east14thstreet.com/tag/lest-we-forget-1918-film/, accessed April 29, 2023.
7. "English Girl With Skinner," *Washington Post*, December 17, 1911, 106.
8. Rita Jolivet's sister, Inez Jolivet, an internationally renowned violinist, became depressed after her husband's drowning death and committed suicide by shooting herself on July 28, 1915.
9. https://11east14thstreet.com/tag/lest-we-forget-1918-film/, accessed April 29, 2023.
10. *Moving Picture World*, May 11, 1918.
11. *The New York Times*, January 28, 1918.
12. *Moving Picture World*, January 19, 1918.
13. *Variety*, February 2, 1918.
14. Larry Wayne Ward, *The Motion Picture Goes to War: The U.S. Government Film Effort During World War I* (Ann Arbor: UMI Research Press, 1981), 55, 56.
15. Charles Reed Mitchell, "New Message to America: James W. Gerard's 'Beware' and World War I Propaganda," *Journal of Popular Film* 4, no. 5 (1975): 275–295.
16. www.silentsaregolden.com/DeBartolorereviews/rdbmyfouryear.html, accessed January 8, 2022.
17. Campbell, *Reel America*, 98.
18. "Gerard Sees His Film, Makes A Speech At Presentation Of 'My Four Years In Germany,'" *The New York Times*, March 11, 1918.
19. *Variety*, March 15, 1918.
20. *Motion Picture News*, March 21, 1918.
21. *Photoplay*, June 1918.
22. www.silentsaregolden.com/DeBartoloreviews/rdbymyfouryear.html, accessed September 23, 2022.
23. www.lonchaney.org/filmography/102.html, accessed September 14, 2022.
24. David Quinlan, *The Illustrated Guide to Film Directors* (Lanham, MD: Limelight Editions, 1992), 70–71.
25. Campbell, *Reel America*, 100.
26. *Moving Picture World*, March 23, 1918.
27. *Exhibitor's Herald*, March 30, 1918, 23.
28. *Photoplay*, June 1918.
29. Campbell, *Reel America*, 100.
30. Plot description from *Exhibitor's Herald* 6, no. 27 (May 18, 1918).
31. Betty Harper Fussell, *Mabel: Hollywood's First I-Don't-Care Girl* (Lanham, MD: Limelight Editions, 1992), 70–71.
32. https://looking-for-mabel.webs.com/joanofpittsburgh.1918.htm, accessed January 12, 2022.
33. *The New York Times*, May 9, 1918.
34. *Exhibitor's Herald* 6, no. 27 (May 18, 1918).
35. John Canemaker, *Winsor McCay: His Life and Art* (New York: Harry N. Abrams, 2005), 195–196.
36. *Motion Picture News*, April 6, 1918.
37. *Ibid.*
38. Campbell, *Reel America*, 100.
39. *The New York Times*, July 1, 1918.
40. *Variety*, July 5, 1918.
41. http://www.tcm.com/tcmdb/title/493/The-Claws-of-the-Hun, accessed January 8, 2022.
42. Brian Taves, "Establishing a Studio," in *Thomas Ince: Hollywood's Independent Pioneer* (Lexington: University Press of Kentucky, 2012), 64–65.
43. Schertzinger had already composed the score for Ince's *Civilization*.
44. *The New York Times*, July 1, 1918.
45. Campbell, *Reel America*, 210.
46. The film also featured Stan Laurel (prior to his partnership with Oliver Hardy) as a German gang member pursuing Larry in the breakneck finale. Frank Cullen, Florence Hackman, and

Notes—Chapter 4

Donald McNally, *Vaudeville, Old & New: An Encyclopedia of Variety Performers in America* (New York: Routledge, 2007), 1006.

47. *Motion Picture News*, September 7, 1918.

48. https://wikimapia.org/37480856/Romayne-Super-Films-Company-Studios, accessed September 12, 2022.

49. *Motion Picture News*, September 7, 1918, 1463.

50. Ward, *The Motion Picture Goes to War*, 127–132.

51. *Exhibitor's Herald and Motography*, September 7, 1918, 50.

52. Horst von der Goltz (born Franz Wachendorf in 1884) was a German counterintelligence agent during World War I. He started working for the German Secret Service in 1911, and on orders from Germany, insinuated himself into Pancho Villa's revolutionary army in 1912. He was recruited by the German consul on Chihuahua to become a member of Franz von Papen's espionage ring. When von Papen set up an office as the new German military attaché in New York City (specializing in sabotage and subversion) at the start of World War I, von der Goltz quickly became a trusted agent. Goltz was involved in a plot to blow up the Welland Canal (a transportation link between the United States and Canada), which ultimately failed. Goltz was then recalled to Germany. In November of 1914, he registered at a London hotel with a fake passport. Apprehended by Scotland Yard as a German agent, Goltz gave them insider information on secret papers being carried by von Papen (leaving the United States) linking evidence of a German conspiracy in the United States to change the American position of neutrality. This was in exchange for his not being shot as a spy by British intelligence. When the British searched von Papen's luggage at sea, they found the documents. Goltz's affidavit, charging von Papen and other co-conspirators, was withheld after consultation with the U.S. State Department. Goltz agreed to appear as a witness in the 1916 court case, and his evidence helped convict a number of German diplomats of espionage, sabotage, and passport offences. For his service, Goltz was interned at Ellis Island and later granted asylum in the United States. He disappeared and was never heard from again. "Von Papen's Aide Here To Confess," *The New York Times*, March 29, 1916. "Von Der Goltz Got Aid From Von Papen," *The New York Times*, April 4, 1916. "Consul Is Indicted On Passport Fraud," *The New York Times*, May 9, 1916.

53. Campbell, *Reel America*, 96.

54. *The Prussian Cur*, http://www.imdb.com/title/tt0009524, accessed September 26, 2022.

55. Campbell, *Reel America*, 96.

56. https://gracekingsley.wordpress.com/2018/08/31/week-of-august-31st-1918/, accessed 23 September 2022.

57. *Moving Picture World*, September 7, 1918, 1455.

58. *The Richmond Herald*, September 28, 1918.

59. *Exhibitor's Herald and Motography*, October 15, 1918.

60. *Exhibitor's Herald and Motography*, September 28, 1918, 28.

61. "Mary Pickford, First Great Film Star, Dies Five Days After Massive Stroke," *Daily Variety*, May 30, 1979, 1.

62. https://catalog.afi.com/Catalog/MovieDetails/1964, accessed September 24, 2022.

63. *Variety*, September 1, 1918.

64. *Moving Picture World*, September 14, 1918, 1610.

65. *Los Angeles Times*, September 16, 1918.

66. Mabel Normand (*Stake Uncle Sam to Play Your Hand*), Douglas Fairbanks, Sr. (*Sic 'Em, Sam*), Mary Pickford (*100% American*), Sessue Hayakawa (*Banzai*), Corinne Griffith (*A Wise Purchase*), Norma Talmadge (*Norma Talmadge in a Liberty Bond Appeal*), Mae Murray (*The Taming of Kaiser Bill*), Marguerite Clark (*The Biggest and the Littlest Lady in the World*), Charles Ray (*Charles Ray in a Liberty Bond Appeal*), Alla Nazimova (*A Woman of France*), William S. Hart (*A Bullet for Berlin*), William Farnum (*William Farnum in a Liberty Loan*

Film), Charlie Chaplin (*The Bond*), Fatty Arbuckle (*Fatty Arbuckle in a Liberty Loan Appeal*). Campbell, *Reel America*, 255–259.

67. Campbell, *Reel America*, 88–89.
68. *Ibid.*, 253.
69. https://www.charliechaplin.com/en/films/14-shoulder-arms, accessed September 23, 2022.
70. Brownlow, *The War*, 38, 39.
71. https://prruk.org/white-feather-for-cowardice-or-bowler-hat-charlie-chaplin-and-the-first-world-war/, accessed January 22, 2022.
72. Campbell, *Reel America*, 23. Brownlow, *The War*, 40.
73. https://silentology.wordpress/2018/08/07/thoughts-on-shoulder-arms-1918/, accessed September 23, 2022.
74. Brownlow, *The War*, 43.
75. *The New York Times*, October 21, 1918.
76. *Variety*, October 21, 1918.
77. *Moving Picture World*, October 19, 1918.
78. Campbell, *Reel America*, 111.
79. *Moving Picture World*, October 19, 1918, 445–446.
80. https://web.stanford.edu/-gdegroat/CKY/reviews/rtd.htm, accessed May 1, 2023.
81. For a full description of Clara Kimball Young and Lewis J. Selznick's business relationship and subsequent dissolution of their partnership, see note 62 in chapter 1.
82. Campbell, *Reel America*, 104.
83. *Variety*, December 20, 1918.
84. *Moving Picture World*, December 21, 1918.

Chapter 5

1. When Charles Hart, recruited from *Hearst's Magazine*, became chairman of the Committee on Public Information's Division of Films in the spring of 1918, he assembled a staff of film editors, writers, and cameramen to supplement and edit footage of American soldiers, shot by the Signal Corps in France, using the material to produce a number of feature-length films. Ward, *The Motion Picture Goes to War*, 95.
2. Ward, *The Motion Picture Goes to War*, 108–109.
3. *Ibid.*, 96.
4. *Ibid.*, 97.
5. *Ibid.*
6. *Ibid.*, 99.
7. *Ibid.*, 103.
8. Ebony Film's model for *Spying the Spy* was the slapstick of the Keystone Cops and not minstrel show stereotypes. The film, shot with Black neighborhoods in mind, was also received well by white audiences. www.weirdwildrealm.com/f-spying-the-spy.html, accessed May 5, 2023.
9. After the war, the Commission on Training Camp Activities (CTCA) transferred the rights for the film to the American Social Hygiene Association (ASHA). The ASHA reached an agreement with Isaac Silverman's Public Health Films to distribute the films to American theaters, with ASHA to receive 25 percent of the profits. Adding an epilogue to the film and retitling it *Fit to Win*, the film was released to the American public on March 2, 1919, where it was met with denunciation and censorship by United States surgeon general Rupert Blue, who withdrew endorsement of the film. The Catholic Church excoriated the film for its graphic content, deeming it unfit due to its advocacy for chemical prophylaxis, and condemning it as an exploitation film. Allan M. Brandt, *No Magic Bullet: A Social History of Venereal Disease in the United States Since 1880*, expanded ed. (Oxford: Oxford University Press, 1987), 207.
10. Ward, *The Motion Picture Goes to War*, 99.
11. https://www.tvguide.com/movies/pershings-crusaders/reviews/2030275911/, accessed September 24, 2022.
12. Walter Niebuhr was born in Illinois and became a journalist, going to Germany to cover World War I. He visited the eastern front in 1915, often accompanying cinematographer Wilbur Durborough, and he appeared in Durborough's film *On the Firing Line with the*

Notes—Chapter 5

Germans. After the end of the war, he set up the American Cinema Corporation, and in the 1930s he worked in documentary production. During World War II, he edited footage shot by the Signal Corps. https://shootingthegreatwar.blogspot.com/2015/11/walter-niebuhr-and-pershings-crusaders.html, accessed September 24, 2022.

13. *Milwaukee Journal*, May 24, 1918.
14. *Variety*, May 31, 1918.
15. Ward, *The Motion Picture Goes to War*, 124.
16. "Army to Investigate Hearst's Tank Film," *The New York Times*, June 25, 1918, 24, c. 2.
17. Ward, *The Motion Picture Goes to War*, 125.
18. "War Film Stopped; Hearst Influence on Creel Blamed," *The New York Times*, June 29, 1918, 1, c. 1.
19. The list included Charles Hart, Edgar Sisson, and Ray Hall, who had worked with various Hearst publications. The remaining men—J.A. Berst, H.C. Hoagland, E.B. Hetrick, Lew Simmons, C.F. Van Arsdale, G.A. Smith, Hubbell, and Donahue—had been associated with the Hearst-Pathé newsreel corporation or with Hearst's International Film Service. *The New York Times*, June 29, 1918, 1, c. 2.
20. The full statement read as follows: "The motion picture, *The Yanks Are Coming*, was refused the necessary official sanctions because every detail of the film's making was in open disregard and even defiance of established procedure. No photographs may be made in any factory doing Government work without formal permits, issued after investigation. Universal did not have these permits and made no effort to get them. Also, after making the pictures without permits, Universal planned a commercial exploitation of the film for its own profit, a privilege denied every other motion picture producer in the United States at one time or another. The only question in issue is whether private greed shall have the power to nullify the Government's efforts to protect military secrets. The charge of Hearst influence is merely an attempt to muddy the water and is absurd as it is indecent. No one in connection with this organization had responsibility in the matter save myself. The decision was my own and others merely carried out my explicit instructions." "Army to Investigate Hearst's Tank Film," *The New York Times*, June 25, 1918, 24, c. 2.
21. https://film.iwmcollections.org.uk/record/570/media_id//1020, accessed September 24, 2022.
22. This film shows the prelude to the Battle of Château-Thierry, which was fought on July 18, 1918 and was one of the first actions of the American Expeditionary Forces (AEF) under General John J. Pershing. The troops fighting consisted of both Army and Marine Corps units, which were the newest troops on the front in France and just barely out of training. On the morning of July 18, the combined French and American forces, under the overall direction of Allied Marshal Ferdinand Foch, launched a general counter-assault on the 25-mile-wide front between Fontenoy and Château-Thierry. The Allies managed to keep the plan of attack secret from the Germans, and the attack at 04:45 took the Germans by surprise. The troops went "over the top" without any preparatory bombardment, and were able to penetrate German lines, with individual American units fighting behind enemy lines. John S.D. Eisenhower, *Yanks: The Epic Story of the American Army in World War I* (New York: The Free Press, 2001), 136–137.
23. Hugo Riesenfeld (1879–1939) born in Vienna, Austria, became a noted American composer who wrote orchestral compositions for silent films. He was one of the creators of modern production techniques where film scoring serves as an integral part of the action on screen. Three of his most notable compositions were for Cecil B. DeMille films: *Joan the Woman* (1917), *The Ten Commandments* (1923), and *King of Kings* (1927). In addition, he was responsible for co-founding the cinema library of music-topical collections of music for silent film orchestra and musicians. https://travsd.wordpress.

Notes—Chapter 6

com/2021/01/26/hugo-riesenfeld-silent-composer/, accessed March 15, 2022.

24. *The New York Times*, July 30, 1918.

25. Ibid.

26. Ward, *The Motion Picture Goes to War*, 105.

27. Campbell, *Reel America*, 91.

28. https://net.lib.byu.edu/estu/wwi/comment/scott/SCh20.htm, accessed March 16, 2022.

29. Between 370,000 and 400,000 African American soldiers enlisted during the First World War. Many served as stevedores and as logistical support, with the 92nd and 93rd Divisions fighting on the front lines under the command of the French Army by order of General John J. Pershing. The famous "Harlem Hellfighters" (given the nickname by the German army), 369th Infantry Regiment, 93rd Division, received the French Croix de Guerre as a unit. Sergeant Henry Johnson of the "Hellfighters" became the first American to receive the Croix de Guerre and was posthumously awarded the Congressional Medal of Honor. Corporal Freddie Stowers of the "Black Devils," 371st Infantry Regiment, 93rd Division, also received the Congressional Medal of Honor posthumously. https://net.lib.byu.edu/estu/wwi/commen/scott/SCh20.htm, accessed September 24, 2022.

30. *The Cleveland Advocate* 5, no. 31 (December 7, 1918): 3.

31. https://shootingthegreatwar.blogspot.com/2018/10/under-four-flags-usa-1918.html, accessed March 18, 2022.

32. https://shootingthegreatwar.blogspot.com/2018/10/under-four-flags-usa-1918.html, accessed March 18, 2022.

33. *The New York Times*, November 18, 1918.

34. On June 30, 1919, the Congress of the United States officially wiped the Committee on Public Information out of existence. Using his own funds, George Creel had the committee's records moved to the Fuel Administration Building. On August 21, 1919, the disbanded organization's records were turned over to the Council on National Defense, where they were saved and stored. Creel continued in public life after the war, out of the public eye. He became a successful writer of nonfiction books, with his best-known book, *War Criminals and Punishment* (published toward the end of the Second World War), advocating for the identification, exposure, and punishment of Axis war criminals. The book was instrumental in the formation of the postwar tribunals in Nuremberg and Tokyo, bringing numerous war criminals to justice for crimes against humanity. George Creel died in 1953. Alan Axelrod, *Selling the Great War* (New York: Palgrave Macmillan, 2009), 211–216.

35. Kaiser Wilhelm II abdicated on November 9, 1918, under pressure from civilian leaders and the leaders of the exhausted German army. On November 10, Wilhelm and his family took a train across the border to neutral Holland, where he was allowed by the Dutch Queen Wilhelmina (1880–1962) to purchase a house in the town of Doorn. Although the Allies wanted to prosecute Wilhelm for war crimes, Queen Wilhelmina refused to extradite him, and he lived out the remainder of his life in Holland, dying on June 4, 1941, at the age of 82. https://www.history.com/topics/world-war-i/kaiser-wilhelm-ii, accessed March 30, 2022.

Chapter 6

1. Louise Chipley Slavicek, *The Treaty of Versailles*, Milestones in Modern World History (Broomall, PA: Chelsea House, 2010), 41–43, 58.

2. Wilson refused to concede to the houses of Congress, taking his case to the American public in the hope that they would call upon their representatives to ratify the treaty. While trying to muster support for the issue, Wilson suffered a serious stroke on October 2, 1918, rendering him an invalid for the remainder of his life.

3. Campbell, *Reel America*, 112.

4. Earl Schenck (1889–1962) bore a remarkable resemblance to Crown Prince Wilhelm and portrayed him

Notes—Chapter 6

in three other 1918 pictures: *My Four Years in Germany, To Hell with the Kaiser*, and *The Kaiser's Finish*. Shortly after the release of *The Great Victory*, Schenck would appear in the movie *The Spirit of Lafayette*, portraying the heroic Marquis de Lafayette, a distinct change from playing the evil German crown prince. This movie was one of the last made under auspices of the CPI and was only screened once in February of 1919. Because the film had Lafayette visualizing a world with a League of Nations, it was regarded as pro–Wilsonian propaganda, and the film industry, now trying to adjust to postwar sentiments and the political opposition to the league, pulled it from distribution to the movie public. Campbell, *Reel America*, 129.

5. *Ibid.*, 112–113.

6. *Moving Picture World* 39, no. 113 (January 4, 1919).

7. Although the underwater scenes were photographed by the Williamson Submarine Film Corporation in the Bahamas, Eugene Gaudio is credited as the cinematographer for his work in inserting the photography into the film.

8. Many people consider Ince's greatest contribution to the war effort to have been his "Smiles Films," which were films of mothers, wives, and sweethearts of soldiers stationed in France. Soldiers saw group shots and close-ups of loved ones or relatives holding signs, or even babies born after their departure. The films were shown in American training camps, theaters, and YMCA huts abroad. Taves, *Thomas Ince*, 144.

9. *Ibid.*, 146–147.

10. *The New York Times*, February 17, 1919.

11. *Moving Picture World*, February 22, 1919, 1026.

12. Bobby Connelly (1909–1922) was one of the first male child stars in motion pictures, already well known for his "Sonny Jim" series of shorts in 1914–1915. He was the first child actor to get his own series of films with his name above the title emphasizing his star billing. Much-loved by his adult peers, he was diagnosed with endocarditis in 1917 and died tragically at the age of 13 of bronchitis in 1922. "'Bobby' Connelly Dead: Child Screen Star Dies of Bronchitis at His Home," *The New York Times*, July 7, 1922.

13. https://www.allmovie.com/movie/v115213, accessed September 24, 2022.

14. Acclaimed writer Rupert Hughes wrote the book on which the film was based in 1918, with the novel becoming an international success. Hughes was also a screenwriter during the silent era, earning an Academy Award nomination for Best Original Screenplay for 1928's *The Patent Leather Kid*. Hughes was the uncle of eccentric millionaire/inventor/producer Howard Hughes.

15. "'The Unpardonable Sin' Attracts Huge Crowds," *Detroit Free Press*, March 5, 1919.

16. "Blanche Sweet Sues Neilan for Divorce," *The New York Times*, September 24, 1929.

17. *The New York Times*, March 3, 1919.

18. *New York Tribune*, August 3, 1919.

19. Race films were films about Black Americans, for Black Americans, and made by Black American directors for distribution to Black theaters in the United States.

20. https:// www.cnet.com/culture/entertainment/black-history-month-2021-how-oscar-micheaux-defied-hollywood-to-make-the-homesteader/, accessed September 24, 2022.

21. https://alcetron.com/Yankee-Doodle-in-Berlin, accessed September 24, 2022.

22. Campbell, *Reel America*, 113–114.

23. *Moving Picture World*, July 4, 1919.

24. *Watertown Daily News Times*, February 5, 1920.

25. https://en.wikipedia.org/wiki/The_Lost_Batttalion_(1919_film), accessed May 9, 2023.

26. Tongs were secret societies or sworn brotherhoods in Chinese communities most often tied to organized crime both in Asia and the United States. Violent disputes between rival tongs (disputes of inter-gang grievances, besmirching another tong's reputation)

Notes—Chapter 7

culminated in the Tong Wars in the big Chinese communities in San Francisco and New York in the early 1900s. Hostilities lasted for over 20 years, finally calming down after the end of World War I.

27. Cher Ami (French for "dear friend") was a carrier pigeon in the United States Signal Corps in France, famed for his courage in delivering the message that saved the Lost Battalion. Although gravely wounded by German fire (shot through the breast, blinded in one eye, and with a leg hanging by a tendon), he managed to take flight and deliver his message. His decorations included the French Croix de Guerre Medal, a (small) version of the Distinguished Service Cross awarded to him by General John Pershing, and the Animals in War & Peace Medal of Bravery. He died of his wounds on June 13, 1919. His body was mounted and stuffed and can be seen today (with his medals) at the National Museum of American History at the Smithsonian Institution in Washington, D.C.

28. https://en.wikipedia.org/wiki/The_Lost_Battalion_(1919_film), accessed May 10, 2023.

29. Campbell, *Reel America*, 129.

30. *The New York Times*, July 3, 1919.

31. https://www.flickeralley.com/the-history-behind-the-door-1919/, accessed April 5, 2022.

32. https://www.flickeralley.com/the-history-behind-the-door-1919/, accessed April 5, 2022.

33. Taves, *Thomas Ince*, 148.

34. *Exhibitor's Herald*, December 14, 1919.

35. *Motion Picture Classic*, January 1920.

36. *Photoplay*, March 30, 1920.

Chapter 7

1. Prohibition (known as the Volstead Act) was the 18th Amendment to the Constitution of the United States, which went into effect on January 17, 1920. It prohibited the manufacture, sale, and transportation of intoxicating liquors. Prohibition gave rise to bootlegging (illegal production and sales of forbidden liquor) and speakeasies (illegal drinking spots).

2. https://www.filmsite.org20sintro.html, accessed April 20, 2022.

3. Rex Ingram (1893–1950) is ranked alongside D.W. Griffith, Cecil B. De-Mille, and close friend Erich von Stroheim as one of the great directors of the 1920s. Educated in Ireland, Ingram immigrated to the United States in 1911. He briefly studied sculpture at the Yale School of Fine Arts, giving him a lifelong fascination with the human body. Moving to Hollywood, he would briefly have a career as an actor. After serving in the First World War, he would return to Hollywood and become a noted director, directing smash hits including *The Four Horsemen of the Apocalypse* (1921), *The Conquering Power* (1921), *The Prisoner of Zenda* (1922), *Scaramouche* (1923), and *Mare Nostrum* (1926).

4. Ruth Barton, *Rex Ingram: Visionary Director of the Silent Screen* (Lexington: University of Kentucky Press, 2014), 71–72.

5. *Ibid.*, 73.

6. *Ibid.*, 85–86.

7. *Ibid.*, 88.

8. *Variety*, February 18, 1921, 40.

9. *The New York Times*, March 7, 1921, 6.

10. *The Los Angeles Times*, March 10, 1921, 4.

11. *Life*, March 24, 1921.

12. Rin Tin Tin (1918–1932) was a male German shepherd born in Flirey, France, during World War I who became an international star in motion pictures. He was rescued as a tiny puppy from a severely damaged Imperial German Army kennel by American Corporal Lee Duncan. At the end of the war, Duncan smuggled Rin Tin Tin aboard a troop ship going back to the United States and then settled in Los Angeles. Warner Bros. cast him alongside actress Claire Adams in 1923's *Where the North Begins* playing a heroic dog raised by wolves who rescues his human friends from evil fur trappers. The film was a tremendous success and was credited from saving Warner Bros.

Notes—Chapter 7

from bankruptcy. He received thousands of fan letters from all over the world and would send back (courtesy of the Warner Bros. publicity department) a glossy portrait of himself signed with his paw print and a message written by his trainer Lee Duncan signed "Most faithfully, Rin Tin Tin." "Rinty," as he was known, also enjoyed visiting traumatized soldiers at veterans' hospitals throughout the United States, where his pictures were often shown, making him an early "service dog." According to some writers, at the first 1929 Academy Awards competition Rin Tin Tin was voted Best Actor by his (human) peers, but the Academy of Motion Picture Arts and Sciences, wishing to appear more serious, removed Rin Tin Tin as a choice and re-ran the vote, giving it instead to German actor Emil Jannings. Rin Tin Tin died at the age of 14 in Los Angeles, and newspapers around the world carried obituaries. He was buried in his native France in the Cimetière des Chiens et Autres Animaux Domestiques, the pet cemetery on the outskirts of Paris. In 1960, Rin Tin Tin was honored with a star on the Hollywood Walk of Fame. Susan Orlean, *Rin Tin Tin: The Life and the Legend* (New York: Simon & Schuster, 2011), 29–30, 46–47, 81, 109–112. "No, Rin Tin Tin Didn't Really Win the First Best Oscar," *The Attic*, February 15, 2017.

13. Caroline Cox, "Invisible Wounds," in *Traumatic Pasts: History, Psychiatry and Trauma in the Modern Age, 1870–1930* (Cambridge: Cambridge University Press, 2001), 295.

14. Michael Wallis, *The Real Wild West: The 101 Ranch and the Creation of the American West* (New York: Macmillan, 2000), 446.

15. *Moving Picture World*, July 1923.

16. https://greatwarfiction.wordpress.com/2014/11/08/the-enchanted-cottage-1924/, accessed April 26, 2022.

17. Although the United States had fought for a relatively short time during the First World War as compared to their French and British allies, they nonetheless had 234,000 soldiers who suffered physical injuries that sidelined them from the front, and roughly 4,000 returned home missing part or all of a limb. Nearly 100,000 soldiers were removed from front line fighting for psychological injuries, and 40,000 were discharged from the service. By 1921, approximately 9,000 veterans had undergone treatment for psychological disability (called "war neurosis") in veterans' hospitals. Ultimately, 224,000 veterans returned home with a permanent physical or mental disability. Through two organizations (the Disabled Veterans of the World War [DAV] and the American Legion), both founded in 1919, public awareness was raised on the plight of disabled veterans, with the United States government being pressured to adopt programs to address rehabilitation and reintegration into American society. Although the Federal Board for Vocational Education had been passed by Congress in 1917, the level of services for disabled veterans varied widely, and attempts to streamline it largely failed. https://blogs.loc.gov/loc/2017/world-war-i-injured-veterans-and-the-disibility-rights-movement, accessed April 27, 2023.

18. https://classicfilmaficiandos.wordpress.com/tag/the-enchanted-cottage, accessed May 3, 2022.

19. *Photoplay Magazine*, May 1924.

20. *Film Daily* review, April 11, 1924.

21. *Variety*, April 16, 1924.

22. *Photoplay Magazine*, May 1924.

23. *The Educational Screen*, June 1924.

24. Mordaunt Hall, "The Enchanted Cottage," *The New York Times*, January 18, 1926.

25. https://en.wikipedia.org/wik/The_Dark_Angel_(1925_film), accessed May 14, 2023.

26. Sheridan Morley, *Tales from the Hollywood Raj: The British, the Movies and Tinseltown* (New York: Viking Press, 1983), 66.

27. Mordaunt Hall, "The Screen: A Blind Hero," *The New York Times*, October 12, 1925.

28. http://historyonfilm.com/big.parade/, accessed May 5, 2022.

Notes—Chapter 7

29. John Baxter, *King Vidor* (New York: Simon & Schuster, 1976), 10–11, 13, 18–20.

30. John Gilbert (born John Cecil Pringle in 1899) was the son of actors. His parents divorced when he was a small child, and his mother re-married a man named Gilbert, who adopted the boy and gave him the nickname of Jack. The marriage also faltered, and his mother died of tuberculosis when Gibert was 13 years old. His stepfather gave him 10 dollars and a ticket to San Francisco. He spent two years working at odd jobs, and then, in 1915, began to get work as an extra player at Thomas Ince's Santa Monica film studio. Within one year, his good looks earned him leading parts. By 1919, he was working with respected Hollywood directors including Maurice Tourneur, Clarence Brown, and Sidney Franklin. By the time Gilbert met Irving Thalberg, he was a veteran of dozens of films and was under contract to Fox Studios. Gilbert was lured over to MGM, and his suave good looks (and pencil-thin moustache) soon earned him the status of one of filmdom's romantic leading men and, by 1925, after his performance as the hot-blooded Prince Danilo in director Erich von Stroheim's hit movie *The Merry Widow*, the title of "The Great Lover." https://silentfilm.org/the-big-parade, accessed May 8, 2022.

31. Renée Adorée (1898–1933) was born in a rural part of Lille, France. The daughter of circus performers, she was a skilled acrobat and bareback rider, performing with her parents throughout Europe. She immigrated to the United States in 1919 and had great success on the 1920 Broadway stage as a dancer/actress in two musical productions: *Oh, What a Girl!* and *The Dancer*. She entered motion pictures in director Raoul Walsh's hit *The Strongest*, a dramatic photoplay written by First World War French prime minister Georges Clemenceau, and then had another hit in *The Eternal Struggle* (1923) before being cast in *The Big Parade* in 1925. She went on to make eight other films with good friend John Gilbert as well as making four films with another film idol, Ramon Novarro. She easily made the transition to sound films, but in 1930 she contracted tuberculosis. Her marriages to actor Tom Moore and businessman William Sherman Gill had ended in divorce, and she died alone in a health sanitorium in October of 1933. For her contribution to films, she was given a star on the Hollywood Walk of Fame. "Renée Adorée, 31, Film Player, Dead," *The New York Times*, October 6, 1933.

32. Brownlow, *The War*, 189.

33. https://silentology.wordpress.com/2018/08/31/thoughts-on-the-big-parade-1925/, accessed May 8, 2022.

34. H. Mark Glancy, "MGM Film Grosses, 1924–28: The Eddie Mannix Ledger," *Historical Journal of Film, Radio and Television* 12, no. 2 (1992): 127–144.

35. Mordaunt Hall, "The Screen: A Superlative War Picture," *The New York Times*, November 20, 1925.

36. "The Big Parade" review, *Life*, December 1925.

37. *Chicago Daily News*, December 29, 1925.

38. "Honors for Arnold," *American Cinematographer*, December 1926, 5.

39. Brownlow, *The War*, 193.

40. https://www.history.com/this-day-in-history/valentino-dies, accessed September 26, 2022.

41. At the first Academy of Motion Picture Arts and Sciences Oscar ceremony in 1929, *Wings* would win the first Academy Award for Best Picture.

42. David W. Menefee, *Richard Barthelmess: A Life in Pictures* (Albany, GA: BearManor Media, 2009), 296.

43. *The Herald Democrat*, February 28, 1920.

44. Dempsey retired from boxing in 1927 after being defeated by fellow heavyweight Gene Tunney, a decorated Marine in World War I. Dempsey redeemed himself in the eyes of boxing fans all over the world through his service in World War II. He joined the Coast Guard Reserve, taught boxing and self defense to sailors, and was eventually promoted to the rank

Notes—Chapter 7

of commander, serving on the transportation ship USS *Wakefield* at the invasion of Okinawa.

45. *The Queens Borough Daily Star*, August 26, 1927, 6.

46. Barthelmess would lose the award to German actor Emil Jannings but would be given a special Academy Award the following year (1928) for his work as both producer and star of *The Noose*. He would make the transition to sound movies, acting in a number of socially conscious movies including the well-reviewed *Heroes for Sale* (1933). His popularity waned in the mid–1930s, and he resorted to plastic surgery to restore his youthful good looks. The surgery instead left deep scars under his eyes. Barthelmess did not act for three and a half years, but, encouraged by director Howard Hawks, he accepted a strong supporting role in the 1939 hit movie *Only Angels Have Wings* (starring Cary Grant and Jean Arthur), earning the best reviews of his late film career. After the United States declared war in 1941, he turned his back on Hollywood and enlisted at the age of 47 in the United States Navy, rising to the rank of lieutenant commander and serving as an aide to Vice Admiral Herbert F. Leary. After the war, he retired completely from films and devoted himself to his charitable work and his family. At the 1957 Academy Awards ceremony, he was honored with the George Eastman Award for distinguished contributions to the art of film. He died of throat cancer at the age of 68 in 1963. Menefee, *Richard Barthelmess*, 136–138, 142–149.

47. *The New York Times*, August 16, 1927, 31.

48. *Variety*, August 17, 1927.

49. Menefee, *Richard Barthelmess*, 297.

50. https://greatwarfiction,wordpress.com/2015/07/12/barbed-wire-and-hall-caine/, accessed May 15, 2022.

51. https://greatwarfiction.wordpress.com/2015/07/12/barbed-wire-and-hall-caine/, accessed May 15, 2022.

52. Panikos Panayi, "Forgotten Prisoners of the Great War," *History Today* 62, no. 11 (2012).

53. *Screenland*, November 1927.

54. *Motion Picture*, November 1927.

55. "The All Time Best Sellers," *International Motion Picture Almanac, 1937–38* (New York: Quigley, 1938), 942

56. Tag Gallagher, *John Ford: The Man and His Films* (Berkeley: University of California Press, 1986), 31.

57. Joseph McBride, *Searching for John Ford* (New York: St. Martin's Press, 2003), 160.

58. www.silentsaregolden.com/featurefolders5/FScommentary.html, accessed May 21, 2023.

59. "The All Time Best Sellers," *International Motion Picture Almanac, 1937–38* (New York: Quigley, 1938), 942.

60. *Variety*, December 31, 1927.

61. https://www.imdb.com/title/tt0020396/plotsummary/, accessed June 3, 2023.

62. "Evasion of Taxes Charged Actress," *The Salt Lake Telegram*, May 23, 1929.

63. *Detroit Free Press*, June 8, 1929.

64. *Motion Picture Magazine*, July 1929.

65. https://www.history.com/topics/great-depression/1929-stock-market-crash, accessed May 20, 2022.

66. https://www.filmsite.org/20sintro.html, accessed September 26, 2022.

67. *Variety*, May 7, 1930.

68. Joseph R. Millichap, *Lewis Milestone* (Boston: Twayne, 1981), 38.

69. Michael Sragow, "The Front Page: Stop the Presses!" https://www.criterion.com/current/posts/4382-the-front-page-stop-the-presses, accessed July 4, 2022.

70. Looks can be deceiving. Because of his rough physical appearance, Louis Wolheim (1880–1931) was relegated mostly to playing thugs or villains in the movies. In actuality, he attended Cornell University, graduating with a degree in engineering, and taught mathematics at Cornell for six years. His pushed-in nose was the result of an injury suffered while playing football for Cornell. A close friend of John, Lionel, and Ethel Barrymore, Wolheim would appear in numerous films with John and Lionel, interspersed with lead roles on the

Notes—Chapter 7

Broadway stage, including *The Hairy Ape* (1922) and his most famous role of Captain Flagg in *What Price Glory?* (1925). In 1927, he appeared in the rollicking *Two Arabian Knights*, directed by Lewis Milestone; the film would win Milestone the 1927 Academy Award for Best Comedy Direction. In 1928, he appeared as the gangster protagonist in Milestone's crime epic *The Racket*. "The Hard-Boiled Samaritan," *Photoplay*, May 1931.

71. Lew Ayres, who had become a star in the 1930s MGM series *Dr. Kildare*, was so affected by his role as Paul Baümer that when America entered the Second World War, he registered as a conscientious objector. He later served bravely under fire as a medic in the Philippines, earning commendations and three battle stars. Although he returned to Hollywood in 1946 and later received a Best Actor nomination for his role as a doctor in 1948's *Johnny Belinda*, he never regained his 1930s star status.

72. Eugene P. Schleh, "All Quiet on the Western Front: A History Teacher's Reappraisal," *Film & History* 8, no. 4 (1978): 66–69.

73. "All Time Film Rental Champs," *Variety*, October 16, 1990, M150.

74. Mordaunt Hall, "Young Germany in the War," *The New York Times*, April 30, 1930.

75. *Ibid.*

76. Irene Thirer, "Raging war and soldier's struggle back home in 'All Quiet on the Western Front,'" *New York Daily News*, April 30, 1930.

77. "Review: 'All Quiet on the Western Front,'" *Variety*, May 7, 1930.

78. Charles Higham, "Select List of Banned Films," in "Film Censorship: The Unnecessary Secrets," *The Bulletin*, November 20, 1955, 18.

79. David Mikies, "Hollywood's Creepy Love Affair with Adolf Hitler, in Explosive New Detail," *Tablet*, June 10, 2013.

80. Only Charlie Chaplin would continue to make silent films into the 1930s: *City Lights* (1930) and *Modern Times* (1936).

81. Beset by personal problems (including binge-eating and alcoholism), Marie Prevost died in Hollywood in 1937 of acute alcoholism. John Gilbert, one of the most popular leading men in the silent era, incurred the ire of MGM studio head Louis B. Mayer, who vowed to destroy his career. Gilbert, under contract to MGM, was deliberately put into a series of inferior films (it's said that Mayer deliberately sabotaged his sound debut in 1929's *His Glorious Night*) in the 1930s. Although he appeared with Greta Garbo in the "A" picture *Queen Christina* in 1933, all of the publicity went to Garbo. Ashamed, humiliated, and demoralized by his treatment at MGM, Gilbert left the studio. He began to drink heavily and suffered two heart attacks, dying in 1936. "Marie Prevost Diets, and Dies," *The Milwaukee Journal*, January 24, 1937, 12. "John Gilbert, Screen Lover, Dies Suddenly in Sleep," *Pittsburgh Post Gazette*, January 10, 1936, 1.

82. "News in Brief," *The Times* (London), no. 45153 (March 16, 1929), 9.

83. Anthony Slide, *Early American Cinema* (Lanham, MD: Scarecrow Press, 1994), 141.

84. "Loretta Young's 'Counselor' a Star, Too," *The Indianapolis News*, May 29, 1951, 10.

85. Earl Schenck's stage and screen career was cut short in 1925 by a condition called "Klieg light eyes," which caused him to nearly go blind. He went to Hawaii to recover and became one of the world's foremost researchers of Polynesian culture, receiving a commission from the Bishop Museum in Honolulu to do research, spending 14 years as an explorer, cartologist, and ethnologist. His research was frequently featured in *National Geographic* magazine during the 1930s. Returning home before the outbreak of the Second World War, Schenck became a college lecturer on the South Seas and during the war years served the United States Navy Department in planning military bases in the Southwest Pacific to assist American troops fighting the Japanese. After the war, he retired to Tahiti and died at age 72 in 1962. Earl Schenck, *Come Unto These Yellow Sands* (Indianapolis: Bobbs-Merrill, 1940).

86. A federally funded New Deal visual arts program set up by President Franklin Roosevelt in the 1930s to put artists and artisans back to work to create murals, sculptures, graphic arts, and scenic designs through the United States for the beautification of the country. American Art Annual Geographical Dictionary of Murals and Sculptures commissioned by the Section of Fine Arts, Public Buildings Administration, Federal Works Agency (American Federation of Arts, 1941), 624–25.

87. Mabel Normand's boyfriend, director William Desmond Taylor, who helped supply her with cocaine, was murdered on February 1, 1922. Police grilled Normand on her possible involvement in the murder but eventually ruled her out as a suspect. Further tarnishing her reputation was the 1924 shooting by her chauffeur, Joe Kelly, of millionaire Courtland B. Dines with Normand's pistol. Although Normand was not involved with Dines, this second scandal would result in her movies being pulled from theaters around the country. Her movie career went into a steep decline; broken in health, she died of complications of pulmonary tuberculosis on February 23, 1930. Robert Giroux, *A Deed of Death: The Story Behind the Unsolved Murder of Hollywood Director William Desmond Taylor* (New York: Alfred A. Knopf, 1990), 232, 236. "Ohio and M.P.T.O.A. Both Bar Normand Films," *Variety* 8, no. 19 (January 10, 1924).

88. Author's note: In 1943, my father, a Polish-born GI, was stationed in Texas prior to being sent overseas. One night, he and his buddies saw the movie *Hi Diddle Diddle* starring my father's favorite (Polish) actress, Pola Negri. He'd seen some of her silent movies (both in Poland and the United States) as a small child and was thrilled to see her in an American musical comedy. He sent her a fan letter written in Polish, and she sent him a picture of herself from the movie and signed it (in Polish) "from one patriot to another." He kept that picture all through his war service in France and Germany, and when he returned home, he had it framed and kept it on his bedside table until he died in 1983.

89. "Silent Film Star Jane Novak Talks at Length About Her Past," *Nevada State Journal*, November 11, 1974, 37.

90. Sessue Hayakawa received a supporting actor Oscar nomination for his portrayal of the Japanese prison commandant Colonel Saito in 1957's blockbuster hit *The Bridge on the River Kwai*, while Erich von Stroheim received a supporting actor Oscar nomination for his portrayal of silent film director turned butler Max von Mayerling in the 1950 classic *Sunset Boulevard*. Ironically, both men appeared together in the 1939 French movie *Macao, l'enfer du jeu* (English title *Gambling Hell*) made just before the start of the Second World War. At that point, von Stroheim had become a French movie star, praised for his acclaimed performance in 1937's antiwar classic *Grand Illusion*, while Hayakawa, unable to click with American movie audiences due to his halting English, had traveled to Europe seeking acting jobs. Von Stroheim (Jewish by birth) fled back to America in 1940 before the Nazi invasion of France, while Hayakawa, separated from his family, was trapped in France and sold his watercolor paintings to support himself during the war.

Epilogue

1. *The Atlantic*, December 4, 2013.
2. The *Cinémathèque Française* is a French nonprofit organization that holds one of the largest archives of film documents and film-related objects in the world and offers daily screenings of worldwide films, both silent and sound.
3. https://filminstitut.se/sv-och-samtela-om-film/cinemateket-stockholm/, accessed July 20, 2023.
4. https://www.goldenglobes.com/articles/out-vaults-civilization-1916, accessed July 20, 2023.
5. 2016 Traverse City Film Festival Program, 20.
6. https://lostmediawiki.com/The_Fall_of_a_Nation_(lost_sequel_

to_"The_Birth_of_a_Nation"_11916), accessed July 20, 2023.

7. The Dawson Film Find was the accidental discovery in 1978 of 372 film titles, preserved in 533 reels of silent-era nitrate film in the Klondike Gold Rush town of Dawson City, Yukon, Alaska.

8. https://centuryfilmproject.org/2017/01/14/joan-the-woman-1916/.

9. 2021 Capitolfest Film Festival Program, 13.

10. www.https://moma.org/collection/works/304742, accessed July 23, 2023.

11. www.https://cineuropa.org/en/newsdetail/802501, accessed July 23, 2023.

12. www.https://silentra.com/people/musicians/Rapsis-jeff.html, accessed July 23, 2023.

13. https://www.archives.gov/research/motion.pictures/ww1, accessed September 27, 2022.

14. https://www.silentfilm.org/preservation/behind the door/, accessed July 26, 2023.

15. The five-piece Mont Alto Motion Picture Chamber Orchestra (founded in 1989 in Colorado) is a chamber music ensemble that revives the tradition of silent film orchestras with period music culled from historical libraries of music.

16. "7,200 Lost U.S. Silent Feature Films (1912–29)," Library of Congress, February 4, 2021.

17. American-born conductor and composer Carl Davis (1936–2023) was internationally known for creating new film scores for silent film classics, including D.W. Griffith's monumental epic *Intolerance* (1916), the restored version of Erich von Stroheim's masterpiece *Greed* (1924), King Vidor's acclaimed *The Big Parade* (1925), Lon Chaney's horror thriller *The Phantom of the Opera* (1925), French director Abel Gance's historical epic *Napoleon* (1927), Cecil B. DeMille's *The Godless Girl* (1928), and Charlie Chaplin's *City Lights* (1931).

18. Richard P. May, "Restoring The Big Parade," *The Moving Picture Image* 5, no. 2: 140–146.

19. www.jonnybest.co.uk/about-me, accessed July 27, 2023.

20. www.cinefile.info/cine-list/2017/4/14/-friday-apr-14-thursday-apr-20, accessed July 28, 2023.

21. The Academy Film Archive is part of the Academy Foundation, established in 1944 with the purpose of organizing and overseeing the Academy of Motion Picture Arts and Sciences educational and cultural activities, including the preservation of motion picture history.

22. https://www.nitrateville.com/viewtopic.php?t=7182, accessed July 28, 2023.

23. Excerpted from an article in the February/March 1998 issue of the Library of Congress's publication "Civilization."

24. *New York Post*, August 3, 2009.

25. Robert Osborne (1932–2017) was the primary host for the cable channel TCM (Turner Classic Movies) and the driving force for the "Silent Sundays" weekly film series, which shows silent films, both national and international, every Sunday evening at midnight. A respected and much-admired Hollywood film reporter and film historian of both the silent and sound era, Osborne selected the 1928 Buster Keaton classic *The Cameraman* as the first silent film shown on TCM on April 17, 1994.

26. The *Frankfurter Allgemeine Zeitung*, one of Germany's most respected newspapers, savaged the film, saying, "The inner plot, the brains of the story, have been removed by Edward Berger and his scriptwriters and replaced with a Hollywood programme." Munich-based *Süddeudsche* movie critic Hubert Wetzel concurred, writing, "You have to ask yourself whether director Berger has ever read Remarque's novel." The German tabloid *Bild* wrote: "There are good literary adaptations and there are bad ones, and then there is 'All Quiet on the Western Front' by director Edward Berger. His version of Erich Maria Remarque's classic is a piece of indescribable impudence. It takes a considerable portion of ignorance, disrespect and Oscar-lust to mess up a masterpiece in such a fashion, to pulverize its content and story so mercilessly." Excerpts of the reviews published by *The Guardian*, January 27, 2023.

Bibliography

"All Quiet on the Western Front." *Variety*, May 7, 1930.

American Art Annual Geographical Dictionary of Murals and Sculptures Commissioned by the Section of Fine Arts, Public Buildings Administration, Federal Works Agency. The American Federation of Arts, 1941.

"America's Answer to the Hun." *The New York Times*, July 30, 1918.

Andrew, Christopher. *For the President's Eyes Only*. New York: HarperCollins, 1996.

Appelbaum, Peter C. *Habsburg Sons: Jews in the Austro-Hungarian Army 1788–1918*. Boston: Cherry Orchard Books, 2022.

Axelrod, Alan. *Selling the Great War*. New York: Palgrave Macmillan, 2009.

"Barbed Wire." *Motion Picture*, November 1927.

"Barbed Wire." *Screenland*, November 1927.

Barton, Ruth. *Rex Ingram: Visionary Director of the Silent Screen*. Lexington: University of Kentucky Press, 2014.

"The Battle Cry of Peace." *Deutsches Journal*, September 1915, section 3.3.

"The Battle Cry of Peace." *The New York Times*, August 7, 1915.

"The Battle Cry of Peace." *Variety*, August 13, 1915.

Baukhage, H. R., and A. A. Hoehling. "The Black Tom Explosion." *The American Legion Magazine* 77, no. 2 (August 1964): 14–15, 49–50.

Baxter, John. *King Vidor*. New York: Simon & Schuster, 1976.

"Behind the Door." *Exhibitor's Herald*, December 14, 1919.

"Behind the Door." *Motion Picture Classic*, January 1920.

"Behind the Door." *Photoplay*, March 1920.

Brewer, Susan A. "Propaganda." In the *Oxford Companion to United States History*, edited by Paul S. Boyer. Oxford: Oxford University Press, 2001.

Brownlow, Kevin. *The War, the West, and the Wilderness*. New York: Alfred A. Knopf, 1979.

Brownlow, Kevin, and John Kobal. *Hollywood: The Pioneers*. New York: Alfred A. Knopf, 1979.

Caesar, Gaius Julius. *The Gallic Wars*. Translated by Carolyn Hammond. New York: Oxford University Press, 2008.

Campbell, Craig W. *Reel America and World War I*. Jefferson, NC: McFarland, 1985.

Canemaker, John. *Winsor McCay: His Life and Art*. New York: Harry N. Abrams, 2005.

Carr, William. *The Origins of the Wars of German Unification*. New York: Longman Group, 1991.

Caves, Roger W. *Encyclopedia of the City*. Milton Park, Abington-on-the-Thames, Oxfordshire: Routledge, 2013.

Cherchi, Paolo Usai, and Eileen Bowser. *The Griffith Project: Films Produced in 1916–1918*. London: British Film Institute, 2005.

Chisick, Harvey. "Pamphlets and Journalism in the Early French Revolution: The Offices of the Ami du Roi of the Abbé Royou as a Center of Royalist Propaganda." *French Historical Studies* 15, no. 4 (1988): 623–845.

"Civilization." *Deutsches Journal*, June 13, 1916, 4.

Bibliography

"Civilization." *Fairbanks Daily News*, September 16, 1916.

"Civilization." *The Fatherland*, June 24, 1916, 4.

"Civilization." *La Crosse Tribune*, October 21, 1916.

"Civilization." *New Yorker Staats-Zeitung*, August 1916, 4.

"The Claws of the Hun." *The New York Times*, July 1, 1918.

Cohen, Esther. "The Propaganda of Saints in the Middle Ages." *Journal of Communications* 31, no. 4 (December 1981): 22–24.

Cox, Caroline. *Traumatic Pasts: History, Psychiatry and Trauma in the Modern Age, 1870–1930*. Cambridge: Cambridge University Press, 2001.

Creel, George. *How We Advertised America*. New York: Harper & Brothers, 1920.

———. *Rebel at Large: Recollections of Fifty Crowded Years*. New York: G.P. Putnam's Sons, 1947.

"The Cross Bearer." *Hattiesburg American*, April 5, 1918, 7.

"The Cross Bearer." *Michigan Film Review*, April 1918.

"The Dark Angel." *The New York Times*, October 12, 1925.

Davis, Paul K. "Marathon." In *100 Decisive Battles From Ancient Times to the Present*. Oxford: Oxford University Press, 2001.

De Volder, Jan. *Cardinal Mercier in the First World War: Belgium, Germany and the Catholic Church*. Leuven: Leuven University Press, 2018.

Dumoulin, Michel. *L'entrée dans le XX Siecle, 1905–1918 (The Beginning of the Century from 1905–1918), Nouvelle Histoire de Belgique*. Brussels: Le Cri Edition, 2010.

Eisenhower, John S.D. *Yanks: The Epic Story of the American Army in World War I*. New York: The Free Press, 2001.

"The Enchanted Cottage." *The Education Screen*, June 1924.

"The Enchanted Cottage." *Film Daily*, April 11, 1924.

"The Enchanted Cottage." *The New York Times*, January 18, 1926.

"The Enchanted Cottage." *Photoplay Magazine*, May 1924.

Everitt, Anthony. *Augustus: The Life of Rome's First Emperor*. New York: Random House, 2007.

Eyman, Scott. *Empire of Dreams: The Epic Life of Cecil B. DeMille*. New York: Simon & Schuster, 2010.

"The Enchanted Cottage." *Deutsches Journal*, June 6, 1916, 4.

"The Enchanted Cottage." *The New York Times*, June 7, 1916, 0.

"The Enchanted Cottage." *Variety*, June 9, 1916, 29.

"The False Faces." *Moving Picture World*, February 22, 1919, 1026.

"The False Faces." *The New York Times*, February 17, 1919.

"The False Faces." *Wid's Film Daily*, February 27, 1919.

Farmer, Hugh David. *The Oxford Dictionary of Saints*, 4th edition. Oxford: Oxford University Press, 1997.

Foner, Phillip S. *The Complete Writings of Thomas Paine*, vol. 2. New York: Citadel Press, 1945.

"The Four Horsemen of the Apocalypse." *The New York Times*, March 7, 1921, 16.

"The Four Horsemen of the Apocalypse." *Variety*, February 18, 1921, 40.

"Four Sons." *Variety*, December 31, 1927.

Frieda, Leonie. *Catherine de Medici, Renaissance Queen of France*. London: Weidenfeld & Nicolson, 2003.

Fussell, Betty Harper. *Mabel: Hollywood's First I-Don't-Care Girl*. Lanham, MD: Limelight Editions, 1992.

Gallagher, Tag. *John Ford: The Man and His Films*. Berkeley: University of California Press, 1986.

Gandelman, Claude. "'Patri-arse': Revolution as Anality in the Scatological Caricatures of the Reformation and the French Revolution." *American Imago* 53, no. 1 (Spring 1996): 7–24.

Garthwaite, Ralph Gene. *The Persians*, 1st edition. Hoboken: Wiley-Blackwell, 2005.

Giroux, Robert. *A Deed of Death: The Story Behind the Unsolved Murder of Hollywood Director William Desmond Taylor*. New York: Alfred A. Knopf, 1990.

Glancy, H. Mark. "MGM Film Grosses, 1924–28: The Eddie Murphy Ledger."

Bibliography

Historical Journal of Film, Radio and Television 12, no. 2 (1992): 127–144.

Godley, Alfred D. *Herodotus: The Persian Wars Wars, Books 3–4*. Cambridge: Harvard University Press, 1921.

"The Great Victory: Wilson or the Kaiser? The Fall of the Hohenzollerns." *Motion Picture World*, January 4, 1919, 113.

Hall, Mordaunt. *"All Quiet on the Western Front." The New York Times*, April 30, 1930.

———. *"The Big Parade." The New York Times*, November 20, 1925.

———. *"The Patent Leather Kid." The New York Times*, August 16, 1927.

Hanley, Wayne. *The Genesis of Napoleonic Propaganda 1796–1799*. New York: Columbia University Press, 2005.

Harrison, Louis Reeves. "Johanna Enlists." *Moving Picture World*, September 14, 1918, 1610.

———. "Womanhood the Glory of the Nation." *Motion Picture World*, April 21, 1917.

"The Heart of Humanity." *The New York Times*, December 22, 1918.

"The Heart of Humanity." *The Ohio State Journal*, May 28, 1919.

"Hearts of the World." *The New York Times*, April 3, 1918.

"Hearts of the World." *Variety*, April 6, 1918.

Higashi, Sumiko. *Cecil B. DeMille and American Culture: The Silent Era*. Berkeley: University of California Press, 2004.

Higham, Charles. "Select List of Banned Films." In "Film Censorship: The Unnecessary Secrets." *The Bulletin*, November 20, 1965, 18.

Hill, Walter K. "The Prussian Cur." *Moving Picture World*, September 7, 1918, 1455.

Horn, John, and Alan Kramer. *Notes on German Atrocities, 1914: A History of Denial*. New Haven: Yale University Press, 2001.

"The Hun Within." *The New York Evening Telegram*, September 7, 1918.

"The Hun Within." *The New York Times*, August 20, 1918.

"The Hun Within." *The New York Times Tribune*, September 7, 1918.

"If My Country Should Call." *Moving Picture World*, October 7, 1916, 96.

Jewett, Garth S., and Victoria O'Donnell. *Propaganda and Persuasion*, 7th edition. Newbury Park, CA: Sage, 2018.

"Joan of Plattsburg." *Exhibitor's Herald*, May 18, 1918.

"Joan the Woman." *Motion Picture News*, January 6, 1917.

"Joan the Woman." *Moving Picture World*, January 13, 1917.

"Joan the Woman." *Variety*, December 29, 1916.

"Johanna Enlists." *Exhibitor's Herald and Motography*, October 15, 1918, 50.

"Johanna Enlists." *Los Angeles Times*, September 16, 1918.

"Johanna Enlists." *Variety*, September 1, 1918.

Johnson, Julian. "Panthea." *Photoplay*, April 1917.

Jules-Verne, Jean. *Jules Verne: A Biography*. Translated by Roger Greaves. London: MacDonald and Jane, 1976.

"The Kaiser, the Beast of Berlin." *Moving Picture World*, March 23, 1918.

"The Kaiser, the Beast of Berlin." *Photoplay*, June 1918.

Kelley, Bruce C., and Mark A. Snell. *Bugle Resounding: Music and Musicians of the Civil War Era*. Columbia: University of Missouri Press, 2004.

Kingsley, Grace. "The Prussian Cur." *Los Angeles Times*, September 1, 1918.

Langer, William L. "The Blunders of Imperial Diplomacy." In *The Diplomacy of Imperialism 1890–1902*. New York: Knopf, 1950.

Langman, Larry. *American Film Cycles: The Silent Era*. Westport, CT: Greenwood, 1998.

Lazenby, John F. *The Defence of Greece 490–479 BC*. Liverpool: Liverpool University Press, 1993.

Lennig, Arthur. *Stroheim*. Lexington: University Press of Kentucky, 2000.

"Lest We Forget." *Moving Picture World*, January 19, 1918.

"Lest We Forget." *The New York Times*, January 28, 1918.

"Lest We Forget." *Variety*, February 2, 1918.

Lipkes, Jeff. *Rehearsals: The German*

Bibliography

Army in Belgium, August, 1914. Leuven: Leuven University Press, 2007.

"The Little American." *Variety*, March 15, 1918.

"The Lost Battalion." *The New York Times*, July 2, 1918.

Louvish, Simon. *Cecil B. DeMille: A Life in Art.* New York: Thomas Dunne, 2007.

Markowitz, Claude. *A History of Modern India 1480–1959.* Anthem South Asian Studies. London: Anthem Press, 2004.

Massie, Robert K. *Dreadnought: Britain, Germany, and the Coming of the Great War.* New York: Random House, 1991.

Mastrangelo, Lisa. "World War I, Public Intellectuals and the Four Minute Men: Convergent Ideals of Public Speaking and Civic Participation." *Rhetoric and Public Affairs* 12, no. 4 (2009): 607–633.

McBride, Joseph. *Searching for John Ford.* New York: St. Martin's Press, 2003.

"Me und Gott." *Motion Picture News*, September 7, 1918, 1463.

Menefee, David W. *Richard Barthelmess: A Life in Pictures.* Albany, GA: BearManor Media, 2009.

Mikies, David. "Hollywood's Creepy Love Affair with Adolph Hitler, in Explosive New Detail." *Tablet*, June 10, 2013.

Millichap, Joseph R. *Lewis Milestone.* Boston: Twayne, 1981.

Mitchell, Charles Reed. "New Message to America: James W. Gerard's 'Beware' and World War I Propaganda." *Journal of Popular Film* 4, no. 5 (1975): 275–295.

Miyao, Dausuke. *Sessue Hayakawa: Silent Cinema and Transnational Stardom.* Durham: Duke University Press, 2007.

Muller, Jan-Dirk. *Spielregeln für den Untergang: Die Welt des Nibelungenliedes.* Tübingen: Niemeyer, 1998.

"My Four Years in Germany." *Motion Picture News*, March 23, 1918.

"My Four Years in Germany." *The New York Times*, March 11, 1918.

"My Four Years in Germany." *Photoplay*, June 1918.

"My Four Years in Germany." *Variety*, March 15, 1918.

"Old Heidelberg." *Variety*, October 8, 1915.

Orlean, Susan. *Rin Tin Tin: The Life and the Legend.* New York: Simon & Schuster, 2011.

"Our Colored Fighters." *The Cleveland Advocate* 5, no. 31 (December 7, 1918): 3.

Panayi, Panikos. "Forgotten Prisoners of the Great War." *History Today* 62, no. 11 (2012).

"The Patent Leather Kid." *Variety*, August 17, 1927.

"Pershing's Crusaders." *The Milwaukee Journal*, May 24, 1918.

"Pershing's Crusaders." *Variety*, May 31, 1918.

"The Prussian Cur." *Exhibitor's Herald and Motography*, October 15, 1918, 50.

Quinlan, David. *The Illustrated Guide to Film Directors.* Lanham, MD: Limelight Editions, 1992.

Quirk, Robert E. *An Affair of Honor: Woodrow Wilson and the Occupation of Veracruz.* New York: W.W. Norton, 1967.

Rhoden, W. Jack. "French Caricatures of the Franco-Prussian War and Commune of the British Library." *FSL Annual Review* 6 (2009–2010): 22–24.

"The Road Through the Dark." *Variety*, December 20, 1918.

Rohl, John C.G. *Young Wilhelm: The Kaiser's Early Life, 1859–1888.* Cambridge: Cambridge University Press, 1998.

Rosenthal, H., and J. Warrack. "Farrar, Geraldine." In *The Concise Oxford Dictionary of Opera*, 2nd edition. Oxford: Oxford University Press, 1977.

Sandburg, Carl. "The Big Parade." *Chicago Daily News*, December 29, 1925.

Schallert, Edward. "The Four Horsemen of the Apocalypse." *Los Angeles Times*, March 10, 1923, III–4.

Schenck, Earl. *Come Unto These Yellow Sands.* Indianapolis: Bobbs-Merrill, 1940.

Schleh, Eugene P. "*All Quiet on the Western Front*: A History Teacher's Reappraisal." *Film & History* 8, no. 4 (1978): 66–69.

Schreckenberger, Max. "Die Wacht am Rhein." In *Germany, The Netherlands,*

Bibliography

and Switzerland—The World's Story (Volume 7): A History of the World in Story, Song and Art, edited by Eva March Tappan. Boston: Houghton Mifflin, 1914.

"The Secret Game." Exhibitor's Herald, December 16, 1917, 28.

"The Secret Game." Moving Picture World, December 15, 1917, 1642.

"She Goes to War." Detroit Free Press, June 8, 1929.

"She Goes to War." Motion Picture Magazine, July 1929.

Sherwood, Robert E. "The Big Parade." Life, December 1925.

_____. "The Four Horsemen of the Apocalypse." Life, March 24, 1921.

Shirley, Wayne D. "A Bugle Call to Arms for the National Defense! Victor Herbert and His Score for Fall of a Nation." Quarterly Journal of the Library of Congress XL (1983): 26–27.

"Shootin' for Love." Moving Picture World, July 1923.

"Shoulder Arms." The New York Times, October 21, 1918.

"Shoulder Arms." Variety, October 21, 1918.

Silverman, David. This Land Is Their Land. New York: Bloomsbury, 2019.

Slavicek, Louise Chipley. The Treaty of Versailles. Milestones in Modern World History. Broomall, PA: Chelsea House, 2010.

Slide, Anthony. Early American Cinema. Lanham, MD: Scarecrow Press, 1994.

_____. The Encyclopedia of Vaudeville. Jackson: University Press of Mississippi, 2012.

Smith, Frederic James. "Behind the Door." Motion Picture Classic, January 1920.

"The South African Concentration Camps." Manchester Guardian, June 19, 1901, 1.

Taves, Brian. Thomas Ince: Hollywood's Independent Pioneer. Lexington: University Press of Kentucky, 2012.

Terry, Virginia. "The Unpardonable Sin." The New York Tribune, August 3, 1919.

Thirer, Irene. "All Quiet on the Western Front." New York Daily News, April 30, 1930.

"Til I Come Back to You." Exhibitor's Herald, September 14, 1918, 33.

"Til I Come Back to You." The New York Times, August 26, 1918.

"To Hell With the Kaiser." The New York Times, July 1, 1918.

"To Hell With the Kaiser." Variety, July 5, 1918.

"The Unbeliever." The New York Times, February 12, 1918.

"The Unbeliever." Variety, February 15, 1918.

"Under Four Flags." The New York Times, November 18, 1918.

"The Unpardonable Sin." The New York Times, March 3, 1919.

Viereck, George Sylvester. "The Battle Cry of Peace." The Fatherland, June 24, 1916, 20.

_____. "The Fall of a Nation." The Fatherland, June 24, 1916, 20.

Von der Goltz, Horst. My Adventures as a German Secret Service Agent. Uckfield, UK: Naval and Military Press, 2014.

Wallis, Michael. The Real Wild West: The 101 Ranch and the Creation of the American West. New York: Macmillan, 2000.

"War Brides." Moving Picture World, December 21, 1916.

"War Brides." The New York Times, November 13, 1916, 0.

Ward, Larry Wayne. The Motion Picture Goes to War: The U.S. Government Film Effort During World War I. Ann Arbor: UMI Research Press, 1981.

Warnack, Henry Christeen. "Civilization." Los Angeles Times, April 18, 1916.

Watts, Steven. The People's Tycoon: Henry Ford on the American New Century. New York: Alfred A. Knopf, 2005.

Weitzel, Edward. "Kaiser's Finish." Moving Picture World, October 19, 1918.

_____. "The Road Through the Dark." Moving Picture World, December 21, 1918.

Whitfield, Eileen. Pickford: The Woman Who Made Hollywood. Lexington: University Press of Kentucky, 1997.

Wollstein, Hans J. Strangers in Hollywood: The History of Scandinavian Actors in American Films. Lanham, MD: Scarecrow Press, 1994.

Bibliography

"Womanhood the Glory of the Nation." *The New York Times*, April 2, 1917.

"Womanhood the Glory of the Nation." *New York Dramatic Mirror*, April 7, 1917.

"Womanhood the Glory of the Nation." *Variety*, April 6, 1917.

Woodward, Kenneth J. *Making Saints*. New York: Simon & Schuster, 1996.

"Yankee Doodle in Berlin." *Moving Picture World*, July 4, 1919.

"Yankee Doodle in Berlin." *Watertown Daily News Times*, February 15, 1920.

Film Reviews: Newspapers, Magazines, Journals

"All Quiet on the Western Front." Review. *Variety*, May 7, 1930.

"An Altogether Exceptional, Extraordinary Picture." Review of *The Cross Bearer*. *Hattiesburg American*, April 5, 1918, 7.

"America Is Invaded Again in the Films." Review of *The Fall of a Nation*. *The New York Times*, June 7, 1916, 0.

"America's Answer Stirs War Spirit." Review of *America's Answer to the Hun*. *The New York Times*, July 30, 1918.

"As a Big Picture, It Is the Poorest One from Every Angle That Has Ever Been Turned Out Over Here." Review of *Lest We Forget*. *Variety*, February 2, 1918.

"Astounding, Laugh-producing, Breathtaking Comedy!" Review of *Yankee Doodle in Berlin*. *Watertown Daily News Times*, February 5, 1920.

"Barbed Wire." Review of *Barbed Wire*. *Motion Picture*, November 1927.

"Barbed Wire." Review of *Barbed Wire*. *Screenland*, November 1927.

Blaisdell, George. "Cecil B. DeMille Belongs in the Front Rank of the Day." Review of *Joan the Woman*. *Moving Picture World*, January 13, 1917.

"Chaplin as Soldier Drops Old Disguises." Review of *Shoulder Arms*. *The New York Times*, October 21, 1918.

"Civilization Is Ince Masterpiece: Picturing Christ." Review of *Civilization*. *La Crosse Tribune*, October 21, 1916.

"The Claws of the Hun." Review of *The Claws of the Hun*. *The New York Times*, July 1, 1918.

"Does Anybody in Pictures Give Us Better, Sweeter, More Wholesome and Natural Comedy Than Mary Pickford." Review of *Johanna Enlists*. *Los Angeles Times*, September 16, 1918.

"An Eloquent Statement of This Country's Reason for Entering the War." Review of *Lest We Forget*. *The New York Times*, January 28, 1918.

"The Enchanted Cottage." Review of *The Enchanted Cottage*. *The Education Screen*, June 1924.

"The Enchanted Cottage." Review of *The Enchanted Cottage*. *Film Daily*, April 11, 1924.

"The Enchanted Cottage." Review of *The Enchanted Cottage*. *The New York Times*, January 1926.

"The Enchanted Cottage." Review of *The Enchanted Cottage*. *Photoplay Magazine*, May 1924.

"The Entire Production Stands Apart from the Eagles Screaming Variety of War Films, Which Are Only Too Common in These Martial Times." Review of *My Four Years in Germany*. *Photoplay*, June 1918.

"Erich Oswald Hans Maria Von Stroheim in Archduke Karl's Regiment Makes His Most Recent Appearance on the Screen in the Heart of Humanity." Review of *The Heart of Humanity*. *The Ohio State Journal*, May 28, 1919.

"The False Faces." Review of *The False Faces*. *Moving Picture World*, February 22, 1919, 1026.

"The False Faces." Review of *The False Faces*. *The New York Times*, February 17, 1919.

"The False Faces." Review of *The False Faces*. *Wid's Film Daily*, February 27, 1919.

"Feeble War Film Shown, Womanhood the Glory of the Nation Is a Plea for Preparedness." Review of *Womanhood, the Glory of the Nation*. *The New York Times*, April 2, 1917.

"The Film as a Whole Is an Achievement Worthy of Respect." Review of *Civilization*. *Deutsches Journal*, June 13, 1916, 4.

Bibliography

"The Film Caricatures German Invaders and Immigrant Traitors." Review of *The Fall of a Nation. Variety*, June 9, 1916, 23.

"The Film Is Harmless in This Realm Compared to What Has Been Achieved by Others." Review of *Civilization. New Yorker Staats-Zeitung*, August 1916, 4.

"A Film Is Now Exhibited Under the Title of 'Civilization.'" Review of *Civilization. The Fatherland*, June 24, 1916, 4.

"For Barthelmess, Perfect." Review of *The Patent Leather Kid. Variety*, August 17, 1927.

"Four Horsemen of the Apocalypse." Review of *The Four Horsemen of the Apocalypse. Variety*, February 18, 1921, 40.

"Fully Dramatic Enough to Make the Ten Reels Pass Tirelessly." Review of *My Four Years in Germany. Motion Picture News*, March 23, 1918.

"Gerard Sees His Film, Makes a Speech at Presentation of 'My Four Years in Germany.'" Review of *My Four Years in Germany. The New York Times*, March 11, 1918.

"German Cruelty Is Driven Home by Erich Von Stroheim in the Role of a Lieutenant of the Prussians." Review of *The Unbeliever. Variety*, February 15, 1918.

"A Good Exhibitor's Prospect." Review of *The Great Victory, Wilson or the Kaiser? The Fall of the Hohenzollerns. Moving Picture World*, January 4, 1919, 113.

Hall, Mordaunt. "A Blind Hero." Review of *The Dark Angel. The New York Times*, October 12, 1925.

——. "Mr. Barthelmess at His Best." Review of *The Patent Leather Kid. The New York Times*, August 16, 1927.

——. "Young Germany in the War." Review of *All Quiet on the Western Front. The New York Times*, April 30, 1930.

Harrison, Louis Reeves. "Johanna Enlists." Review of *Johanna Enlists. Moving Picture World*, September 14, 1918, 1610.

——. "'Womanhood' is in every respect a finer example of artistry than 'The Battle Cry of Peace.'" Review of *Womanhood the Glory of the Nation. Moving Picture World*, April 21, 1917.

Hill, Walter K. "Another Picture Created to Foment the Proper Determination in the Hearts of the Allies to 'Treat 'Em Rough.'" Review of *The Prussian Cur. Moving Picture World*, September 7, 1918, 1455.

"In 'Hearts of the World' D. W. Griffith Makes His Principal Love Story a Fleshless Skeleton on Which to Hang a Large Number of Brilliant War Scenes, in an Effort to Show the Horrors of War at Close Range." Review of *Hearts of the World. Variety*, April 6, 1918.

"In Shoulder Arms Chaplin Is a Doughboy. At the Finish He Captures the Kaiser, the Crown Prince and Hindenburg." Review of *Shoulder Arms. Variety*, October 21, 1918.

"In This Story the Representatives of the Two Countries Are Not at Odds, They Are Working Hand-in-hand Against a Common Enemy ... Germany." Review of *The Secret Game. Moving Picture World*, December 15, 1917, 1642.

"It Is a Story of the Conflict in Europe Under the German Reign of Terror." Review of *Till I Come Back to You. Exhibitor's Herald*, September 14, 1918, 33.

"It Is Impossible to Describe in Detail What Producer DeMille Accomplished with Such a Wealth of Material." Review of *Joan the Woman. Variety*, December 29, 1916.

"It's a Film That Will Come in for Nationwide Discussion." Review of *The Battle Cry of Peace. Variety*, August 13, 1915.

"It's a Pickford. 'Nuff Said." Review of *The Little American. Variety*, July 6, 1917, 8.

"It's Once Again the Dreadful 'Hyphens' who are cast as the villains." Review of *The Fall of a Nation. Deutsches Journal*, June 6, 1916, 4.

"Joan of Plattsburg, Mabel Norman Picture, Opens." Review of *Joan of Plattsburg. Exhibitor's Herald*, May 18, 1918.

"'Johanna Enlists' Is an Attractive,

Bibliography

Refreshing and Original a Picture as One Would Care to See." Review of *Johanna Enlists. Variety*, September 1, 1918.

Johnson, Julian. "One of the Best Screenplays in Screen History." Review of *Panthea. Photoplay*, April 1917.

"The Kaiser Is Less a Photoplay than a Dramatic Presentation of the Crimes of Germany Dominated by the Satanic Sneer of Her Leader." Review of *The Kaiser, the Beast of Berlin. Photoplay*, June 1918.

Kingsley, Grace. "An Absorbing Story Thread That Runs Throughout." Review of *The Prussian Cur. Los Angeles Times*, September 1, 1918.

"Large Audience Is Thrilled by Ince Spectacle." Review of *Civilization. Fairbanks Daily News*, September 16, 1916.

"Latest Kaiser Film Is a Farce." Review of *To Hell with the Kaiser. The New York Times*, July 1, 1918.

"A Laugh Riot, with Many of the Resident Keystone Comics as Slapstick Huns." Review of *Yankee Doodle in Berlin. Moving Picture World*, July 4, 1919.

"Lost Battalion on Screen. Gen. Alexander Sees First Showing of Film of Argonne Defense." Review of *The Lost Battalion. The New York Times*, July 2, 1919, 0.

"The Main Interest of the Producers, and They Have Adhered to It Admirably, Was to Give the Server a Look at the Private and Public Life of This Human Monster." Review of *The Kaiser, the Beast of Berlin. Moving Picture World*, March 23, 1918.

"Me Und Gott." Review of *Me Und Gott. Motion Picture News*, September 7, 1918, 1463.

Milne, Peter. "'Joan the Woman' is a triumph for Geraldine Farrar but ... equally for Cecil B. DeMille." Review of *Joan the Woman. Motion Picture News*, January 6, 1917.

"'My Four Years in Germany' Purports to Depict Events in Berlin." Review of *My Four Years in Germany. Variety*, March 15, 1918.

"Nazimova in Film Of War Brides Play, Makes First Appearance as Movie Star." Review of *War Brides. The New York Times*, November 13, 1916. 0.

"New York Shelled on Movie Screen." Review of *The Battle Cry of Peace. The New York Times*, August 7, 1915.

"Official Film Tells How War Was Won." Review of *Under Four Flags*. November 18, 1918.

"One Paramount Special That Is Special." Review of *Behind the Door. Exhibitor's Herald*, December 14, 1919.

"Our Colored Fighters." Review of *Our Colored Fighters. The Cleveland Advocate* 5, no. 31 (December 7, 1918): 3.

"Pershing's Crusaders." Review of *Pershing's Crusaders. The Milwaukee Journal*, May 24, 1918.

"Pershing's Crusaders." Review of *Pershing's Crusaders. Variety*, May 31, 1918.

"The Production Is Magnificent in the Amazing Effectiveness of Its Fine Realism and in Its Utter Simplicity." Review of *Four Sons. Variety*, December 31, 1927.

"The Prussian Cur." Review of *The Prussian Cur. Exhibitor's Herald and Motography*, October 15, 1918, 50.

"Reaches a Tragic Height Never Before Attained by a Motion Picture." Review of *War Brides. Moving Picture World*, December 21, 1916.

"The Road Through the Dark." Review of *The Road Through the Dark. Variety*, December 20, 1918.

Sandburg, Carl. "And Oh! It's Something to Talk About." Review of *The Big Parade. Chicago Daily News*, December 29, 1925.

Schaller, Edward. "Reviews." Review of *The Four Horsemen of the Apocalypse. Los Angeles Times*, March 10, 1921, III–4.

"The Screen: The Heart of Humanity a Distinct Achievement of Motion Picture Creation." Review of *The Heart of Humanity. The New York Times*, December 22, 1918.

"The Screen: A Superlative War Picture." Review of *The Big Parade. The New York Times*, November 20, 1925, 0.

"The Screen: Review of *The Four

Bibliography

Horsemen of the Apocalypse." *The New York Times*, March 7, 1921, 0.

"'The Secret Game' Is a War Play That Shows No Fighting and One That Holds the Attention of Spectators from Beginning to End." Review of *The Secret Game*. *Moving Picture World* 5, no. 28 (December 16, 1917).

"A Sensational Photoplay, by Far the Most Tremendous Film." Review of *The Battle Cry of Peace*. *Deutsches Journal*, September 12, 1915, Section 3, 3.

"Several Scenes Depict Prussian Brutality in Realistically Ugly Form." Review of *The Unbeliever*. *The New York Times*, February 12, 1918.

Sherwood, Robert E. "The Big Parade." Review of *The Big Parade*. *Life*, December 1925.

——. "The Four Horsemen of the Apocalypse." Review of *The Four Horsemen of the Apocalypse*. *Life*, March 24, 1921.

Smith, Frederic James. "Hobart Bosworth Is Decidedly Strong in This Role." Review of *Behind the Door*. *Motion Picture Classic*, January 1920.

Terry, Virginia. "The Unpardonable Sin." Review of *The Unpardonable Sin*. *The New York Tribune*, August 3, 1919.

"There Are Few Directors in This Country Who Have DeMille's Ability to Make Pictures." Review of *Till I Come Back to You*. *The New York Times*, August 26, 1918.

Thirer, Irene. "Raging War and Soldier's Struggle Back Home in 'All Quiet on the Western Front.'" Review of *All Quiet on the Western Front*. *New York Daily News*, April 30, 1930.

"This Is a He-picture, No Pap for Puking Infants." Review of *Behind the Door*. *Photoplay*, March 20, 1920.

"This Rather Harrows the Feelings at Times." Review of *If My Country Should Call*. *Moving Picture World*, October 7, 1916, 96.

"The Unpardonable Sin." Review of *The Unpardonable Sin*. *The New York Times*, March 3, 1919.

"An Uplifting Story of Courage and Faith in the Face of a Ruthless Enemy." Review of *The Cross Bearer*. *Michigan Film Review*, April 1918.

"Valiant Doughboys Battling Menacing Huns." Review of *She Goes to War*. *Detroit Free Press*, June 8, 1929.

Viereck, George Sylvester. "An Abortion Whose One Purpose Is to Traduce the German Race and Make the German People Appear as Enemies of the United States." Review of *The Fall of a Nation*. *The Fatherland* 4, no. 20 (June 24, 1916).

——. "Atrocity bankrolled by a 'secret British propaganda fund.'" Review of *The Battle Cry of Peace*. *The Fatherland* 4, no. 20 (June 24, 1916).

"Vitagraph in 'Womanhood' Has Overshot the Mark and Overplayed the Game." Review of *Womanhood the Glory of the Nation*. *Variety*, April 6, 1917.

"The War Scenes Showing Soldiers Advancing in Tanks Through Liquid Fire Are About the Most Exciting Thing Ever Seen on the Screen." Review of *She Goes to War*. *Motion Picture Magazine*, July 1929.

"War Vividly Seen in Griffith Film. Hearts of the World Also Tells a Story That Quickly Stirs The Emotions. It Begins Before The Conflict. Germans Advance with Fury Upon A French Village Harboring a Romance of Boy and Girl." Review of *Hearts of the World*. *The New York Times*, April 5, 1918.

Warnack, Henry Christeen. "Drama: Not Daring, Violates Good Taste. Artistic Touch Is Absent from Story of War Picture." Review of *Civilization*. *Los Angeles Times*, April 18, 1916.

Weitzel, Edward. "Kaiser's Finish." Review of *Kaiser's Finish*. *Moving Picture World*, October 19, 1918.

——. "The Road Through the Dark." Review of *The Road Through the Dark*. *Moving Picture World*, December 21, 1918.

"Whoever Is Directly Responsible for the Casting Is a Positive Genius for Selecting 'Types.'" Review of *Old Heidelberg*. *Variety*, October 8, 1915.

"With Many Thrilling Scenes." Review of

Bibliography

Lest We Forget. Moving Picture World, January 19, 1918.

"'Womanhood the Glory of the Nation,' Greater Vitagraph's militant film spectacle." Review of *Womanhood the Glory of the Nation. New York Dramatic Mirror*, April 7, 1917.

"A Wonderful Mix of Comedy and Drama." Review of *Shootin' for Love. Moving Picture World*, July 1923.

"A Wonderfully Effective Propaganda Picture." Review of *To Hell with the Kaiser. Variety*, July 5, 1918.

Index

Abbott, George 145
Academy Film Archives 151, 154, 184
Across the Pacific 20
Adamson, Barry 156
Adoree, Rene 130, 133, 180
Aeschylus 7
AFI Silver Theatre and Cultural Center 142, 152, 153
Albert, King of the Belgians 57, 59, 78
Alexander, Ben 65, 67, 142
Alexander, Maj. Gen. Robert 113, 114
All Quiet on the Western Front 2, 5, 142, 144, 145, 158, 159, 182
Alpha Video Studio 152, 153, 154, 155, 156, 158
Amazon 158
The American 40
American Cinema Commission 99
American Civil War 9
The American Expeditionary Forces 53, 124, 175
The American Film Institute 151
The American Indian Gets Into the War 97
The American Revolution 8
American Society of Cinematographers 106
American Symphony Orchestra 157
America's Answer 15, 100, 101, 154
Anderson, Maxwell 145
Anglo-Boer War 9, 10
Apple TV 157
Arbuckle, Fatty 88, 174
Argonne Forest 114, 115
Arlen, Richard 135
Arms and the Girl 51
Army and Navy Sports 46
Artcraft Pictures 49, 50
Astra Films 63
The Atlantic Magazine 149, 183
Attila, King of the Huns 55
The Aviator Spy 20
The Aviator Traitor 20
Axt, William 156
Ayres, Lew 142, 144, 145, 152

The Bad Buck of Santa Ynez 20
Baker, Sec. of War Newton D. 44, 100
Bambrick, Gertrude 110
Banky, Vilma 127, 128, 129
Bara, Theda 107
Barbed Wire 137, 157
Barbican Theatre 153
Barthelmess, Richard 3, 4, 16, 28, 124, 126, 127, 135, 136, 137, 165, 171, 181
Bartlett, Trevor 157
Baruch, Bernard 85
Basevi, James 133
Bates, Blanche 42
The Battle Cry of Peace 11, 12, 21, 22, 36, 150, 151
Battle of Messines 128
Battle of Saint-Mihiel 103
Baynes, Capt. George 95
Beaton, Kenneth 103
Behind the Door 116, 117, 147, 155
Belgian Cinémathèque 157
Belgium, in war films 56, 57, 59, 69, 77, 78, 79, 82, 108, 109, 110
Belleau Wood 131, 132, 133
Beery, Wallace 109, 116, 119, 146
Behistun Inscription 7
Bernstorff, Count Johann von 26, 85, 164
Best, Jonny 157
BFI Film & Television 154
Biddle, Maj. Nicholas 100
The Big Parade 2, 5, 130, 133, 134, 135, 156, 180, 184
Bild 184
Biograph 19, 149
The Birth of a Nation 1, 26, 108, 110, 122, 184
Black Tom Island-espionage plot 27, 164
Blackton, J. Stuart 19, 22, 35, 162
Blaisdell, George 34
Blasco-Ibanez, Vincente 121
Blind Husbands 116
Blue, Monte 87
Blue Sky DVD 156
Boardman, Eleanor 140, 141, 146
The Bond 90

195

Index

Bond, Fred 85
Borderlands Film Festival 155
Bosworth, Hobart 31, 116, 117, 130, 146, 147
Bow, Clara 16, 135
The Boxer Rebellion 55, 169
Brandeis, Justice Louis 43
Brady, William A. 47
Brand, Neil 157
Brenon, Herbert 29, 30
Brewster's Millions 50
British Film Institute 154, 155, 157
British War Office Cinematograph Committee 65
Broekmann, David 145
Broken Blossoms 112, 120
Brook, Clive 137, 138
Browne, Bothwell 2, 112
Brownlee, Frank 85
Brulier, Nigel de 32, 76, 84, 85, 119, 122
Bryan, William Jennings 26
The Bureau of War Expositions 46
Byrne, Robert 155

Caesar, Gaius Augustus 7, 8
Caine, Hall 138
Camille 123
Campbell, Douglas 100
Capitolfest Film Festival 153, 184
Castle, Irene 52, 169
Cavell, Edith 106
Cecil B. DeMille Archives 153
Chaplin, Charles 1, 2, 10, 12, 20, 48, 79, 80, 88, 89, 90, 107, 147, 174, 182
Chaplin, Sidney 89, 153
Château-Thierry, Battle of 15, 100, 103, 175
Chautauqua Silent Film Series 159
The Cheat 23, 53, 163
Cheney, Lon 15, 27, 28, 76, 108, 109, 115
Cher Ami 113, 178
Chicago Daily News 134, 180
Chicago Film Society 157
Chicago Herald 44
Chicago Tribune 23
Children in Bondage 43
Chinn, Private Henry 114
Cinderella 50
Ciné Lumière Festival 153
The Cinemateket Svenska Film Institutet 150
Cinémathèque Française 149, 152, 153, 183
Cinémathèque Royal de Belgique 154
Civilization 11, 24, 25, 26, 51, 83, 107, 108, 127, 163
Clara Kimball Young Corporation 93
Clark, Marguerite 79, 88, 173
Claws of the Hun 14, 83, 84, 152
Cleveland Advocate 103, 176

Cochrane, Robert H. 111
Cohen Media Group 153
Colman, Ronald 127, 128, 146
Columbus Evening Dispatch 102
Commission on Training & Camp Activities 99, 174
Committee on Public Information 1, 39, 44, 46, 47, 48, 56, 76, 86, 94, 95, 96, 97, 98, 99, 100, 101, 102, 103, 104, 176, 177
Congdon, Christopher 157
Connelly, Bobby 35, 92, 94, 109, 177
The Conquering Power 123
Cooper, Miriam 85, 86
Cops 123
Cosmopolitan 41
Courtot, Marguerite 63, 64
The Coward 83
Coward, Noël 66
Creel, George 1, 39, 40, 41, 42, 43, 44, 47, 76, 98, 100, 101, 102, 167, 176
The Cross Bearer 12, 56, 153
The Crowd 141
Crowley, Adrian 156
Cullen, Capt. William J. 113
Cunard, Grace 20
Cusack, Thomas 45

Daddy Long Legs 112
The Daily Mail 90
Dane, Karl 74, 81, 130, 134
Daniels, Sec. of the Navy Josephus 44
The Dark Angel 127, 128, 130, 156
A Daughter of Uncle Sam 72
DAV–Disabled Veterans of the World War 126, 179
Davis, Carl 156, 184
Dawson Film Find 150, 155, 184
Dean, Louis 74, 91
The Deeds of the Divine Augustus 8
DeGrasse, Joe 28
The Delicious Little Devil 112
DeMille, Cecil B. 6, 12, 13, 31, 47, 49, 50, 57, 58, 71, 116, 151, 153, 163, 166, 168, 169, 170
Demille, William 52, 53, 38, 169
Dempsey, Jack 136, 180, 181
The Denver Post 40
Department of the National Archives, Still Holdings 154
Detroit Free Press 141, 177, 181
Deutsches Journal 23, 26, 27, 163, 164
The Division of Advertising 45
The Division of Civic and Education Cooperation 45
The Division of Films 46, 94, 95, 96, 97, 98, 99, 174
The Division of News 44
The Division of Pictorial Publicity 44

Index

The Division of the Four Minute Men 46
The Division of War Expositions 46
The Division of Work with the Foreign Born 46
Dixon, Bryony 155
Dixon, Thomas E., Jr. 26, 164
Dixon Studios 26, 150
Doing Their Bit 51, 81
Donahue, Robert 96
Douane, Maj. John H. 100
Downing Film Company 102
The Dragon Painter 116
Duell, Charles 126
Durborough, Lt. W.H. 96, 174
Dwan, Allen 62

Eagels, Jeanne 56, 57
The Eagle's Eye 72
Ebony Films 97, 174
Edison, Thomas Alva 19, 43
Edison Company 149, 153
Education Film Corporation of America 81
The Educational Screen 127, 179
Elliot, Chris 157
Ellis Island 61
Emcee Film Library 154
Emerson, John 62, 63
The Enchanted College 5, 6, 16, 124, 126, 156
England's Menace 20
Espionage Act of 1917 47, 167
Evening Journal 40
Evening World 40
Exhibitor's Herald 53, 58, 59, 78, 79, 81, 86, 87, 117, 169, 170, 172, 173, 178
Exhibitor's Trade Review 96
The Exquisite Little Thief 111

Fairbanks, Douglas 12, 48, 62, 63, 79, 88, 107, 173
The Fairbanks Daily Times 25, 123, 163
The Fall of a Nation 26, 150, 164
The Fall of France 20
The False Faces 15, 108, 155
Famous Battles of Napoleon 20
Famous Lasky Players 50, 57, 67, 87, 137
Farnum, William 88, 173
Farrar, Geraldine 31, 166
The Fatherland 23, 25, 27, 162
Faulwell, Marvin 156
Favorite Son 83
Federal Art Project 147, 185
Feeding an Army 96
Feeding the Fighter 14, 96
Ferguson, Helen 106, 147
The Film Detective Studio 154
The First Thanksgiving 8
Fisher, George 25

Fit to Fight 97
Fitzmaurice, George 63, 127, 128
Flicker Alley 155
Fonda, Henry 146
Foolish Wives 123
For France 63
For Liberty 51
Ford, Guy Stanton 45
Ford, Henry 26, 164
Ford, John 139, 181
Ford Peace Ship 164
Foreign Film Service 99
The Foreign Language Newspaper Division 45
The Foreign Press Bureau 45, 46
Fosdick, Raymond B. 99
Four Horsemen Exhibition Corporation 121
The Four Horsemen of the Apocalypse 2, 5, 16, 118, 121, 147, 155, 156
Four Sons 16, 139, 157, 158
Fox Film Corporation 85, 139, 152
France, in war films 9, 11, 20, 63, 64, 65, 82, 120, 121
Franco-Prussian War 9, 20
francs tireurs 55
Frankfurter-Allgemeine Zeitung 184
French Revolution 8
Frohman, Charles 73, 74
From Hand to Mouth 117
Fun Factory 112
Funkhouser, Maj. Metallus Lucillus 76

Garbo, Greta 144
Garde Civique 55
Gaudio, Eugene 107, 177
The Geezer of Berlin 84
The George Eastman House International Museum 149, 150, 152, 153, 154, 155, 157
Gerard, Ambassador James W. 14, 74, 75, 76, 85, 152
German Americans, perceptions of in war films 14, 49, 67, 69, 84, 116, 171
German atrocities, World War I 20, 55, 56
German espionage in the United States-First World War 21, 27
The German Side of the War 23
Germany in war films 11, 23, 26, 28, 29, 48, 49, 51, 52, 64, 65, 74, 75, 77, 78, 82, 84, 85, 90, 91, 92, 106, 112, 119, 120, 131, 138, 139, 140, 142, 143, 144
Germonprez, Valerie 64, 68, 69, 170
Gerson, Harry 109, 110
Gettins, Wyndham 84
The Ghost Busters 50
Gibson, Charles Dana 44
Gibson, Hoot 123, 124
Gilbert, John 130, 132, 133, 134, 146, 180, 182

197

Index

Ginoris, Marie 96
A Girl's a Man for N' That and A' That 97
Gish, Dorothy 65, 66, 67, 68
Gish, Lillian 4, 65, 66, 67, 110, 147, 171
Glennon, Bert 157
Goebbels, Joseph 146
Goldman, Emma 41
Goldstein, Bruce 159
Goldstein, Robert 168
Goltz, Capt. von der Horst 85, 86, 152, 173
Goldwyn, Samuel 129
Goldwyn Pictures Corporation 79, 80, 81
Google Play 158
Gosfilmofond Russian State Archives 155
Gottschalk, Louis F. 121
Grant, Lawrence 81, 82, 146
Granville, Fred LeRoy 107
Grape Vine Video 152, 154, 157
Die Grazer Handelsakadamie 60
The Great Depression 142
The Great Victory, or Wilson or the Kaiser? The Fall of the Hollenzollerns 105, 106, 146, 154, 155, 177
Great War 1, 104, 118, 120
Griffith, Corinne 88, 173
Griffith, D.W. 1, 6, 12, 13, 47, 65, 70, 71, 107, 110, 149, 171
Griffith, Lt. Edward H. 97
Griffith, Raymond 143, 145, 146
The Guardian 184
Gymnasium 61

Haghe Film Digitaal 151
Hale, Alan 118, 122
Hall, Mordaunt 127, 136, 145, 179, 180, 182
Hammond, Dr. Michael 157
Handschiegel color process 34, 166
Hanson, Einar 137, 138
Happiness 132
Harlem Hellfighters ("Hollenkamp") 103, 176
Harper's Weekly 42
Harrison, Louis Reeves 38, 39, 88
Hart, Charles S. 46, 95, 96, 97, 174
Hart, William S. 12, 20, 48, 88, 173, 175
Hatrick, E.B. 47
The Hattisburg American 57, 88, 170
Hayakawa, Sessue 12, 20, 23, 48, 50, 52, 53, 116, 147, 163, 169, 173, 183
Hearst, William Randolph 10, 21, 23, 26, 27, 40, 41, 52
Hearst Pathé Newsreel Company 99, 175
The Heart of Humanity 5, 69, 70, 107, 140, 154
Hearts Adrift 20, 50
Hearts of the World 5, 13, 65, 69, 70, 122, 153, 154
Her Country's Call 51

Herbert, Holmes 126, 150, 164
Herbert, Victor 26, 164
His Hour 122
His Only Son 124
His Prehistoric Past 20
The History of the World's Greatest War 10, 21
Hitler, Adolf 146
Hoagland, H.C. 96, 97, 175
Hofberg Palace 60
Hoff, James 96
Holland, John 140, 141
The Hollywood Foreign Press Association and the Film Foundation 150
Holmes, Stuart 118, 147
Holt, Jack 49, 52, 53, 92, 94, 146
Holubar, Alan 69, 70
The Homesteader 111
Hooligan, Happy 81
Horne, Stephen 155
Horrible Huns 55, 56, 58, 59, 69, 71
Horrors of War 21
Houdini, Harry 114
Houston, Herbert 45
How Uncle Sam Prepares 51
Hughes, Charles Evans 31
Hughes, Rupert 110, 141, 177
The Hun Within 13, 67, 69, 153
Huns and Hyphens 84
Hyphens 27, 164

I Run the Biggest Life Insurance Company on Earth 14, 97
Ibanez, Vincente Blasco 121
If My Country Should Call 27, 150
If Your Soldier's Hit 101
I'll Help Every Willing Worker Find a Job 14, 97
"I'm Giving You to Uncle Sam" 83
In Again, Out Again 62
Ince, Thomas 12, 25, 48, 83, 107, 108, 109, 116, 117, 127, 163, 177, 180
The Independent 40
Ingram, Rex 118, 121, 122, 123, 156, 178
Inspiration 23
Inspiration Pictures 124, 126, 140
International Silent Film Festival 150, 154, 155, 157
Intolerance 122, 184
Israelitische Kultusgemeinde 60
Italian Film Journal 95
Italy, in war films 20, 103
iTunes 158

James, Dennis 156
Jaxon Film Corporation 72
The Jazz Singer 138, 146
Jef Films 151

198

Index

Jewel Productions 81
Joan of Plattsburg 79, 81, 152
Joan the Woman 31, 50, 151, 175
Johanna Enlists 87, 88, 107, 152
Johns, William H. 45
Johnson, Jane Stannard 96
Johnston, William 96
Jolivet, Rita 14, 73, 146, 173
Jolson, Al 138
Julian, Rupert 1, 76, 78
Julius Caesar 7

Kaiser, Lt. Augustus 113
The Kaiser, the Beast of Berlin 1, 14, 76, 152
Kaiserphobia 1, 71, 72
The Kaiser's Finish 14, 91, 92, 152, 177
The Kaiser's New Dentist 89
Kansas City Film Festival 156, 157
Kearney, James 97
Keaton, Buster 123
Keckeisen, Bob 157
Kee, Sgt. Sing Lau 114
Keep 'Em Singing 97
Keystone Cops/Keystone Studios 112
Keystone Film Company 114
Kicking the Germ Out of Germany 84
Kid Auto Races 20
Kineto Company 95
King, Burton L. 113, 114
King, Henry 126, 140, 141
King-Lorber Films 153
Kingsley, Grace 86
The Kiss 144
The Klansman 26
Knox, Margaret 61
Knudtson, David 156
Krotoshinsky, Private Abraham 113

Labor's Part in Democracy's War 46
The La Crosse Tribune 25
Laemmle, Carl 48, 144, 145
La Giornate del Cinema Muto 151
Langlois, Henri 149
Lansing, Sec. of State Robert 44
The League of Nations 105
Lee, Ivy Ledbetter 43
Lee, Rowland V. 137, 138
Less Than Dust 31, 50, 62
Lesser, Sol 70, 112
Lest We Forget 14, 73, 74, 146, 151
Leuven (Louvain) 21, 56, 163
Levering, Joseph 49
Lewiston Evening Herald 72, 172
Liberty Loan Campaigns 56, 74, 79, 88, 90, 134
Library and Archives of Canada 154
Library of Congress 17, 149, 150, 151, 152, 153, 154, 155, 156, 157, 158

Life Magazine 134, 178, 180
Lillian Gish Trust Fund for Film Preservation 154
Limerick, Lou 159
Lincoln, Elmo 76, 92, 94
The Little American 12, 49, 151
The Little Patriot 51
Lloyd, Harold 31, 84, 117, 123
London National Film Theatre 157
Los Angeles Times 25, 86, 88, 122, 178
The Lost Battalion 15, 113, 114, 115, 155, 177
Louis B. Mayer Conservation Center 149
Love, Montagu 56, 57, 146
The Lucille Love, Girl of Mystery 20
Ludlow Massacre 43, 167
Lufberry, Raoul 100
Luke's Preparedness Preparations 31
Lusitania, sinking depicted in war films and cartoons 10, 21, 26, 73, 76, 78, 81, 85, 108

MacArthur, Douglas 44
Mac Erlaine, Sean 156
Mack, Hughie 139, 140
Mack, Louis B. 46
Mack Sennett-Keystone Cops 80
MacManus Corporation 114
MacPherson, Jeanne 33
Majestic Studios 62
Making a War Poster 51
Making of Big Guns 46
Making the Nation Fit 102
Male & Female 116
Maltin, Leonard 155
The Man Who Was Afraid 51
Mann, Margaret 139, 140
Manning Our Navy 51
Mare Island Naval Shipyard explosion 35
Marion, Frances 88, 128
Mary Pickford Film Festival 151
Mason. Leslie 96
The Master Murder Mystery 114
Mathis, June 121, 122
Mayer, Louis B. 132, 182
McAvoy, May 124
McCay, Winsor 81
McKee, Raymond 63, 64
McKeogh, Lt. Arthur F. 113
Mercier, Cardinal Désiré-Joseph 56, 153, 170
Me Und Gott 14, 84, 152
The Merry Widow 132, 180
Metro-Goldwyn-Mayer 130, 132
Metro Pictures Corporation 73, 105, 118, 121
Mexican-American conflict 11, 19, 28, 44
Micheaux, Oscar 111
The Michigan Film Review 57, 170
Microsoft 158

Index

Milestone, Lewis 142, 144, 145
Milne, Peter 34
Milner, Victor 107
Milwaukee Journal 98, 175, 182
The Miracle Man 115
The Miser 123
Miss Jackie of the Navy 51
Miss USA 51
Modern Husbands 112
Monto Alto Motion Picture Orchestra 156, 159, 184
Motion Picture Classic 117, 178
Motion Picture Magazine 138, 141, 181
The Motion Picture News 28, 34, 50, 76, 85, 165, 166, 169, 172, 173
The Motion Picture World 34, 86, 166, 169, 172, 177
Moving Picture News 96
Moving Picture World 28, 29, 31, 37, 38, 39, 53, 78, 88, 92, 93, 96, 106, 109, 113, 124, 165, 167, 169, 171, 173, 174, 179
Muckraker 40, 167
Munson, Audrey 23
Murnau, F.W. 139
Murphy, Kevin 156
Murray, Mae 88, 173
Museum of Modern Art, New York City 149, 150, 151, 153, 154, 157
Mutt & Jeff 88, 89
My Adventures as a German Secret Agent 86
My Four Years in Germany 74, 92, 152, 177

Nanook of the North 123
Napoleon Bonaparte 8, 9
National Archives 150, 154
National Association of the Motion Picture Industry (NAMPI) 47
National Convention of the General Confederation of Women's Clubs 75
The National Film Archives of Canada/Ottawa 150
National Film Preservation Board 149, 151, 152
National World War One Museum 151
Nautilius 31
Navarro, Ramon 4
Nazi Germany 146
Nazimova, Alla 28, 29, 30, 31, 88, 123, 146, 165, 173
Negri, Pola 137, 138, 147, 183
Neilan, Marshall 109, 110, 122, 177
New York American 30
New York Daily News 146, 182
New York Evening Telegram 69, 171
New York Film Festival 151
New York Film Forum 159
New York Herald Tribune 110

New York Institute of the Blind 126
New York Journal 40
New York Motion Picture Journal 40
The New York Post 159, 184
The New York Times 22, 23, 26, 30, 35, 36, 37, 58, 64, 67, 68, 70, 74, 75, 76, 81, 82, 83, 84, 91, 101, 103, 104, 109, 110, 113, 114, 115, 122, 127, 128, 129, 133, 134, 136, 145, 162, 164, 165, 167, 170, 171, 172, 174, 175, 176, 177, 178, 179, 180, 181, 182
The New York Times Dramatic Mirror 37, 38, 167
The New York Times Tribune 68, 177
Newhard, Robert 107
Niebuhr, Walter 98, 174, 175
94th "Hat in the Ring" Pursuit Squadron 100
Nolan, Matthew 156
Normand, Mabel 3, 79, 80, 88, 121, 147, 152, 173, 183
Nothing Can Lick 'Em 97
Novak, Jane 83, 116, 147, 183

O'Brien, Tom 130, 133, 134
O'Day, Molly 135, 137
The Official Bulletin 44
Official War Review 95, 96
Ogle, Charles 52, 53
The Ohio State Journal 70, 171
Ohlheiser, Abby 149
Oland, Warner 52, 169
Old Heidelberg 12, 62, 170
Old Wives for New 57
On the Farm Where the Food Comes From 51
On the Firing Line With the Germans 21, 175
Orandorff, Marguerite 127
Osbourne, Robert 159, 184
Our Colored Fighters 6, 15, 102, 103, 154
Our Fighting Forces 51
Our Four Days in Germany 89
Our Horses of War 102
Our Wings of Victory 101
Out Yonder 117
Over There 51

Panthea 62
Paramount Bray Pictographs 79, 97
Paramount Pictures Corporation 23, 31, 53, 65, 87, 96, 108, 109, 110, 116, 137
Paris Peace Conference 105
Passaga, General 100
The Patent Leather Kid 135, 136, 137, 157, 177
Pathé News 52, 96
Patria 52
Patriotic Auntie 51

Index

Patterson, Joseph 23
Patterson, Sen. Thomas M. 41
Peckham, David 153
Peg o' My Heart 132
Pelham Bay Naval Training Station 101
Perry, William 154
Pershing, Gen. John J. 98, 100, 103, 165, 176
Pershing's Crusaders 15, 97, 98, 154
The Persians 7
Phillips, Dorothy 27, 69, 70
Photoplay 62, 76, 79, 83, 117, 127, 170, 172, 178, 179, 182
Photoplay Magazine Medal 135, 140
Pickford, Mary 10, 12, 20, 31, 48, 49, 50, 62, 76, 79, 87, 88, 107, 110, 121, 146, 152, 168, 173
Poole, Ernest 46
The Poor Little Rich Girl 50
Pordenone Silent Film Weekend 154
Powers, Patrick A. 99, 100
Preer, Evelyn 111
The Pride of the Clan 50
Provost, Marie 112, 146, 182
The Prussian Cur 14, 85, 152, 173
Purviance, Edna 89

Queen Catherine di Medici 8
Queen Elizabeth 1, 8

Radio City Music Hall 157
Rapsis, Jeff 154, 184
Ratisbonne, Edmund 95
Ray, Charles 83, 88, 173
Rebuilding America's Merchant Marine 51
Reclaiming the Soldier's Duds 97
Reel Vault Studios 154
Rehfeld, Curt 121
Reid, Wallace 91, 166
Reilly, Leigh 44
Reisenfeld, Hugo 101, 121, 175
Remarque, Erich Maria 144, 145
Richard, Albert 96
Richmond Herald 173
The Richmond Palladium 86
Riefenstahl, Leni 1
Rin Tin-Tin 123, 178, 179
RLJ Films Entertainment Home Video Distributor 151
The Road Through the Dark 14, 92, 152
Robin Hood 123
Roche, Josephine 11, 41, 46
Rockefeller, John D. 43
The Rocky Mountain News 11, 41, 42, 43
Rogers, Buddy 135
A Romance of the Redwoods 50
Romayne, Henry Y. 84
Romayne-Super Film Company 84
Roosevelt, Theodore 22, 35, 37, 107

Rose of the Rancho 50
Rosen, Phil 107
Rosher, Charles 88, 107
Rowland, Richard A. 107, 121
Ruckner, Joseph 96
Ryerson, Donald 47

Safety Last 123
St. John, Al 141
St. Patrick's Silent Film Festival 156
San Francisco Film Festival 151, 155, 156, 157, 159
San Francisco International Asian-American Film Festival 151
Sandburg, Carl 134
Sanger, Margaret 28
Santell, Edwin 122
Saving the Food of a Nation 51
Scaramouche 123
Schallert, Edwin 122
Schenck, Earl 74, 81, 91, 92, 106, 147, 176, 177, 182
Scott, Dennis 157
Screen Classics, Inc. 81
Screenland 138, 181
The Sea Wolf 117
The Secret Game 6, 12, 52, 53, 58, 151
Secret Service 52, 53
Selznick, Lewis J. 29, 48, 74, 93, 165, 174
Selznick Pictures 28, 30, 62, 92, 152
Semon, Larry 84
Sennett, Mack 112
Sepoy Rebellion of 1857 9
The 75 Mile Gun 81
She Goes to War 16, 140, 158
Sheboygan Press 29, 165
Sheen, James M. 99
The Sheik 123
Shell 43 150
Shelton, Col. George Henry 100
Sherley, Rep. J. Swager 98
Shertzinger, Victor 25, 83, 163, 172
Sherwood, Robert 134
Shootin' for Love 123, 156
Shoulder Arms 2, 14, 89, 153
Siegmann, George 65, 66, 70
Signal Corps 96, 97, 174
Silent Film Society of Chicago 153
Sinking of the Lusitania 81
The Slacker 51
The Slacker's Heart 51
The Slanted Screen 151
Smith, Albert E. 19
Smith, Frederic James 117
The Social Secretary 13, 62
Soldiers of the Sea 51
Solving the Farm Problems in the Nation 14, 96

201

Index

Souls for Sale 151
Spying the Spy 97, 174
The Squaw Man 50
The Staats-Zeitung 25, 162, 163
Standing, Wyndham 127, 130
Stannard, Jane 96
Stanwyck, Barbara 147
Steele, Rufus 96
Sterling, Ford 112
Stone, George 57, 59
Storm of Steel 102
Stowell, William 69
Stroheim, Erich von 1, 6, 12, 13, 54, 59, 60, 61, 62, 63, 64, 65, 66, 67, 68, 69, 70, 71, 116, 123, 139, 147, 170, 180, 183, 184
Stuart, Kathryn 93
The Student Prince 62
Submarines 46
Suddeudeutsche 184
The Sussex Pledge 24
Swanson, Gloria 116
Sweet, Blanche 109, 110, 146, 177
Swickard, Joseph 118, 122
Sylvia of the Secret Service 63

Tarbell, Ida 45
Talmadge, Constance 63
Talmadge, Norma 22, 62, 63, 88, 121, 146, 173
Tarkington, Booth 45
Tarnish 129
Taylor, Laurette 132
Taylor, William Desmond 87, 183
Terry, Alice 119, 122, 146
Tess of the Storm Country 50
Thalberg, Irving 132, 180
A Thief in Paradise 128
Thirer, Irene 146, 182
369th New York Infantry Regiment (93rd Division) 102, 176
'*Til I Come Back to You* 12, 57, 153
Tillie's Fractured Romance 20
To Hell with the Kaiser! 14, 81, 82, 92, 152, 177
Tol'able David 126, 127
The Toledo Ohio Commerce Club 82
Tollaire, August 139, 140
Tongs 113, 177
Tracy, Virginia 110
Traverse City Film Festival 150, 183
Treasury of Chicken Cookery 147
Treaty of Versailles 105, 176
Triangle Film Corporation 24, 114
Triumph of the Will 1
Tunney, Gene 136
Turner Classic Movies (TCM) 152, 155, 159
20,000 Leagues Under the Sea 31, 107

Tyler, Ralph W. 102, 103
The Typhoon 20, 53

U Boat 21, 162
UCLA Film and Television Archives 151
The Unbeliever 13, 63, 64, 69, 152
United Artists 107, 158
United States Army Air Corps 135
United States Army 143rd Regiment of Field Artillery 88
United States Army Signal Corps 94, 95
United States Film Registry 155
Universal Film Manufacturing Company 97
Universal Pictures 69, 70, 76, 78, 123, 124, 142, 145, 152
University of Chicago 154
The Unpardonable Sin 15, 109, 155, 177

Valentino, Rudolph 4, 118, 121, 122, 123, 135, 147
Valles, Chaplain John B de 100
Vance, Jeffrey 156
Vardamon, Sen. James K. 41
Variety 26, 27, 34, 37, 50, 64, 74, 76, 83, 88, 91, 93, 98, 122, 127, 136, 137, 140, 146, 162, 164, 166, 167, 169, 170, 171, 172, 173, 174, 175, 178, 179, 181, 182, 183
Verne, Jules 31
Vernon, George Ley 73
Vidor, Florence 52, 53, 57, 58, 59
Vidor, King 130, 132, 133, 134, 184
Viereck, George Sylvester 23, 25, 27, 162, 164
Vitagraph Studios 19, 22, 35, 36, 93, 158, 162
Vitagraph Theater 25
Volksoper Wien 60
Voluntary Censorship Program 47, 105, 167, 168

Wagon Tracks 115
Walsh, Raoul 85, 86
Walthall, Henry B. 108, 109, 146
War and the Woman 51
War Brides 6, 11, 28, 29, 150
War Cooperation Committee 47
War Department 100
The War Industries Board 85
War to End All Wars 1
Warnack, Henry Christeen 25, 163
Warner Brothers 75, 91, 123, 152
Warner Home Video 156
The Warrens of Virginia 50
Washburn, Bryant 57, 58, 59
Washington, Gen. George 8
Watertown Daily News Times 113, 177
Way Down East 126

Index

Ways and Means Committee 99
We Can't Have Everything 57
Weigle, Edwin F. 23, 96
Weitzel, Edward 31, 93
Wentworth, Marion Craig 29
Western Electric Sound System 145
What Price Glory 132
When the Call Came 51
When the Clouds Roll By 117
Where the North Begins 123
Whittlesey, Lt. Col. Charles W. 113, 114, 115
Wicked Darling 117
Wid's Film Daily 109
Wife of the Centaur 132
Wife to the Conqueror 20
Wild Oranges 132
Wilderness Trail 115
Wilhelm, Crown Prince of Germany 33
Willat, Irvin 108, 109, 116, 117
Wilson, Woodrow 12, 21, 25, 26, 31, 35, 39, 43, 44, 46, 47, 52, 53, 66, 75, 85, 86, 98, 99, 101, 105, 106, 107, 163, 165, 167, 168, 176
Wilson and the Issues 12, 44
Wings 135, 180
The Winning of Barbara Worth 128
Winning with Wheat 51
Winslow, Alan 100
Wisconsin Center for Film and Theater Research 157

Withey, Chester 67, 68
Witzke, Lothar 35, 166
Wolheim, Louis 142, 144, 145, 181, 182
The Woman of Knockaloe 138
Womanhood, the Glory of the Nation 12, 35, 151
Woman's Part in War 46
Women's Work in Wartime 51
Wood, Major General Leonard 22, 37
World Films 56, 153, 165
World War 1 2, 3, 9, 19, 31, 35, 55, 63, 65, 75, 83, 108, 117, 118, 124, 128, 142, 167

Xerxes 1, 7

Yankee Doodle in Berlin 2, 15, 112, 113, 154, 177
The Yanks Are Coming 99, 100
Yellow Peril 53, 169
Yorkshire Film Festival 157
Young, Clara Kimball 92, 93, 94, 146, 152, 165, 174
Young, Loretta 147
YouTube 153, 154, 156, 158

Zeitgeist 27, 164
The Zeppelin's Last Raid 51
Zeus Film Archives 157
Zimmermann Telegram 11, 35, 166
Zukor, Adolph 50, 87

www.ingramcontent.com/pod-product-compliance
Lightning Source LLC
Chambersburg PA
CBHW021354300426
44114CB00012B/1231